M000166646

THE TOWER

THE TOWER

A Chronicle of Climbing and Controversy on Cerro Torre

KELLY CORDES

patagonia

THE TOWER

A CHRONICLE OF CLIMBING AND CONTROVERSY ON CERRO TORRE

At Patagonia, we publish a collection of books that reflect our pursuits and our values— books on wilderness, outdoor sports, innovation, and a commitment to environmental activism.

Copyright 2014 Patagonia
Text © Kelly Cordes
Photograph copyrights held by the photographers
End sheets art © Jeremy Collins

All rights reserved. No part of this book may be used or reproduced in any manner whatsoever without written permission from the publisher and copyright holders. Requests should be mailed to Patagonia Books, Patagonia, Inc., 259 W. Santa Clara St., Ventura, CA 93001-2717

First Edition
Editor: John Dutton
Photo Editor: Kelly Cordes
Book Design and Production: Haruna Madono

Route maps are for reference only. This is not a climbing guide.

Printed in the United States on Cascade Enviro 100% post-consumer-waste recycled paper, except for photo inserts.

ISBN 978-1-938340-33-8
E-Book ISBN 978-1-1938340-34-5
Library of Congress Control Number: 2014947861

p. 1   Cerro Torre's west ridge from the Col of Hope. Photo: Kelly Cordes
pp. 2–3   Cerro Torre. Photo: Mikey Schaefer
pp. 4–5   The Chaltén Massif. Photo: Kelly Cordes

Cerro Torre. Photo: Mikey Schaefer

The famous wind-carved tunnels in Cerro Torre's rime ice mushrooms.
Photo: Rolando Garibotti

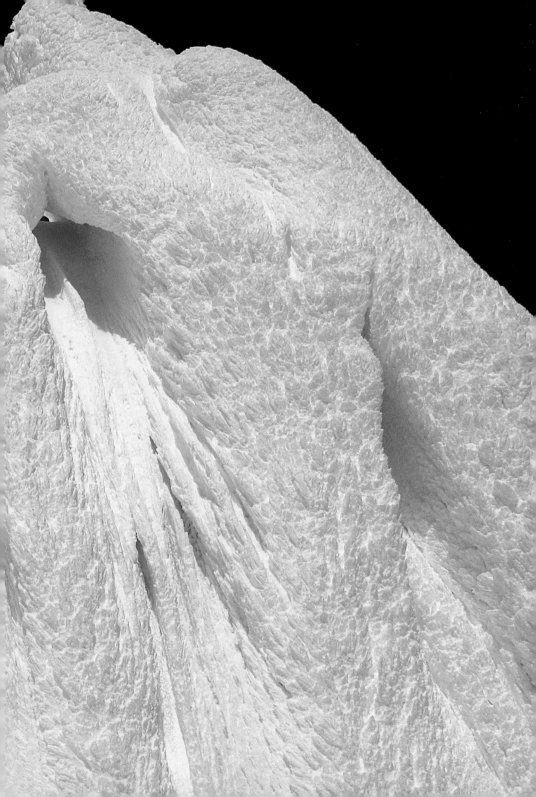

Headlamps high on Cerro Torre's southeast ridge, as seen from the Torre Valley. Photo: Mikey Schaefer.

The eastern side of the Torre group. Photo: Rolando Garibotti

The Chaltén Massif from the east. Photo: Alexandre Buisse

El Arca de
los Vientos

THE HELMET ◀

Ragni Route

COL OF CONQUEST
▼

COL OF HOPE
▼

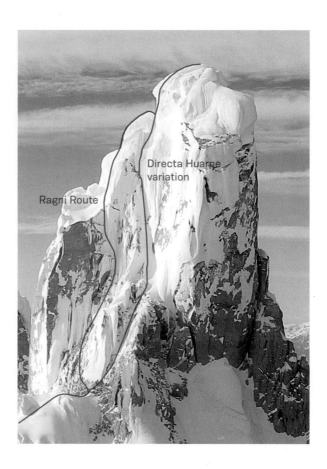

CERRO TORRE FROM THE WEST

Dots represent hidden portions.

left El Arca de los Vientos (Beltrami-Garibotti-Salvaterra, 2005), which approaches
from the east, and the Ragni Route (Chiappa-Conti-Ferrari-Negri, 1974).
Photo: Dörte Pietron

right Upper headwall, showing Ragni Route on left and Directa Huarpe variation
(Fava-Sánchez-Treu, 2013). Photo: Dani Ascaso

Southeast
Ridge

Quinque Anni
ad Paradisum

COL OF CONQUEST

El Arca
de los Vientos

Pekleneska
Direttissima

COL OF PATIENCE

CERRO TORRE FROM THE EAST

Dots represent hidden portions

Southeast Ridge

Alimonta-Claus-Maestri to near summit, 1970; Brewer-Bridwell
to summit, 1979. Both via Compressor Route, which was removed
in 2012. Line shows current state, with variations (see page 304/305):

Kennedy-Kruk headwall	on left
Lama-Ortner headwall	on right
Lama-Ortner	mid-height variation on left

Peklenska Direttissima   Fistravec-Jeglič-Karo-Knez-Kozjek-Podgornik, 1986.
Quinque Anni ad Paradisum   Beltrami-Rossetti-Salvaterra, 2004.
El Arca de los Vientos   Beltrami-Garibotti-Salvaterra, 2005.

Photo: Rolando Garibotti

CERRO TORRE'S UPPER HALF FROM THE NORTH

Seen from the ice cap in snow-plastered conditions. El Arca de los Vientos (approached from east to Col of Conquest; Beltrami-Garibotti-Salvaterra, 2005). Photo: Dörte Pietron

Southeast
Ridge

Corkscrew
linkup

COL OF HOPE ▼

Southeast
Ridge

Infinito Sud

COL OF PATIENCE ◄

Southeast
Ridge

The Long Run start
to Southeast Ridge

South Face

What's Love Got to Do with It

Los Tiempos Perdido

CERRO TORRE FROM THE SOUTH

Los Tiempos Perdidos	Marsigny-Parkin, 1994; Cordes-Haley to summit via Ragni Route, 2007.
South Face	Jeglič-Karo, 1988, to junction with Southeast Ridge.
Infinito Sud	Manni-Salvaterra-Vidi, 1995, to junction with Southeast Ridge.
What's Love Got To Do with It	Jeglič-Lukič-Praprotnik, 1994, to junction with Southeast Ridge.
Southeast Ridge	Approached from northeast to Col of Patience; see pages 18/19 and 304/305 for details.
The Long Run	Start to Southeast Ridge (Koch-Potter-Prezelj, 2006).
Corkscrew linkup	Lied-Saeland, 2008.

Photo: Rolando Garibotti

SOUTHEAST RIDGE

THE HELMET

COL OF HOPE

SOUTH FACE

THE UPPER HALF OF CERRO TORRE FROM THE SOUTH
Photo: Dani Ascaso

*"The world of dew
is the world of dew
And yet, and yet..."*

Kobayashi Issa
(1763–1828)

Cerro Torre enshrouded in storm, 1972. Photo: Leo Dickinson

Contents

A view from the southern end of the Torre Valley, with the prominent Cerro Torre and Torre group on the left, and the Fitz Roy chain on the right. Photo: Mikey Schaefer

previous spread Cerro Torre. Photo: Mikey Schaefer

above Colin Haley below the gargoyled west ridge of Cerro Torre.
Photo: Kelly Cordes

chapter 1

LOST
TIME

The howling Patagonian wind calmed to a whisper. The afternoon sun beat down and I blinked hard against a haze of exhaustion, the kind of blink where a black screen seems to linger behind your eyelids and you wonder how much time you lost.

I stared past thousands of feet of golden granite disappearing beneath me. A vertical mile below flowed the Torre Glacier, bending, cracked, cracking—growing and shrinking with the years. At its terminus, only a short way down valley, it calves into Laguna Torre and flows into rivers feeding forests and rolling pampas. Scattered estancias dot a landscape where not long ago pumas and wild horses roamed. A giant condor soared overhead, riding the thermals. Sheep grazed on the barren grasslands that extend eastward to the Atlantic Ocean.

A hundred feet above, enormous structures of overhanging, aerated ice, vestiges of Patagonia's brutal storms, held guard over Cerro Torre's summit. They loomed like multi-ton sculptures pulled from a land of fairy tales, like whipped cream frozen in place, jutting wildly outward in gravity-defying, wind-forged blobs. On the opposite side of the mountain Cerro Torre faces the Hielo Continental, an Antarctic-like world comprising massive sheets of flat glacial ice that spill into the Pacific Ocean.

Just before sunrise, thirty-some hours earlier, we had started climbing. We raced up ephemeral ice beneath a sérac, then weaved through gargoyles of rime. We fell short of the summit as the sun set and the wind roared, and we shivered away the night in a snow cave in the starlit blackness of Cerro Torre's upper crest. Come morning we struggled over the summit, and then started down the other side. Both of us carried only ten-pound backpacks, but we also carried fantasies, a dose of self-delusion, and a shred of hope. Without those, we'd have never left the ground.

I blinked again, and my gaze returned across the landscape, from the distant pampas to the beech forests surrounding Laguna Torre, to the golden granite falling away beneath my feet. And then to the rusting engine block on which I stood. The only stance on Cerro Torre's headwall. A 150-pound, gas-powered air compressor, a god-damned jackhammer lashed to the flanks of the most beautiful mountain on earth. Above and below ran an endless string of climbing bolts—ancient two-inch pegs of metal drilled into the rock and spaced to be used like ladders—courtesy of the compressor and a man possessed, that for four decades allowed passage up this impossible tower.

The wind remained at a whisper. Exhaustion pulsed through my bones and I stared into a clear, cobalt sky, and knew that we'd been lucky. Calm around Cerro Torre never lasts.

Colin Haley in a world of wild, wind-sculpted rime below
Cerro Torre's summit. Photo: Kelly Cordes

Cesare Maestri (left) and Walter Bonatti during a chance
encounter near the summit of Cerro Adela Sur in 1958.
Photo: Folco Doro-Altán collection

chapter 2

IN THE BEGINNING

For all of the spectacular images of dramatic mountains and coastlines, Patagonia is a largely barren, arid, and sparsely populated region covering a million square kilometers in southern Argentina and Chile. But over the course of the last sixty-five million years, erosion has worn away soft surrounding rock to reveal a compact cluster of granite spires just inland from the Pacific Ocean at forty-nine degrees south latitude. The Chaltén Massif juts from the earth like parallel rows of sharpened teeth.

The massif and its surroundings embody a range of contrasts. The massive Hielo Continental (Southern Patagonia Ice Cap) spans 240 miles north–south. Fjords snake inland from the Pacific only thirty miles to the west, while a few miles to the east, vast grasslands and plains extend 200 miles to the Atlantic. Just south, giant lakes—Lago Viedma and Lago Argentino, forty-five and sixty miles long—could be mistaken for seaways. A bit farther south, from the tip of the South American continent, 400 miles of ocean leads to Antarctica.

The massif's location subjects it to ferocious oceanic weather; cold air currents race across the narrow ice cap with little resistance, carrying moist air that coats the summits in rime ice. The Chaltén Massif comprises two parallel rows of north–south mountains: the Torre group and the Fitz Roy chain. The Torres are bordered on the west by the ice cap, thus they bear the brunt of the incoming weather and acquire outrageous rime ice formations. The eastern aspects of the Torres drop precipitously into narrow, glaciated valleys then rise into the Fitz Roy chain. Despite being in the same compact massif, sitting only two and a half miles apart, these two mountain groups experience different conditions. The Fitz Roy chain is usually considerably warmer and drier than the Torres.

Continuing just east of the Fitz Roy chain, in the narrow space between the mountains and the scrub-brush pampas, flourishes a sanctuary for birds and mammals. *Lenga* and *ñire* trees, stout and strong against the ever-present wind, blend with *calafate* bushes and *manzanillas* that sit low to the ground with berries and thistles. The textured landscape alternates between sparse and dense forests.

The weather in the rain shadow, where the town of El Chaltén sits, is often mild—breezy, a mix of sun and mist shifting and swirling every thirty seconds—while in the mountains, even contemplating climbing would be unthinkable. The wind up there lifts people off the ground and slams them down. The severity is almost beyond description. Many a would-be hardman has visited the massif thinking the tales exaggerations, thinking they could deal with the notorious weather. Those foolhardy enough to harbor such illusions are rapidly sent scampering away.

Unlike other storied alpine ranges, the challenges of Patagonia have nothing to do with altitude. Cerro Torre's summit rises to 10,262 feet. Fitz Roy, the highest peak in the massif, rises 11,168 feet.

Cerro Torre isn't like the perfect pyramidal mountains children draw. It's more sheer, more vertical, with summit mushrooms of snow and ice spilling beyond the walls below, resembling the top of a shaken champagne bottle, its exploding contents frozen in place. The general public calls "vertical" what devoted climbers call slabs. Vertical is, properly, ninety degrees—telephone-pole vertical. Give it some wiggle room and today's climbers might call vertical anything steeper than eighty or eighty-five degrees. Regardless, nowhere on Mount Everest or K2—not even on their hardest routes—nor on any of the alpine ice routes in the Alps, will you find such sustained vertical climbing as on Cerro Torre's *easiest* route.

Cerro Torre's reputation was defined in a 1972 *Mountain* magazine passage, written by the editors: "To climbers it has come to represent the epitome of the unattainable icy peak—a savage fang of rock, falling away on all sides for thousands of feet, encrusted in a fragile armour of ice, and constantly battered by the winds and storms that sweep across the Patagonian Ice Cap. This diminutive yet formidable mountain has come to embody the whole spirit of super-alpinism."

NOBODY KNOWS FOR CERTAIN when the first humans laid eyes on Cerro Torre. The Tehuelche Indians roamed the land around today's El Chaltén for some ten thousand years before colonialization, disease, and assimilation rendered them virtually extinct. The plumes of wind- and storm-driven clouds that have forever streamed from the top of Fitz Roy led the Tehuelches to believe it was a volcano. The word *chaltel*, or *chaltén*, loosely translates to "smoking mountain."

Magellan's famous sixteenth-century voyage sparked interest among explorers in the region that we now call Patagonia, perhaps named after a mythical beast known as the Grand Patagon. Myths enshrouded the region. When Sir Francis Drake came to Patagonia in 1578 seeking riches but experiencing only atrocious storms, he blamed the natives: "They built great fires and then cast upon them heaps of sand, as a sacrifice to the devils."

The first westerner known to see the striking peaks of the Chaltén Massif was Spanish explorer Antonio de Viedma in 1782. One of his diary entries provides the earliest suggestion of Cerro Torre's name, when he describes a prominent peak as "una torre"— a tower.

In the centuries that followed, Europeans visited in increasing numbers, though the waterways held a constant threat from pirates. Charles Darwin sailed to Patagonia on British astronomer and explorer Robert FitzRoy's *Beagle*. FitzRoy spent nearly a decade mapping the coastal areas. Later, the Argentine explorer Francisco "Perito" Moreno named the massif's highest mountain in his honor (the Argentine spelling of the mountain became Fitz Roy), overriding or ignoring the original Tehuelche name, Chaltén.

By the late 1800s, settlers colonized the plains—the mountains, devoid of game and unsuitable for farming, were of little use. Gauchos tended their livestock on horseback and navigated at night by the stars of the Southern Cross.

While nearby Tehuelche rock paintings date back some five thousand years, it wasn't until the early 1900s that European settlers began living near the area we now call El Chaltén. A 1915–16 expedition led by Swiss Alfred Kölliker was the first to explore the massif, charting much of its southern and western portions, and making several nontechnical ascents of nearby peaks. His team published a book, which was later followed by a personal account from Kölliker. Knowledge spread slowly in those days. But with a significant and growing community of European immigrants in Argentina, it's no surprise that interest in exploring the massif arose among those not only in Buenos Aires but also across the Atlantic. Starting in the 1930s, expeditionary interest grew and, along with it, competition to climb the area's peaks.

One of the most influential European explorers, at least in terms of climbing, was the Italian missionary (and devoted mountaineer, geographer, and photographer) Alberto María De Agostini. He made the first of his multiple expeditions to the area in 1932. In 1937, an Italian team, led by the well-connected Count Aldo Bonacossa, made the first attempt on Cerro Fitz Roy. In 1941, the genie was officially out of the bottle when De Agostini published his book, *Andes Patagónicos*. Quite naturally, it caught the eye of many top European alpinists.

Inspired by De Agostini's images, a French team led by Guido Magnone and Lionel Terray made plans to attempt Fitz Roy. According to rumor Argentina's president was so excited by the publicity of such a feat that he offered them a helicopter to the summit. The climbers declined; even back then, when siege-style expeditions were the norm, the idea was to actually *climb* the mountain. It was an early harbinger that would resonate years later on Cerro Torre, where use of technology would prompt questions about the difference between climbing a mountain and merely getting to the top.

On February 2, 1952, Magnone and Terray stood on the summit of Fitz Roy. They'd made an impressively rapid ascent weaving up the line of least resistance along the cold south buttress. (In the Southern Hemisphere the sun warms the northerly aspects, while south faces remain shaded.) Utilizing a minimal number of fixed ropes, their climb was a nod toward the future in an era of siege-style ascents.

From the summit, Terray looked over at Cerro Torre and declared, "Now there's a mountain worth risking one's skin for!" After their ascent of Fitz Roy, Terray gave a presentation at the Italian Alpine Club branch in Buenos Aires at which he mentioned seeing the most beautiful mountain in the world. Magnone and Terray publicly labeled Cerro Torre "impossible," but their words only whetted the interest of the day's top alpinists. The challenge of the future was clear.

CESARE MAESTRI, a young climber in the autonomous Trentino

province of Northern Italy, was making a name for himself, soloing up and often back down some of the most daunting faces in the Dolomites—an incredible assortment of difficult routes up to three thousand feet tall. Soloing—climbing alone, usually without a rope—was considered the mark of a loner, a characterization that fit Maestri's upbringing. His mother died when he was seven, and his father ran a traveling theater. The elder Maestri was condemned to death and hunted when the Nazis overtook Trento in World War II; he, as well as young Cesare, had sided with the Italian partisans against the Nazis and Mussolini's fascist movement. They fled to the plains of the Bologna region, where they wandered for a year until returning toward the end of the war.

In post-war 1950s, climbers were celebrities in Northern Italy, often recognized on the streets and featured in newspapers. Maestri's was a rags-to-riches story. He soon became known as Il Ragno delle Dolomiti (The Spider of the Dolomites) for his free solos. On the occasions that he roped up with a partner, he insisted on leading every pitch. Cesare Maestri would follow nobody. His skill was as legendary as his determination. Climbing was his obsession. He trained, went to bed early, followed a strict diet—climbing

The Chaltén Massif, jutting skyward from the pampas.
Photo: Mario Conti

consumed him. "Even when I made love to a girl, I did it in the press-up position to strengthen my arms," he said.

But Maestri was excluded from the large 1954 Italian K2 expedition. He was snubbed for reasons that remain unclear but suggest expeditionary politics and his anarchistic mindset. He was denied the greatest honor an Italian climber could have at the time. Maestri responded by enchaining thirteen peaks in the Brenta Dolomites, climbing both up and down, ropeless, totaling some twelve thousand vertical feet—the same height from base camp to the summit of K2. Maestri completed this enchainment in a mere sixteen hours. The feat made the news and soon after, Cesarino Fava, a Trentino climber who'd emigrated to Buenos Aires after the war, saw a magazine spread featuring a photo of Maestri during his enchainment. Though Fava and Maestri were from nearby villages, they'd never met. Fava wrote Maestri a letter describing Cerro Torre: "Come here, you will find bread for your teeth"—an Italian saying meaning a mountain worthy of your reputation.

Of course the beautiful and daunting Patagonian tower, declared impossible by none other than Terray and Magnone, had already generated a buzz among the daring and competitive alpinists of the day.

Maestri left Italy in late 1957 on a Cerro Torre expedition led by the renowned Trentino explorer and expedition veteran Bruno Detassis. Fava met them in Buenos Aires and they headed south in early 1958.

Around the same time, the Italian Alpine Club of Buenos Aires adventurer and Italian émigré Folco Doro-Altán had already explored the ice cap three times. He provided a natural logistical link between the bewitching landscape of Patagonia and some of the top climbing talent on earth, back home in Italy. Doro-Altán insisted that the original idea for attempting Cerro Torre (Fava had never been to Patagonia), and even for inviting Maestri, were his. As things played out he invited the great alpinist Walter Bonatti, who invited Carlo Mauri. Bonatti and Mauri were from Italy's Lombardy region (though around that time Bonatti was moving west, to Courmayeur), and frequently climbed together in the Grigna Spires, near Lecco. They were two of the hottest climbers in Europe. In 1959, they would make what was, at the time, the hardest technical ascent in the Himalaya with their first ascent of Pakistan's 26,001-foot Gasherbrum IV.

While the relationship between Doro-Altán and Fava and their respective teams isn't perfectly clear, in Doro-Altán's unpublished autobiography (he died in 1999) he describes the infighting and competition. Climbing was huge in Italy, and provincialism—extending to competition among expats—ran deep.

"Any climbers from two different parts of Italy would have been competing as if they were from different hemispheres," said Marcello Costa. Costa, now seventy-three years old and an M.D. and neurophysiology researcher in Australia, was born and raised in Italy. He immigrated to Buenos Aires, where he explored the ice cap in the late 1950s, was a member of the alpine club, and became acquainted with Doro-Altán and Fava. He remembers both men: "Folco [Doro-Altán] was the opposite of Cesarino [Fava]. Folco was an ambitious, sophisticated entrepreneur while Cesarino was an old-fashioned mountaineer, full of that 'pseudo-poetry' of mountaineering that mixes morality of 'a good mountain treats well good people.'"

WHEN THE TWO GROUPS MET in the shadow of the

Chaltén Massif, it became apparent that there would be no joining of forces.

Members from Detassis's Trentino team, including Fava, had already made an aerial reconnaissance of Cerro Torre and planned to climb from the east side. Protected from the initial brunt of storms that rage off the Pacific to the west, the east side has a less hostile climate and has far easier logistics. Due to travel infrastructure, both teams would start from the east.

Bonatti's team, however, would try to climb the west face. This would require a grueling forty-mile approach hike, crossing the north–south ridge of glaciated mountains into the full fury of the storms blasting across the ice cap.

"The storms which burst over the mountain are terrifying," Bonatti wrote. "Sometimes gusts of wind laden with sleet and ice crystals reach the terrific velocity of one hundred and twenty miles an hour and form permanent ice encrustations, even under roofs and overhangs, which jut out further than one would imagine. The white and bluish ice, which covers the rocks, can reach thicknesses of over ten feet, assuming fantastic and terrifying forms. Everything is of gigantic size and seems to hang miraculously in space."

Bonatti and Mauri got about halfway up the icy west face. Along the way, they fixed ropes and camped at a prominent col just south of Cerro Torre. "Our surroundings were fantastic, though absolutely terrifying. We were optimistic, so much so that we didn't recognize that merely to reach the col we were already overcoming difficulties comparable to those on the most taxing climbs in the western Alps," Bonatti wrote.

Above the col, in the face of daunting terrain considered difficult and serious even by today's standards, Bonatti and Mauri valiantly climbed on, navigating around overhanging mushrooms of rime with painstaking techniques. They knew they had no chance. Still they inched onward, periodically staring out to the vast emptiness of the ice cap. Above loomed a thousand feet of significantly harder climbing.

When they retreated, Bonatti said it was like waking from a dream and entering the real world. "We were beaten. We got back down to the col and stayed there, sitting down for a long time, in silence."

Armed with knowledge of the mountain, they promised themselves they would return. In that spirit they named the saddle where they sat the Col of Hope.

AT THE SAME TIME, on the other side of the mountain, when they saw Cerro Torre up close, Detassis prohibited his team from even attempting it, declaring, "The tower is a mountain impossible, and I do not want to endanger anyone's life. Accordingly, in my capacity as leader of the expedition, I forbid you to attack the tower."

Maestri remained undeterred. The proud Spider of the Dolomites had envisioned a potential line up the lower east face of Cerro Torre to a prominent col, then continuing up the north face to the summit. He began planning his return. Later he would bestow a name upon this col: the Col of Conquest—a pointed dig at Bonatti and Mauri's Col of Hope. "In the mountains," Maestri wrote, "there is no such thing as hope, only the will to conquer. Hope is the weapon of the weak."

Toni Egger. Photo: Alpenraute—Lienz, Austria

chapter 3

TONI, TONI, TONI

It was February 2013, and raindrops darted intermittently through the air, carried by the only constant in the village of El Chaltén, Argentina: the wind. The Patagonian wind so scours the landscape that in some regions people call it la escoba de Dios—the broom of God.

Melodic sounds of Latina singers floated through the air in Patagonicus restaurant, one of El Chaltén's most popular spots, owned by one of the town's prominent families. Archival photos—origin stories—hang from its walls. I sat at a rustic wooden table, sipped my espresso, and waited for César Fava.

César's father, Cesarino, is the man who wrote the letter to Cesare Maestri, inviting him to attempt the mountain that would provide "bread for his teeth." The elder Fava died in 2008 at the age of eighty-seven; Maestri, born in 1929 and now in his eighties, lives in a mountain village in Italy. He refuses to talk about the mountain that made him famous. I wanted to talk with César because he is one of the last living links to Cerro Torre's early, complex history. I wanted to ask him about 1959.

After his failure in early 1958, Maestri returned in 1959. With the elder Fava's help, he and Austrian climbing ace Toni Egger made the first ascent of the tower previously deemed impossible. Egger and Maestri's rapid climb of Cerro Torre's daunting north face was such a quantum leap in standards that serious alpinists then considered it the greatest ascent of all time. But Egger died on their descent and questions arose about the veracity of Fava and Maestri's story.

I GOT UP AND WANDERED over to stare at the photos that

line Patagonicus's walls. Dozens of grainy black-and-whites of Fava and Maestri's late 1950s expeditions. Photos of everything, that is, but the actual climb of 1959.

The images depict a different world, another time within the same place. My mind short circuits at the audacity of even trying the north face of Cerro Torre back then. It was astronomically harder than anything yet climbed; it took forty-seven years and dozens of attempts by the finest alpinists of each succeeding generation before another party would successfully climb Cerro Torre from the north.

In those old photos Maestri looks comfortable, happy, at peace. But in 2012, at the age of eighty-two, he said, "If I could have a magic wand, I would erase Cerro Torre from my life."

A WOMAN'S VOICE pulled me from my reverie. "César will be

here in a minute," she said. I went back to my chair, opened my notebook and took another sip of espresso.

"Hi, I am César," he said, as he approached my table. He was forty-six years old, appeared fit, stood five foot eight—a few inches taller than his famous father, Cesarino. They share similar features: wavy hair, strong cheekbones, sturdy build.

Within minutes César's eyes sparkled and grew wide, his face glowing as he reminisced about the mountains and the past: simple times, days of passion. "My father always tell me, 'Follow the passion.'"

His father grew up a peasant, one of twelve children, in the Trentino province of war-torn Italy. After serving five years in the war, like so many Italians he left the homeland, landing in Buenos Aires where he worked odd jobs between trips to the mountains, eventually earning a living as a street vendor. Along with other immigrants he founded the Argentine branch of the Italian Alpine Club and became a prominent conduit to Italian climbers, especially those visiting the Andes from Trentino. A simple, hard-working, and humble man known for his sincerity and charm, Cesarino Fava balanced a tireless work ethic with his passion for the mountains and, later, the demands of raising a family.

As with so many connected to the elder Fava, Maestri, and old-school Trentino climbing, César's reverence for the past seems ingrained in his DNA.

César recalled his first trip to this area in 1983, when, as a teenager, he helped carry gear on one of his father's expeditions. There was no town, no bridge, and they rode horses across the river and camped in the beech forests. Those days were modern compared to 1959, but ancient compared to today.

"If you take Maestri," he said in accented English with a deep, soft intonation, "and even Egger, before they started climbing, they had very strong childhoods and a lot of stories of their lives that are amazing. You understand how they *forged* their character even from their childhood. My generation, and the new generation, are very strong climbers, but we have not been forged the same. It's much easier today, and it's OK…. It's a different time."

His voice dropped to a measured, deliberate tone. "So you have to respect the story. And to respect the story you have to know not only what they have done, but always what they were and what they are. The *man* they were, the *man* they are."

He said it's a pity that Maestri is only known for Cerro Torre. Again his tone changed, and he reached out and lightly touched my forearm. "Cesare Maestri made over *three thousand* first ascents, *one thousand* of them made by *himself*, in solo."

I dropped the direct question: "What do you think happened in 1959?"

"About what?" he replied, taken aback.

"Do you think that Egger and Maestri climbed to the top?"

There was a brief but distinct pause as César sat upright, raised his eyebrows, and gesticulated with his hands saying, "Well. Well, yes, of course. This is my opinion."

Given the sheet of ice that covered the north face, he said, certainly they could have reached the summit. That ice doesn't form nowadays, but conditions have changed so much—he looked out the window to the mountains, his posture again relaxing, and rattled off examples. In some years, he explained, patches of snow cling to the north face of the Torre, but never the continuous ice sheet of

1959, which is important because Egger was known as a virtuoso on ice. "What Maestri was able to climb on rock," he said, again sitting upright, "Toni could climb on ice."

He's puzzled by the way people get stuck on trivialities and details of the 1959 climb, the number of pitons found or not found, the rope. "I want to say, 'You don't understand the spirit, the way of doing mountains in those years.' Maestri, with three thousand routes, he could not even remember the route on Cerro Torre he made. They didn't think about how was this, 6b or 6c grades, they just, they *climb*. Was another concept."

While he may be right, of all the mountains in the world, I can think of none other whose history has been so heavily influenced by one man who refuses to discuss anything beyond vague details of his greatest achievement.

We were an hour in and César's face still glowed.

He told me about February 3, 1959. His father left the snow cave on the upper Torre Glacier for the last time. Egger and Maestri had been gone for too long. Six days, the last three in a raging storm. Thousands of feet above, the wind roared like fighter jets, sending plumes and trailers across the sky, obscuring the soaring granite summit. Time and again, through brief clearings, Fava had gazed up at the Torre looking for his friends, only to return to the dark and cold snow cave, his mind flickering between hope and despair, agonizing over when to go, when to leave them for dead. Finally, Cesarino Fava began the somber hike down to tell the others.

"Then the last time he turned up to look, he saw something different in the snow," César said, his voice dipping to a hushed tone. Through the swirling clouds and falling snow, on the upper Torre Glacier, just below the towering walls, his father saw a dark object. But only one. In desperation he raced up the snow slope. As he drew nearer, he could see: It was a person. He hurried to the crumpled body, calling out. Still alive, but only barely, the great Cesare Maestri lifted his head from the snow.

César Fava leaned forward, gently grasped my forearm, and whispered, "My father say the only words of Cesare were, 'Toni, Toni, Toni...'"

Cesare Maestri (left) and Cesarino Fava in a bivy cave on the Torre Glacier, 1959.
Photo: Fava collection

THERE WAS LITTLE PHYSICAL EVIDENCE to support
the 1959 claim—Toni Egger's camera disappeared along with his body.
Only a leg bone (presumably Egger's), some strands of rope, and some
climbing gear below the Col of Conquest were ever found. But Maestri
had his word, and Fava's too.

The doubts about the 1959 ascent so enraged Maestri that he
returned to a different aspect of Cerro Torre in 1970, the southeast ridge, infused with vengeance and obsession. He strung up
thousands of feet of fixed rope and winched along several hundred
pounds of hardware in the form of a gasoline-powered air compressor
that he used to drill around four hundred bolts into the rock. It was
as close to a scaffolding project as anybody had ever done in the
remote mountains. The bolts, little metal studs with a hole in the
end, were spaced close enough to be used as ladders, no climbing
engagement with the rock necessary—clip bolt, stand up in your
portable ladders, repeat. Vertical lines of hundreds of bolts, an
arm's reach apart, now headed toward the summit.

Maestri's tactics were reviled by the vast majority of the climbing
world. But over the ensuing decades, the bolt ladders enabled
hundreds of climbers to clip their way past the hardest portions
of the immaculate Cerro Torre on what became known as the
Compressor Route.

Jason Kruk approaching the Col of Patience and Cerro Torre's
southeast ridge. Photo: Hayden Kennedy

chapter 4

JANUARY 2012

On January 15, 2012, fifty-three years after Cesare Maestri's claimed first ascent of the north face of Cerro Torre with Toni Egger, two young men cruised through the crevassed approach to Cerro Torre's southeast ridge— home to the Compressor Route and Maestri's infamous 1970 bolt ladders. They took their time climbing moderate mixed terrain to a landmark called the Col of Patience. No rush, they were saving their energy for the difficult climbing they anticipated ahead. At the col they pitched their compact bivy tent and lounged away the afternoon, staring across the valley to the peaks of the Fitz Roy chain—the hulking Cerro Fitz Roy, Agujas Desmochada, Poincenot, Rafael Juárez, and Saint-Exupéry, jagged and sharp along the skyline. The sun set; they snoozed through their 11:00 p.m. alarm and woke at 2:00 a.m.

AMERICAN HAYDEN KENNEDY and Canadian Jason Kruk were only twenty-one and twenty-four years old at the time. But they were far from rookies—this was their seventh trip to the massif between them—mostly with other partners, though together they'd climbed the five-thousand-foot Supercanaleta on Fitz Roy two seasons prior. They're proverbial next-generation alpinists, adept on all terrain, from bouldering and sport climbing to big mountains. They arrived in El Chaltén in December 2011 without a specific agenda and started ticking summits in every weather opening. First, Cerro Standhardt. Then Punta Herron and Torre Egger. Next weather window, a jaunt to the other side of the Torre Valley, where they climbed the classic Chiaro di Luna on Aguja Saint-Exupéry, and then established a 1,300-foot new rock route on Aguja de l'S. In a month they'd tallied a lifetime's worth of routes for mortals. The boys were on a roll. Only one torre left, and they'd do something unthinkable in the days of Old Patagonia: Climb all of the Torres in a single season.

In the old days, the logical way up Cerro Torre would be the line of least resistance, the bolt ladders of the Compressor Route. In New Patagonia, Kennedy and Kruk would do things a little differently.

As they approached the southeast ridge of Cerro Torre they had an idea. Not a new idea, but one dating back to before Maestri came along with his gasoline-powered compressor. It also reflected an ideal embraced by a handful of parties who had been willing to strap on blinders, ignore Maestri's unnecessary bolts, and treat the southeast ridge like a natural climbing line: Climb it by the century-old term of "fair means." Climb not the Compressor Route, but the southeast ridge. Turn it into a proper name: the Southeast Ridge Route. Getting to the top is no big trick—Terray understood that when he declined the Argentine government's offer of a helicopter ride to the summit of Fitz Roy before his 1952 first ascent. But climbing the line by fair means—without the Compressor Route's bolt ladders—would be a big trick.

Kennedy and Kruk have got nothing against bolts. Bolts allow some of the finest climbs in the world; they connect natural features or protect the climber when there are no options for placing gear. The problem with these particular bolts is, nobody—neither Maestri nor his closest supporters—pretended that the rock on the southeast ridge was unprotectable. Those nearly four hundred wholly unnecessary bolts, drilled into the most beautiful alpine spire on the planet, were a different story. And a bizarre story not just in itself, but in how it gradually came to be accepted, even among many of the hard-line stylistas of the alpine climbing world, who eschew bolts where rock can be naturally protected.

THEY WOKE AT 2:00 A.M. on January 16, brewed coffee, and forty-five minutes later began climbing. Shouts of joy escaped as they swiftly climbed the moderate lower flanks of the ridge, their frozen breath drifting through the beams of their headlamps, perfect cracks leading them to the first major decision point. They'd more than made up for oversleeping, and sat and waited for daylight. Orange alpenglow fluttered low on the horizon, spread out like baseline fires on the curve of the earth.

At dawn they saw the first of Maestri's bolt ladders, some one hundred bolts, two feet apart, heading up and to the right. Just above them was a natural weakness—a laser-cut seam in the flawless granite. Kennedy alternately free climbed and aided through the crack using small cams and the occasional knifeblade piton. Higher, the rock unveiled perfect 5.10 edges at ideal intervals. The daunting and frigid south face fell away for four thousand feet to his left. Kennedy short-fixed the rope while Kruk jumared behind. They moved with well-tuned efficiency and soon gained the ice towers.

Kruk was the team's ice specialist—he's Canadian, after all—and he smoothly led through ice and mixed terrain, still not clipping any of Maestri's bolts, looking at the line like it was a natural alpine route. Where another of Maestri's bolt ladders angled up rightward, around the corner to the left was a brilliant chimney of perfect, solid ice. The ice pitch brought them to the base of Cerro Torre's famed headwall faster than anybody could have imagined.

Kennedy took the lead again and floated up steep, positive holds, now nearly a mile above the twisting Torre Glacier, going left, then back right, piecing it together, guided by natural features and ignoring the bolt ladders. He climbed flakes and face holds, protected the intermittent cracks, foregoing protection when he had to—nothing more than alpine climbing, really.

After a wild pendulum, using tension from the rope to run across the vertical wall, he latched a fingertip-edge and climbed to a stance where he set a belay. Discontinuous features rose above, with blobs of rime inexplicably stuck to the ninety-degree reddish-orange rock. Kennedy kept climbing, hanging on the occasional cam to clean ice from the cracks, switching between free and aid, connecting delicate face climbing traverses. Just below and to their right hung the 150-pound engine block, where it had been for four decades.

Hayden Kennedy leads the headwall on natural protection while ignoring
a row of Maestri's controversial bolts to his right. Photo: Jason Kruk

Suddenly, Kennedy let out a wild series of hoots; he'd topped out the headwall, completing a vision that began before Maestri came along with his compressor. A feat imagined for more than forty years: a fair-means ascent of the gorgeous Southeast Ridge of Cerro Torre. Theirs was a reification of a philosophy of how you climb mountains. In ignoring Maestri's bolt ladders, they had climbed the line in a style that lived up to anybody's standard—the way that, one suspects, it would have been climbed had Maestri not come along with his drilling machine. Together they hiked up the easy summit cone, found a flat spot to set down their gear and unrope, and climbed to the summit with one ice tool each.

They'd left their tent at the Col of Patience, 2,600 vertical feet below, merely thirteen hours before. It was only midafternoon. The weather was perfect. They could see forever across the ice cap to the west and to the timeless plains to the east.

Within the fuzzier realms of climbing's mores, they had earned a sort of exclusive "right" by climbing the controversial line cleanly, by proving what had long been suspected: that Maestri's interminable bolt ladders were unnecessary. Now, it was proven. They spent thirty minutes on the summit, relaxing and talking. An idea came to mind, one that had lurked in the minds of alpinists the world over since Maestri drilled his way up Cerro Torre in 1970.

"We had an opportunity to remove the bolts unlike anyone else previously," Kruk reflected later. "If opportunity presents itself, you must seize it."

AND SO, ON THE WAY DOWN, they seized the moment and cleaned all of Maestri's progression bolts from the headwall, and more below. Kennedy and Kruk made it back to their tent at the col with 120 of Maestri's old bolts on a string in their pack. The next day they returned at a leisurely pace to their bivy camp on the Torre Glacier, where they stayed through unsettled weather. A couple of days later, after a storm left the tips of the spires coated in rime that glowed orange in the sunlight, they loaded their packs and hiked to town. By early evening they finished walking the dusty trail to El Chaltén. Kruk dropped his pack and headed to a nearby phone center, while Kennedy ordered some food, showered, and waited in their rental cabin.

Little did they know that word of their de-bolting the Compressor Route had already made it to town, enraging a group of local climbers —and, soon, plenty more around the globe. By the time Kruk reached the call center, he found himself surrounded by some twenty angry locals. A police car arrived and took Kruk back to the cabin, but the mob grew, shouting and gathering around the pair's house. Then, to the applause of the crowd, the cops hauled Kennedy and Kruk off to jail. While sitting in the police car, one local came to the car and screamed through the window at Kruk, "I will fuck you in the ass like you fucked me in the ass!"

This tiny, relaxed village in beautiful southern Patagonia immediately became the focus of a global climbing controversy widely considered the biggest in the last decade. Because of some old bolts? It seems absurd, except the roots of the story connect to an outsized mythology that began fifty-odd years earlier, fueled by something more than little pieces of metal, and ignited by the power of anger.

Soon afterward, in what could be called prescience, Hayden Kennedy's father told him, "Some will call you and Jason heroes. Others will call you villains. Don't buy into either narrative. Remember one thing: All this noise is someone else's story, not yours."

The removed bolts, back at camp on the Torre Glacier. Photo: Mikey Schaefer

PART TWO

previous spread The Torres, as seen from just below the summit
of Fitz Roy. Photo: Kelly Cordes

above Preparing to cross the Río de Las Vueltas, early in the
1958/59 expedition. Photo: Gianni Dalbagni

PART TWO

chapter 5

1959

In an era known for large, nationalistic sieges of the highest peaks of the Himalaya—the 1950s were called the Golden Age of Mountaineering—a different undercurrent was emerging among the vanguard. The top mountaineers began looking at steeper, more technical mountains and climbing them in lightweight style. Alpine style meant climbing as a small, self-sufficient team, carrying all of their gear with them, starting at the bottom and climbing to the top without employing fixed ropes and pre-stocked camps. It was a sort of enlightenment compared to the military-style campaigns that focused on getting a member to the top by any means necessary. This evolution of climbing style—climbing as more of an art form and less of a conquest—opened alpinists' eyes to beautiful lines on steep peaks and a philosophy in which they relied more on their climbing abilities than on industrial-scale labor.

Granted, on more remote and desperate objectives, fixed ropes were still often used and accepted. With climbing, there's always an interaction between style and difficulty. As climbing skills improved, the definition of a difficult objective and the methods required to climb it—and the willingness to employ by-any-means tactics—shifted. By then it had been shown that with enough equipment and manpower (back then mountaineering was an almost exclusively male endeavor), getting to the top of tall mountains was practically a foregone conclusion.

Around this time, the spires of Patagonia became the talk of top alpinists in Europe. "In the pubs and huts where the best alpinists gathered, the chat took on a special electricity when Patagonia came up," wrote author and climbing historian David Roberts in *Great Exploration Hoaxes*. And nothing in Patagonia—or anywhere—compared to Cerro Torre.

GIVEN THE EVOLUTION of climbing culture at the time, it's no

surprise that Cesare Maestri had turned his attention toward Cerro Torre. A year after his disappointing initial journey, he was back for another round.

On December 21, 1958, Maestri and Toni Egger met the rest of their team in Buenos Aires. They had kept their intentions secret, knowing that Bonatti and Mauri had also planned to return. Bonatti and Mauri had been open about their plans, thinking they might avoid the competition of the previous season. When they discovered that Egger and Maestri were already in Argentina, Bonatti and Mauri cancelled their trip just before their scheduled departure from Italy—likely put off by the competition.

Cesarino Fava was again enthusiastically involved with Maestri's expedition, perhaps enthralled by a sense of purpose and excitement for such a momentous undertaking, particularly one connected to his homeland.

After a week of driving dusty, desolate roads through Argentina's barren scrub-brush deserts, they arrived at the Estancia Fitz Roy and promptly got to work. Four young college students from Buenos Aires accompanied the climbers, serving as porters and base camp support. The team crossed the river and over the next ten days installed three camps: one at Laguna Torre, a second below El Mocho (a stout, stump-like rock tower that branches off the tail of Cerro Torre's southeast ridge), and a snow cave some six hundred feet below the base of Cerro Torre's east wall.

Below its southwest, southeast, and northern aspects, Cerro Torre has high cols—geographic saddles separating the spire from the next formation. The southwestern saddle was reached by

Bonatti and Mauri the previous year on their attempt from the west. The one they optimistically named the Col of Hope.

The saddle to the north is the one Maestri later dubbed the Col of Conquest. Although he hadn't set foot on the mountain the previous year, Maestri's plan remained the same: Climb the lower east face to the Col of Conquest, then take a ninety-degree left turn and climb the sheer north face to the summit. This time, Maestri had nobody holding him back, and he had the Austrian ace Toni Egger as his partner.

After seeing Cerro Torre up close the prior season, the Spider of the Dolomites knew that he needed a great climbing partner. Maestri was a self-proclaimed anarchist who bragged that he had never climbed second on a rope. He always led, if he used a rope at all; but even Maestri wouldn't dare try to solo Cerro Torre. And for all of his prowess on rock, ice climbing—of which there was plenty on Cerro Torre—was a different game for Maestri. Just over the border in Austria lived Toni Egger, rumored to be among the finest ice climbers in the world.

Egger and Maestri knew each other by reputation and had a chance encounter in a mountain hut in the Dolomites. Egger was aware of Maestri's 1958 trip and his planned return, and, though the two fought on different sides of the war, Egger wrote to Maestri: "Dear Cesare, I offer you all my help and hope that I may be able to join you. It's time the Torre was climbed."

TWO THOUSAND vertical feet of mostly rock, and some ice, lead from the base of the wall to the Col of Conquest. The col separates Cerro Torre—its summit still another two thousand feet higher—from an almost equally impressive tower to the north, which would soon bear Egger's name. The col is only some twenty feet wide (east to west) and one hundred feet long. The walls towering thousands of feet above make the col akin to a narrow, uneven, icy walkway perched between skyscrapers dividing different worlds. To the east is a harrowing drop into the Torre Valley, and to the west a nearly vertical plummet into the ice and snow of the Hielo Continental.

Upon arrival at base camp, Egger suffered a foot injury that became infected, forcing him to sit out the initial weeks. During

this time Maestri charged ahead, leading all of the pitches with
Fava following in support. Over an eleven-day period, they spent
four days climbing and fixing ropes toward the Col of Conquest,
getting almost a thousand feet up. They left a cache of gear just
below a small, prominent landmark then and still known as the
"triangular snowfield."

The terrain, though some of the more moderate of the route, was
still extremely hard. "Below me are 300 meters of difficult climbing,
another obstacle that we have surpassed, but at this point I am
completely exhausted.... I have continuous cramps in my arms, and
my hands are totally trashed...." A worn-down Maestri fell ill for
several days.

Fava later praised Maestri's prowess: "From the way he climbs
it looks relatively easy, he goes up about 150 meters, then tells me
to follow him. I cling to the twelve millimeter hemp rope which will
remain fixed to the wall, do a pendulum swing to get myself over to
a point beneath the vertical, and start. From the way I climb, belayed
to Cesare, I am made fully aware of his extraordinary ability."

Back at base camp, atrocious weather ravaged the massif. For
weeks they waited and talked about home, climbing, women, the
war. When the storm finally broke, a layer of rime ice plastered the
mountains. By now, with the help of a course of antibiotics, Egger's
foot had healed and they eagerly returned to their snow cave below
the route.

On their march up the Torre Glacier, infused with optimism
after the prolonged lag in base camp, they studied the northern
aspect. The upper face, substantially steeper and more technical
than anything yet climbed in the mountains anywhere in the world
(it averages close to eighty degrees for well over a thousand feet
before continuing into enormous, overhanging summit mushrooms),
was cloaked in a layer of ice. Egger was an "artist" on ice—as
Maestri would later praise him—and the sheet of ice was like a gift
from the storm.

Along the approach to the snow cave, they discussed strategy.
From the end of their fixed ropes another three thousand vertical
feet of climbing remained to the summit. Maestri, given his relative
lack of ice climbing experience, wanted to fix more ropes above

Toni Egger (left) and Cesarino Fava (white shirt), on the truck heading south, at the start of the ill-fated 1958–59 expedition. To the right are Angelo Vincitorio, Augusto Dalbagni, and Juan Pedro Spikermann, the young college students who eagerly assisted the expedition. Photo: Gianni Dalbagni

the triangular snowfield, to hedge the odds further in their favor. Egger disagreed.

According to Fava: "Toni thought the best technique would be that already used on Jirishanca; to go up with everything we needed and be independent for five or six days. He said it would be quicker and less tiring." Fava must have been referring to the final day of Egger and Siegfried Jungmeir's impressive first ascent of Jirishanca, a remote 19,993-foot mountain in Peru's Cordillera Huayhuash, made less than two years earlier. The pair, along with three other climbers, fixed ropes for three weeks from the peak's shorter northern side to a point high on the mountain's east ridge, and then, from atop their fixed ropes, made a one-day dash to the summit and back. The ascent received much deserved praise and was a testament to Egger's boldness and skill. But on Jirishanca their fixed ropes went high enough that their final dash was only six pitches to the summit.

In the snow cave they packed their gear for the climb. Fava said he asked Egger what he thought. "Look, Cesarino, I don't think it's harder than Jirishanca," came the reply, but without arrogance.

Egger's insistence and confidence prevailed. To climb steep and difficult terrain with five or six days worth of supplies on your back is difficult even with today's ultralight equipment, much less the gear of 1959. Their packs weighed well over fifty pounds each. But they were strong, young, and keen. On January 28, 1959, they left their snow cave and began ascending the fixed ropes.

At one point Egger left the rope and traversed onto the ice— he was known for his boldness. Fava asked Egger what he was doing. Egger replied that he wanted to see, and to feel, if it would hold him—he was testing the surface with a mind toward the much more difficult terrain looming thousands of feet overhead. Maestri cracked, "Actually, I want to know what happens if that snow doesn't hold you." Egger climbed over and tied back in.

Above the triangular snowfield and their previously fixed lines, Egger and Maestri led while Fava followed behind, faithfully carrying supplies to support his more skilled friends.

By the time they'd made it to the Col of Conquest, it had become apparent to Fava, who lacked the technical prowess of Egger and Maestri, that he could be of no further use. Perhaps his feet were

holding him back—he'd had all of his toes amputated as a result
of a heroic attempt to rescue a stranded American climber high
on Aconcagua in 1953. Late in the day he began his descent, alone,
back to the snow cave. This was before speedy and efficient
mechanical ascenders were *de rigueur* for ascending fixed lines—the
prevailing method was to prusik, and sometimes even hand-over-
hand the rope. Fava had lugged the heaviest pack all the way to the
col in this manner. This was also before rappel devices. Fava would
descend by using, presumably, the Dulfersitz method (a way of
wrapping the rope around your body to descend).

All considered, Fava made truly phenomenal time—no modern
climber even reached the col in a day until 1999. "I arrived at the
glacier at dark, as the highest point of Fitz Roy was still glowing
with the last rays of sun," he wrote. Likewise, it's a testament to
Egger's contribution to the partnership that, after Maestri and Fava
took four days to fix ropes up the initial thousand feet to the triangular snowfield, the team raced up the remaining thousand feet to
the col in less than a day.

The next five days rank among the most mythical in climbing history. Cesare Maestri, for the first time ever, relinquished most of the
leading. A delicate crust of ice, thirty centimeters to one meter
thick, coated the face. They were loaded down, anticipating difficult
climbing. "We take a 200-meter rope, which we use doubled, ten
étriers, thirty pitons, one hundred bolts, thirty ice-screws, wooden
wedges, thirty meters of cord, food for three or four days, and all
the bivouacking equipment. The packs are very heavy, weighing
some twenty-five kilograms [fifty-five pounds]," Maestri wrote.

As the sun rose over the pampas and with clear skies out to the
ice cap, Egger took the sharp end, making masterful use of his
long wooden ice ax and piton hammer, climbing brilliantly and boldly.
"At each step, the whole crust made a dull noise like a low whistle,
it cracked and broke and large pieces fell off," Maestri described.
"The ice pegs [pitons] went in like butter and gave us only an illusion
of security. At each pitch we made a small platform, so that we
could dig through to the rock, where we found not the slightest
trace of a crack; so we had to drill holes for expansion bolts, and
each hole needed five hundred hammer blows."

But Egger floated up the face, which Maestri said was "not as steep as you might expect"—averaging "about forty-five to fifty degrees, I suppose."

High on the face, after a big day of climbing, they found a small ledge to sit through the night and wait for daylight. They dozed between shivers and sleep.

Their speed, due largely to Egger's expertise, was phenomenal. That day, Maestri says, they placed thirty bolts. All told he said they placed approximately seventy bolts, sixty of them above the col. Most, if not all, were placed as belay and rappel anchors. He reported that each bolt took thirty-five to forty minutes to drill, which adds up to between seventeen and twenty hours of drilling. Because each anchor would have to be drilled before the second could safely follow, there was little time left for climbing and virtually none for sleep. "For Toni Egger, Cerro Torre was nothing—a Sunday stroll." Maestri said.

Indeed, to cover a thousand feet of climbing could happen quickly with the right climber and the right conditions. "From the technical point of view," Maestri later recalled, "it was one of the easiest climbs of my life. It was certainly the most dangerous, and the only deadly one, but technically it was just a race, a race over a snow sheet."

Come morning on their third day they climbed into the wild formations speckled high on the face, formations so amazing they seemed plucked from a fantasy. Egger sometimes burrowed into the rime, digging tunnels with his long ax. Maestri reported that Egger placed only twenty pitons while climbing eight hundred feet of terrain, which Maestri reported as a "variable slope between fifty and sixty degrees."

It had to be a once-in-a-millennium performance, one of those unequaled moments that become legendary in every pursuit.

On the huge, mushroomed shelf atop the north face, only a few hundred feet below the summit, they stopped for their third bivouac. On their fourth morning the weather began to shift; their urgency escalated. Egger led a two-hundred-foot wall of vertical ice, where Maestri reported that Egger placed pitons, despite the incredibly thick walls of rime known to exist in these sections. The process must have been desperate: climbing vertical rime with a long,

Toni Egger, one of the finest alpinists of his era, atop Peru's Jirishanca on its first ascent in 1957. Photo: Alpenraute—Lienz, Austria straight-picked bamboo ax, and digging through until hitting rock, then hammering in pitons.

But Egger persevered in the lead and Maestri followed through the tremendous gargoyles of the upper ridge, the opaque curtain of clouds opening and closing, shifting the view of where they were and how far they had to go to the top. The wind changed to a hot foehn, signaling the incoming storm, building to an unrelenting violence. They climbed faster, as fast as they could, and Egger caught a glimpse through the clouds and paused to scream back to Maestri: "La cima!"

"The summit was completely surrounded by cornices which threatened to break off at any moment. I climbed down over them without the least bit of emotion and without the slightest trace of disgust or fear," Maestri said.

Finally, exhausted and strained, on January 31, 1959, they stood on Cerro Torre's impossible summit, snapped some photos and left a tin with a note, surely knowing that the wind would soon whisk it away. Maestri later wrote of a sentiment known to many climbers, a sort of emptiness that comes with achieving a long-sought goal: "It seems impossible. I'm not happy, this is a top like the others. How much effort, how much risk, many factors unrelated to climbing gave me the strength to climb. No! I'm not happy."

The wind escalated, the sky obscured in constantly shifting hues of gray from the clouds, wind smashing them with pellets of rime as they rappelled back to their bivy from the night before.

"The wind continues. It seems that above us continuously runs a train. Small avalanches begin to fall from the top. The night goes bad: We knew we could expect more below."

On their fifth morning they continued rappelling from bollards carved into the rime. Horrifying rappels given that on the ascent the rime was too fragile to trust for anchors—the reason they drilled bolts. But desperation grew with the raging tempest. Nobody knows why they didn't return to the same anchors they bolted on their ascent. But in a full-blown storm you can't always see the place that you just passed—it might be virtually invisible minutes later. The lower they got, and the closer to safety, the ice sheet had melted away, revealing only smooth rock slabs. No cracks for pitons. "We had to abseil down and hang on the end of the rope, while we drilled a hole for an expansion bolt for the next abseil," Maestri recalled. "Finally, we bivouacked under a small mushroom, tied to expansion bolts."

They shivered through the night, speaking little as they listened to the rumbles of avalanches, small at first, increasingly tumbling and exploding off Cerro Torre and the surrounding peaks. The warm wind of the freak storm melted the mushrooms, dissolved the ice, and added its own snow to the heights: more fuel for the terrifying avalanches roaring down the walls. They huddled close for warmth through the long night, listening to the howling wind and the horrible thunder of the avalanches. In the darkness, Egger muttered to Maestri, "I hope we don't die a white death."

After another sleepless night they rose. They continued rappelling pitch after pitch toward the triangular snowfield and the security of their fixed lines. The day crept along in a blur. Later, as the sun dropped low, only a couple hundred feet above their fixed ropes they decided to stop at a tiny ledge covered with snow. It would be a grim bivy, but it would have to do. Then Egger thought he saw a better place just below. Maestri began to lower him.

The sound came first, rumbling from the clouds far above "with a whistle of death," and then a horrible, massive wall of white raced down the walls.

Maestri screamed a terrified warning, "Toni, look!" The white wave roared past as Maestri flattened himself against the wall for protection, saved by a tiny overhang. Moments took on endless dimensions as the avalanche exploded down the flanks below, rumbling onto the glacier and echoing throughout the cirque. Maestri faithfully kept his hands on the belay rope, holding Egger. "Then everything stops," he said. "I feel only the howl of the wind, while the rope recoiled without weight."

Ice climbing on Cerro Torre. Photo: Kelly Cordes

chapter 6

AFTERMATH 1959

It was time to go. Cesarino Fava left the snow cave on the upper Torre Glacier for the last time. Egger and Maestri had been gone for too long. Fava looked up into the clouds enshrouding the Torre one last time and began the somber walk down to base camp.

Maestri had endured a hellish night, distraught and alone on the tiny ledge where he had been lowering Egger when the avalanche roared down. Come morning, using the remnants of the rope, he continued down. Finally, he gained the security of their fixed lines. Somewhere near the bottom, in per-haps a moment of inattention from fatigue and stress, he slipped off the ropes and fell. Miraculously, he didn't hit any rock ledges and landed in deep snow at the base of Cerro Torre. When the clouds parted for a moment, Fava saw the dark object in the snow and climbed up to drag Maestri down the glacier. Afterward, he hurried back to camp for help.

One of the four young students from Buenos Aires who had come on the trip to support the climbers was Juan Pedro

Spikermann. He turned eighteen at Laguna Torre and was seventy-three years old when I met with him in Buenos Aires. He recalled the trip with great joy, but he also remembered when Fava came to get their help, and how destroyed Maestri looked, foam coming from his mouth, able only to mumble, his hands and wrists swollen. Fava and Maestri spoke to each other in a Trentino-specific dialect that Juan Pedro and the others didn't understand, but Fava passed along whatever they needed to know. After caring for Maestri, the next day they searched for Toni Egger's body, but they couldn't find it in the raging storm. They had no choice but to leave him to the glacier.

While the climbing world mourned the loss of Egger, the ascent also garnered immediate acclaim. None other than Lionel Terray, the Frenchman who made the first ascent of Fitz Roy, said: "The ascent of Cerro Torre, the more difficult neighbor of Fitz Roy, by Toni Egger and Cesare Maestri, seems to me the greatest mountaineering feat of all time."

It was so far ahead of the standards that, despite the dearth of ascents in Patagonia back then, an editor's note in the *American Alpine Journal* read: "Our correspondent, Sr. Vojslav Arko, points out that with this ascent the Golden Age of Patagonian mountaineering has ended."

History would validate its futuristic nature; it would take forty-seven years, with countless attempts from the best climbers of each ensuing era, before another party would climb Cerro Torre from the north.

When the twenty-nine-year-old Maestri stepped off the airplane in Rome, traumatized and weary, a crowd greeted him: fans, family, photographers, and reporters. Back home, up north in the mountains of Trentino, presentations and meetings were held in Maestri's honor. He was praised in the streets and in the press, hailed by his peers, interviewed on television. He accepted lucrative book offers and received a medal for bravery. The man already renowned as the Spider of the Dolomites was embraced as a true hero.

"One thing for sure, Cerro Torre made Maestri. It elevated him to a much greater standing and produced much greater financial rewards," said the venerable Lindsay Griffin when he was an editor at the British magazine *Climb*.

Italian journalist Giorgio Spreafico, in his latest book about the Torre, *Cerro Torre—La Sfida* (Cerro Torre—The Challenge, 2013), describes the fanfare, including the official reception for Maestri in the provincial capital of Trento, which included the mayor, city officials, and mountaineering dignitaries:

"When it's his turn to take the floor to respond in the warmth of his surroundings, Cesare Maestri opens his heart: 'Cerro Torre has not given me the joy I thought when I first set foot on its summit. The only joy is to be here among you and receive your affection, which is greater than I had known. This is my joy, and it helps to ease the pain of the loss of Toni.'"

IN QUIET CORNERS OF THE CLIMBING WORLD, some

surely whispered doubts. There were reasons to question the fantastic ascent. But back then you always took a climber at his word. In few other endeavors is trust as deeply ingrained in the fundamental essence of the activity as with climbing mountains. You and your partner are tied together, trusting your lives to one another in pursuit of an overtly meaningless prize. It implies a code of honor, an unending loyalty to one another, a morality of the mountains and of men embodied in the enduring phrase, "The brotherhood of the rope."

With Egger's death—he had been carrying the camera that contained the summit photos when that terrible whistle of death swept him away—taking Maestri at his word became that much more intriguing.

1968

The southeast ridge of Cerro Torre, showing the 1968 high point
and Maestri's Compressor Route (dots for hidden portions).
Photo: Rolando Garibotti

chapter 7

DOUBT, RAGE, AND A GAS-POWERED COMPRESSOR

"I return and attack their routes, the routes they were not able to climb. I will humiliate them, and they will feel ashamed of having doubted me," Cesare Maestri said about his return to Patagonia in 1970. On his previous trip, eleven years earlier, he claimed the first ascent of Cerro Torre via the north face. This time, he would attempt a different aspect: the southeast ridge. And he would bring not only his fierce attitude and his incredible determination— but, as climbing equipment, an internal combustion engine. To further prove his point, he went in winter.

In 1970, the general public still believed Maestri's 1959 story, and most climbers did as well. Evidence against his claim had yet to emerge, so people took him at his word. The doubts expressed by climbers who had been in Patagonia, however, surely stung the worst. These were his peers, those who had stood below the magnificent tower and who knew firsthand of its unfathomable difficulties. At any rate, the ultimate tipping point for one of the most controversial climbing routes in history, the Compressor Route, arrived by way of a telegram.

THE SOUTHEAST RIDGE OF CERRO TORRE looks like

a flying buttress between the massive south and east faces. The farther the line drops from the summit, the more it emerges into a spine protruding between the adjacent faces, lessening in steepness the lower it goes until reaching a narrow col, a skywalk of snow and ice. From afar, its shape resembles a hockey stick. On the south side of the col, a hanging glacier calves tons of ice down dead-vertical walls for nearly two thousand feet. The most logical way to gain the col is from the northeast, weaving through the crevassed upper Torre Glacier, passing beneath the towering east face and then climbing two thousand feet of moderately difficult mixed snow, ice, and rock. From the col, the ridge proper begins its ever-steepening, 2,600-vertical-foot rise to the top of Cerro Torre.

The first—and only previous—attempt on the southeast ridge came in early 1968 from the strong Anglo-Argentine team of José Luis Fonrouge (Argentina) and Brits Martin Boysen, Mick Burke, Pete Crew, and Dougal Haston (reporter Peter Gillman was also on the trip). In the face of the vicious storms and obviously hard climbing, the team fixed ropes as they went. At the col, which they named the Col of Patience, they dug a snow cave and stocked supplies for their attempt on the serious difficulties above. Over the course of several days of climbing spread between storms, they came upon an impasse two-thirds of the way up the ridge. The climbing had been hard, requiring much aid, but on terrific, highly featured rock that readily accepted natural protection. They hadn't needed to place a single bolt.

Dougal Haston leading on the 1968 Anglo-Argentine attempt at the southeast ridge. They retreated at two-thirds height, without placing any bolts. In 1970, by the same approximate height, Maestri had drilled nearly two hundred bolts. Photo: Mick Burke

At that point, the difficulties increased substantially, and their pace slowed. They aided up a razor-thin seam and continued with a mix of aid and free climbing. Haston wrote: "Dainty tiptoeing on sky-hooks with no retreat as the wind blew the unused one off the rock. One such move with the bolt kit fleeing from my pocket into the ever-open crevasses 3,000 feet below. Day's end. Down. Up on the morrow with Martin, Mick and I summit-bound. Onward with a hard pitch by Martin and then a blank section with no bolts and the rock needing bolts."

The blank section was a sixty-foot slab rising above, absent even the smallest cracks for natural protection. The team hadn't placed a single bolt to this point, but they needed them now. Just a couple of protection bolts would make the pitch reasonable. Climbers, even the traditionally bolt-averse Brits, had long accepted sparing use of bolts when natural protection wasn't possible, partic-ularly in order to connect short sections of climbable features. But Haston had accidentally dropped the bolt kit. Boysen and Haston tried for seven hours to climb the section without protection, but it was too dangerous. Burke sat perched at the belay, clouds racing overhead, singing songs with refrains about "the man who dropped the bolts on Cerro Torre."

A thousand vertical feet of desperately steep climbing remained above. They retreated, and a storm arrived that lasted for what seemed an eternity.

The '68 team had included some of the world's best alpinists, and when they returned from their prolonged effort at what was clearly an easier line than the one Maestri claimed in 1959, they expressed doubt about Egger and Maestri's three-and-a-half-day dash to the summit.

What wounded Maestri's pride more than doubts cast by Brits and an Argentine, however, was a comment made in early 1970 by fellow Italian and rival Carlo Mauri.

CARLO MAURI had an extraordinary sense of daring and adven-ture. In 1956, he made the first ascent of the remote and stormy Monte Sarmiento, a mountain that, at least when visible, had prompted Charles Darwin to call it "the most sublime spectacle in Tierra del Fuego." In 1958, Mauri and Walter Bonatti made the groundbreaking first ascent of Pakistan's 26,001-foot Gasherbrum IV, considered the hardest Himalayan climb to date. Later in his life, Mauri would retrace Marco Polo's route in Asia and explore the Amazon. In 1969 and 1970, he was part of the famous Norwegian explorer Thor Heyerdahl's attempts to sail across the Atlantic Ocean in a replica of ancient Egyptian vessels made of papyrus reed.

Mauri and Bonatti made their failed attempt on Cerro Torre's west face in early 1958, just as Maestri was making his initial foray on the opposite side of the mountain. In 1970, after twelve years, Mauri was back, again trying the rime-mushroomed west face. Early on, he found himself feeling a sentiment familiar to alpine climbers on hostile objectives: "Sitting on the Col of Hope and munching dried prunes, I let my eye roam down to the space between me and the pampas and wondered what force it was that drove me away from the world of men to such a God-forsaken spot. The Col of Hope seemed a funny name at that moment."

Come late January, after fixing ropes and preparing the route, his team launched a final attempt. About six hundred feet below the summit, the climbing appeared impossible. Then the weather broke bad, sending them hurrying down their ropes to their tent perched atop an office-building-sized rime ice formation they called El Elmo (The Helmet).

"Towards evening the wind started to rise, and before the night was old it had reached its usual pitch of fury. We were soaked to the skin and frozen inside our tent, and the noise was such that it was impossible even to think clearly, let alone hold a conversation," Mauri reported. All five of them huddled inside, but as the walls seemed ready to tear apart, they remembered a natural snow cave they'd seen off to one side. "The cave was already deep in snow and the risk of being buried alive was real enough, but we preferred even that to being flogged to death by the wind."

The following day, they emerged from the cave to find little sign of their tent, and descended through the storm, a "nightmare," as Mauri put it. "The wind threatened to carry us bodily off the mountain, while the stinging ice particles pelted us pitilessly and blinded us every time we opened our eyes."

top Remnants of Maestri's work. Photo: Rolando Garibotti

bottom Maestri's compressor, bolted to the headwall. Photo: Ermanno Salvaterra

One of Mauri's team members, Casimiro Ferrari—who would later make history on Cerro Torre—recalled the moment of their retreat: "I take one last look at the west wall shrouded in clouds and at that time I feel that I will not have peace until I can deal with it again. Because Cerro Torre is a mountain you'll never forget."

In Buenos Aires on their way home, Mauri sent what, in Cerro Torre terms, could be considered the telegram heard 'round the world. When published in one of Italy's biggest newspapers, *Corrière*, the message carried a pointed implication: "We return safe and sound from the impossible Cerro Torre."

ONLY A FEW MONTHS AFTER MAURI'S TELEGRAM,

in May 1970, the proud Cesare Maestri returned to Patagonia. These words, which he boasted later that year, reveal insight to his motives: "Impossible mountains do not exist, but only mountaineers who are not able to climb them."

That might depend on how you define "climb."

For his trip, Maestri had secured major sponsorship from an industrial equipment company, Atlas Copco. Their support paid for the trip—and came with a 150-pound gas-powered air compressor. When Maestri visited the headquarters in Milan, according to rumor, the company manager handed Maestri the drilling gun—with the hoses going to the compressor hidden behind a curtain—and let him drill a hole in the granite floor. It went in like butter. They handed him a check and then lifted the curtain. The compressor would allow him to place bolts quickly and easily, notwithstanding the laborious issue of hauling it up the mountain. Including fuel, tubes, winches, and various equipment for hauling, Maestri reported that the kit weighed nearly four hundred pounds.

The bolts were "pressure bolts," sometimes called "pressure pitons" or, in Argentine-Italian climber slang, "nails." The climber drilled a small hole into which a round metal stud was pounded, with a hanger on the outer eye of the stud for clipping. The compressor essentially allowed Maestri to drill a bolt anyplace, anywhere, any-time—so long as there was available rock. He could ascend any rock by simply drilling bolts close enough to use them as ladders.

Maestri's initial plan was to take the compressor to Torre Egger. But then, after Mauri's thinly veiled doubts about 1959 were publicly broadcasted across Italy, it seems Maestri snapped. He would return to Cerro Torre again, but not to the west face, where Mauri had failed. The compressor wouldn't work in rime. Instead, he would attack the line where the 1968 Anglo-Argentine team, who had also expressed doubts, had failed: the southeast ridge.

Maestri's fellow Italians Ezio Alimonta and Carlo Claus would help him on the wall, along with a support crew that included Renato Valentini, Pietro Vidi, and his reliable expat ally Cesarino Fava. The team and their gear—including a wooden hut—were delivered by helicopter to the Torre Glacier. They got to work on the southeast ridge.

They spent fifty-four days working on the route, enduring the Patagonian winter. Fava told American climber Charlie Fowler that they were consecutive days (Maestri's text in a 1971 *Mountain* magazine says the same); but other reports, including another of Maestri's, said that they regularly returned down their fixed ropes to the hut when bad weather came or they needed a break.

They battled the storms and the cold and the snow (Maestri reported that sixty feet of snow fell during their expedition), reaching a point 1,600 feet above the Col of Patience. It was here that Maestri began jackhammering bolts into the flanks of Cerro Torre in a manner that nearly defies description. In the climbing below, he added only scattered bolts, mostly around belay stances, as if he were testing the machinery.

Then he reached the difficult section the 1968 team described. Not surprisingly, rime covered the thin crack that they'd climbed—dealing with variable conditions is inherent in alpine climbing. But, armed with the compressor, there was no need to contend with such difficulties. Maestri fired up the compressor and drilled a hundred bolts to the right, across blank rock. To see it today makes you wonder about the switch that seemingly tripped in his mind. The rising line of bolts became known as the "ninety-meter bolt traverse."

"Cesare, stop!" Fava shouted high on the wall. But Maestri would not relent.

Fava considered the compressor a hassle, a burdensome hunk of metal, hoses, gasoline, and smoke. He seemed to further consider it an ethical breach; but those views collided with his allegiance to Maestri.

In his 1999 autobiography, *Patagonia: Terra dei Sogni Infranti* (Patagonia: Land of Broken Dreams), with a preface by Cesare Maestri, Fava disapproved of facing a mountain "as if it were a trench to conquer." He alluded to the sieges on Mount Everest, imploring for restraint: "Excess technology enriches a few and destroys every-thing: the moral and spiritual values, ideals that are the essence, the very basis, of alpinism. And the lack of these values allows the climber, or pseudo climber, the indiscriminate use of artificial means. This way of going to the mountains trivializes any ascension."

Yet in his next paragraph, he backpedaled: "But this is not the case of the compressor, which has not facilitated the ascent, but it has created major problems whose solution required great sacri-fices and risks, and an enormous amount of energy."

Fava wrote that he repeatedly suggested that Maestri throw the heavy equipment in a crevasse and climb in a less cumbersome manner. Maestri would have none of it—Atlas Copco had paid for the trip. "I have made commitments and I don't intend to betray them for any reason," Maestri would reply.

After the monumental bolt traverse, a thousand feet below the summit, they retreated. The winter attempt was over, but Maestri's determination was not. He waited until summer, and, in December 1970 (often mistakenly reported as 1971), Maestri returned.

This time, Fava declined. Maestri recruited another support crew, while Alimonta and Claus were still game to accompany him on the wall. They returned up the fixed ropes, replaced the motor on the compressor, and planned their final assault.

The remoteness remained remarkable, the immaculate mountain a symbol of such beauty that it drew them like it did the time before, and the time before that. Maestri's tenacity didn't blind him to moments of appreciation. In this brief passage, he describes waking from a bivy: "The day breaks forth in all its beauty, sweep-ing away the ghosts of fear of the night."

IL GIORNALE DI CAMPIGLIO   dicembre 1970

IL TRIONFO DI MAESTRI SUL CERRO TORRE

ped. Campiglio 70 - Il Vittoria del Cerro Torre - Montagna dell'impossib

A newspaper clipping of Maestri's heroic welcome after the Compressor Route, 1970.
Courtesy of Giorgio Spreafico

A curious mix of anger, awe for the natural landscape, and unrelenting drive seemed to do battle within Cesare Maestri. On the headwall, it's as if Maestri was utterly uninterested in actually climbing the rock. Though desperately steep and serious climbing (especially for the time), there were cracks and flakes off to the sides of his direct line most of the way, providing possibilities for both climbing and natural protection. He said they had mistakenly left their pitons at a camp down below, so he had no choice but to drill.

Nobody knows exactly what drove Maestri, whether it was commitment to his corporate sponsor or something deeper. Regardless, he drilled a plumb line of more than a hundred bolts up the final headwall, spaced so closely that he never had to use his hands or feet to climb the actual rock. Clip the étrier ladder to the bolt, step up, clip the next. By the time he was finished, he'd placed somewhere around four hundred bolts.

Atop the headwall, ice slopes angled back toward the steep summit mushroom.

"I place the last 'pressure bolts' and I attack the ice securing myself with very long pitons manufactured by ourselves," Maestri wrote, adding that the weather kicked up, with snow and wind. "I have inside me the terror that everything will happen like many years ago. Then, at that time, the tragedy started in the same way. I carry on going up. Now the slope is less steep, but I place anyway my long pitons. The rope finishes. I look around. This is the summit."

The storm rose as Maestri began descending. "[A] devilish plan comes into my mind: I'll take out all the bolts and leave the climb as clean as we found it. I'll break them all, so that whoever tries to repeat our route won't even be able to benefit from the holes we've drilled." On rappel, Maestri began chopping his bolts; he disabled the compressor, and "toss[ed] down the face anything that might be helpful to others: pitons, carabiners, ropes." (The pitons that he said they forgot, hence the drilling.)

Maestri once explained what drove him to dedicate his life to climbing: "I wished to use climbing as a way of imposing my personality." With this ascent, he no doubt succeeded.

Alimonta and Claus screamed at Maestri—the wind howled, clouds raced overhead, and snow fell, semaphores of the impending storm—they would leave him if he didn't stop this madness.

Maestri relented. The compressor remained bolted to the wall nearly a mile up Cerro Torre, where it hangs to this day. In the ceaseless wind they began their descent to the Torre Glacier, from where they trudged to the security of the beech forests and then the rolling hills and across the river to the road, and to Buenos Aires and, eventually, back to the motherland of Italy.

When he got off the plane in Milan to a crowd of waiting supporters, he made a statement that he would repeat multiple times throughout the years, in multiple variations: "Impossible mountains do not exist, but only mountaineers who are not able to climb them."

His return to his hometown in the Trentino province was the stuff of legends. He was the only man alive to have climbed the impossible Cerro Torre, not only once but twice. The marching band and parade were dazzling as he and his companions rode in a jeep convoy between fire engines and a sea of waving flags. Cesare Maestri, Il Ragno delle Dolomiti, hero of Cerro Torre.

Working toward Cerro Torre's upper reaches on the first ascent
of the Ragni Route. Photo: Mario Conti

chapter 8
RAGNI DI LECCO

"The summit of the mountain looked like a giant cone which had been overfilled with ice cream and then pressed downwards, so that the ice cream spilled out further and further over the edges: but in the process of spilling, it had been frozen into immobility. As the west wind added more and more ice to the structure, it began to twist under the strain and distort itself into a crazy, upside-down labyrinth of ice, until gravity took over and blocks of ice the size of houses crashed down the smooth granite walls below." That's how Carlo Mauri described the view toward the summit from high on Cerro Torre's west face in 1970.

One of Mauri's team members, a young Lecco climber named Casimiro Ferrari, couldn't get Cerro Torre out of his mind. Come 1974, when Ferrari was selected to lead twelve Ragni di Lecco—the Lecco Spiders, the famed and exclusive branch of the Italian Alpine Club—on an elite ascent to commemorate the club's hundredth anniversary, his choice of a mountain was easy.

In the first paragraph of his feature story in the September 1974 issue of *Mountain* magazine, Ferrari wrote: "In our case the overriding reason for going to Cerro Torre was the desire to re-establish the name of our group, the Lecco Spiders, by carrying out an expedition of note.... Mountaineering in Lecco had for too long been in the doldrums and was badly in need of a new stimulus."

Ferrari set his sights on the west face, where he had been on the 1970 attempt with Mauri. He chose a strong young climber named Mario Conti to be his lead partner. Those two would lead all of the technical terrain, and the remaining climbers would assist by ferrying supplies up fixed ropes.

The impetus to represent Lecco, and the terrific public backing they enjoyed, borne of local pride both before and after their trip, offers a glimpse into the Italian climbing culture of the time. In Argentina, the émigré community supported them as well.

Ferrari seemed to intentionally avoid any public polemic surrounding Maestri's adventures on Cerro Torre, though he did mention both the 1959 claim and the 1970 Compressor Route (if not by name) in his book. He handled them diplomatically, adhering to the romantic ideal that climbers should always be taken at their word. "I think that getting into these controversies is not in the spirit of the mountaineer: To question what one says is to question all mountaineering history."

In reference to what could only be Maestri's compressor, he gently wrote what some in the climbing world had strongly expressed, and what many had felt: "My friends and I remain of the opinion that the use of certain technical tools on the wall diminishes the actual value of an enterprise; it is much greater the more the man uses only traditional methods."

FERRARI AND HIS TEAM of Ragni left Italy on November 17, 1973. In Argentina they drove dirt roads, forded rivers, transported gear on horses and on their backs up the Río Túnel valley, around Laguna Toro, and over Paso del Viento. Then they walked thirty miles, sometimes with huge packs, and, upon reaching the glacier, dragged sledges on the ice cap.

Finally, more than a month after leaving home they were established on the glacier, a world of ice and rock. And wind. Some days they could barely leave the tent for fear of being carried away.

"Still, there came a day when Cerro Torre was outlined like crystal against a clear sky, so near it seemed we could reach out and

THE HELMET

COL OF HOPE

The Ragni di Lecco Route. (Dots represent hidden portions.) Photo: Simone Moro

touch it," Ferrari described. "We could hardly believe the sight of its white walls reaching up to a sky of a blueness such as we had never seen in Italy. It sent a shock through us, and we could feel enthusiasm flowing into our veins. A stupendous vision and an unforgettable sensation."

On December 24, they began working the route to the Col of Hope, two thousand vertical feet below the summit, with all available team members helping.

Above the Col, some six hundred feet of moderate ice leads to a series of rime and snow towers stacked side by side, their tops projecting outward in a series of otherworldly formations. Aided by Ferrari's experience in 1970, the team wove through the maze, finding the line of least resistance. The climbing still included time-consuming

Ascending fixed lines on the first ascent of the Ragni Route.
Photo: Mario Conti

pitches of insecure vertical rime and snow.

With rime, which usually has the consistency of aerated sugar, your axes slide right through; you wonder how the hell something so friable can form so steeply. You plunge the shafts of your tools into the wall, horizontally above your head. If they don't hold, you plunge your arms straight in to your armpits and kick your entire foot into the slope—which makes the vertical wall feel overhanging. In a futile fight you hump your body into the wholly unconsolidated snow, dig, curse, and thrash, and all the while your protection is worthless.

In some places on the west face, seemingly based on nothing more than the whims of the wind, a slight turn, or a different slope angle, you find consolidated, protectable ice to climb. Not often enough, though.

The team fixed ropes and ladders along the way, frequently retreating back to base camp when the storms rolled in across the ice cap from the Pacific. By evening on December 26, their third day of hard work, they pitched a tent inside a hollowed-out area atop the distinctive feature called the Helmet.

They waited. "As the wind began to pound us again, we soon came to realize that merely to resist for any length of time would require new moral fiber and reserves of strength." When supplies ran low, hunger took over. In the interest of rations, they made the difficult decision for all but four to descend. This would be their summit team.

On January 6 the four caught a brief break in the weather and headed up. They climbed beyond the 1970 high point, getting half-way up the ice headwall, below the surreal and mushroom festooned summit ridge. But they were again shut down by a storm, sent back to their snow cave, where shades of gray and darkness were broken only by their flickering candles. Eerie organ pipes played outside, haunting music created by wind racing through the ice chambers of the tower. They stayed in the cave for another week.

January 12 was the last day they could spend at the Helmet. One day's worth of food remained.

"How often has the course of history been changed by a last-minute reversal of fortune?" Ferrari wrote. "Some might speak of miracles, but that is a personal way of viewing things. Be that as it may, when we woke on the 13th there was no mistaking the fact

top Members of the 1974 Ragni di Lecco first ascent team build
a snowman atop Cerro Torre.

bottom Daniele Chiappa on the summit of Cerro Torre.
Photos: Mario Conti

that better weather had come. Not brilliant, but good enough."

They quickly ascended the fixed ropes to their previous high point, but weather moved in just as quickly. It seemed barely manageable and they kept climbing. The overhangs guarding the summit on that side were unlike anything imaginable; hundred-foot masses bulged outward like balloons, improbably held in place. In comparing photos, the summit mushrooms looked bigger back then and devoid of the tunnels of recent years, when clearer and warmer weather seems to have melted away some of the rime, leaving more solid ice.

They spent precious time excavating into a twenty-five-foot protruding mushroom, inching upward into the horrifying rime, hearts in throats.

Back home they had created a special tool for anchors in the precarious medium: a shaft with angled-out fins, rigged in a way that the fins would expand in the rime. Conti had been working in a machine shop and had made twenty of the devices.

They were only a hundred feet below the summit, but another monstrous mushroom blocked their way. Ferrari led two more pitches, traversing to the right, looking, seeking, trying to find a passage.

A groove between the obstructions offered a way. Up they went, climbing, traversing, even descending before going back up again. As clouds and mist drifted between the bulbous towers, at 5:45 p.m. on January 13, 1974, Daniele Chiappa, Mario Conti, Casimiro Ferrari, and Pino Negri emerged on the summit of Cerro Torre. They built a Ragni di Lecco snowman—complete with a club sweater, helmet, ice ax, and flag—snapped photos, and then cut short their celebration in the interest of survival.

The storm was mounting fast, "showing every sign of assuming the unmitigated violence to which we had become accustomed," Ferrari wrote. It took another three days to reach base camp.

The team returned to Lecco triumphant, to celebrations and overwhelming enthusiasm. To this day, in the historical overview section of the Ragni di Lecco website, one passage reflects the pride that the ascent brought to Lecco: "Cerro Torre has almost always been considered a pillar belonging to Grigna and not a distant spire of a distant ocean."

ON A BEAUTIFUL FALL DAY IN 2012, at a cafe below the Grigna Spires, Mario Conti told me about their expedition, as our mutual friend Fabio Palma (also an accomplished Ragni) translated. Conti, the last surviving member of the group's lead climbing team, looked younger than his sixty-eight years. He spoke softly and sparingly, a man of few words with a humble demeanor. He still sport climbs 5.12 and works as a mountain guide and guide instructor. When Ferrari invited Conti to join his team, Conti had never been to Patagonia. He has since returned seventeen times.

"It was a total adventure," he said. Back then, they had no weather forecasts, little infrastructure and no chance of outside assistance. "El Chaltén didn't exist. Patagonia at that time was different from the Patagonia of today." He showed me photos from their expedition: old sweaters and wool mittens, wooden ice axes and strap-on crampons, and climbing through massive bulges of rime. The summit photos show their triumphant, smiling faces beside their snowman, with a backdrop of deteriorating weather.

Toward the end of our conversation, I told Conti that many people consider their climb to be the first ascent of the mountain. Insiders have argued that the Ragni di Lecco team are the real heroes of Cerro Torre and have never received proper credit. I knew he'd heard it before. Surely he's thought it through himself.

"First of all, I was not present in 1959. So I can't judge if they summited or not," he said. "Secondly, if they really managed to do the climb, in my opinion it's one of the greatest climbs in the history of alpinism." I told him that I agreed.

"Third, only the idea of going there in '59 to climb alone, as a team of two, Cerro Torre, only to have the idea is something absolutely fantastic." Again, I agreed.

"Fourth, if he didn't climb the top, for him it must be a nightmare, because his partner died and he has to live with a lie. So I prefer not to enter this private debate, because if he really didn't climb it's a sort of private nightmare, to tell the lie over such an incredible attempt. I prefer not to judge."

"We normally trust in everything said by the alpinist because otherwise... well, it's a matter of trust, yes or no. It's difficult."

I nodded and considered the burden of proof, which remains quite low. A photo isn't even required—many climbs are accepted on

Approaching the Chaltén Massif, late 1973. Photo: Mario Conti

a plausible description of events and terrain. The Compressor Route didn't help Maestri's cause. After all, in 1959 if Maestri climbed a far more difficult route in terrific style, why would he need to return eleven years later to bolt his way up an easier line?

Conti said that he's a friend of Maestri's, but he admitted that in 1970 Maestri trashed the mountain: "He made a big mistake to come back and do that route. He made Cerro Torre accessible to most of the people, and in my opinion 90 percent of the climbers of Cerro Torre couldn't climb the mountain without the bolts."

Once again I agreed, and mentioned that without Maestri's bolt ladders, Cerro Torre was one of the most difficult mountains in the world.

"Now [after the bolt removal by Kennedy and Kruk]," Conti said, "again it is one of the most difficult."

If Conti resents Maestri, he didn't show it. Our conversation wrapped up, and he invited me to lunch with a bunch of his friends, many of them Ragni. Honored, I eagerly accepted.

Before we left, he said, "I know what I did, and that is enough."

Brian Wyvill upon finding Egger's lower leg, rope, and ice ax.
Photo: Ben Campbell-Kelly

chapter 9

BODY OF EVIDENCE

Any doubts surrounding the 1959 ascent were, at first, theoretical. Cerro Torre simply seemed too hard. Too ahead of the standards of the day—astronomically so, considering the style and speed that Maestri reported. But nobody had repeated what Maestri said they'd climbed, and Egger's body had never been found. There were no hard facts, only Maestri's word and Fava's faithful corroboration.

That began to change with two expeditions in the mid-seventies.

IN EARLY NOVEMBER 1974, American climbers John Bragg and Jim Donini were at the end of the road and out of food. They'd gotten to Patagonia the long way. Donini arrived first by a few weeks, traveling with another friend who, after enduring some bad weather, bailed for supposed "girlfriend maintenance."

Bragg was broke, traveling on the cheap, and found Donini when he got there. Bragg had connected with a crazy Brit. "'Tiger' Mick was, without a doubt, one of the funniest humans I have ever met, and he was an amazing ladies' man," Donini recounted. As evidence, joining Tiger Mick Coffey on the journey was his soon-to-be none-too-pleased brand-new girlfriend. The pair met Bragg in New York City, where they'd scored a free ride to Miami delivering an elderly couple's Cadillac to their warm-weather luxury digs. From Miami, they got twenty-five-dollar flights to Bogotá, Colombia. From there they hopped a series of busses to Quito, Lima, Lake Titicaca, somewhere in between that Bragg can't remember, and La Paz. After a couple of train rides, they made it to Buenos Aires, and, finally, Río Gallegos.

After a series of long, sweltering-hot or freezing-cold bus rides, countless shitty hotels, and a month of travel hell, the trip from Río Gallegos was easy: Hitch a ride with the mailman. The mailman headed in twice a month to what we now call El Chaltén. The town was still a decade away, but the post serviced some falling-down army barracks. The three-hundred-mile drive took two days, in part because of the old gravel and dirt roads, in part because the mailman stopped at every estancia. Eventually, Bragg tracked down Donini.

They spent some time in the mountains but soon ran low on food and hiked back out, forded the river, and stood at the end of the road. Cold clouds hung low, shrouding the earth in a ceiling of gray. Wind strafed the grasslands with intermittent drops of rain. Bragg and Donini hitched a ride in the back of a gaucho's truck to the military garrison.

They'd given the mailman a shopping list and paid him to bring a resupply of food. On the appointed day the soldiers were there, but no mailman—or food. So they waited. A week passed, then ten days. Naturally, the weather had cleared, revealing perfect climbing conditions. Their last scraps of food gone, they started walking the dirt road along Lago Viedma, casting occasional, heartbreaking glances back to the spires silhouetted against a cloudless sky. They were heading to Tres Lagos, a small outpost with groceries seventy-five miles away.

"We'd walked fifteen or twenty miles, and all of a sudden we saw a Volkswagen bus—there'd been a lot of snowmelt and for about a hundred-yard section the road had become a swamp. That's why the mailman hadn't come. On the other side of the swamp was this Volkswagen bus with two people." Donini said.

"We were trying to drive around the flood when we saw these two very hairy hitchhikers," recalls Brian Wyvill. "Since we were a very long way from any kind of civilization, we were wondering how safe they were, when one of them (Donini) puts his head in the open window and says: 'Well, well, Brian Wyvill and Ben Campbell-Kelly!'"

They'd met in Yosemite a couple of years before, even climbed a route together, but the two Brits didn't initially recognize Donini. Wyvill and Campbell-Kelly had traveled by boat to Buenos Aires with their Volkswagen Kombi, which they then drove for five days to the end of the road. Their more than nine-thousand-mile journey took them five weeks—and they had plenty of food. Together they spent the rest of the day rigging a makeshift moving bridge to get the bus across the flooded section of road. Under still-clear skies, Bragg and Donini were back at the end of the road, this time with food.

The newly formed team waded the Río Fitz Roy and soon entered the beech forests. Through the woods they reached the Torre Glacier and spent the night in a snow cave beneath the spires. The following day they climbed a few pitches on the then-unclimbed Cerro Standhardt.

Then the typical Patagonian storms came. "Endless storm and wind swept down for three weeks, the snow level crept down to the pampas and we sat frustrated, cold, and eager. Each attempt to return to the valley was rebuffed as the winds charged down and threw us bodily to the ground, and a momentary clearing of the sky showed ice encrusted walls as if lifted from a giant deep-freeze," Campbell-Kelly wrote.

The three weeks stretched into months with only short breaks. In the brief openings between storms and clouds they made recon-noiters and ambitious attempts before retreating to their base camp in the forest. On one of their attempts, on the "sheltered" east wall of Standhardt, they endured ninety mile per hour wind gusts. Back in the trees, life at base camp was more relaxed.

Campbell-Kelly summarized the emotional roller coaster of Patagonia's then-unpredictable weather:

"Unfortunately, good days are so infrequent that one is obliged to keep trying rather than sit and wait for a good spell which might never appear. This soul-destroying attitude resulted in endless marches in and out of the Torre Valley with nothing to show but blisters. One became thankful for a real storm, when we knew that it would be pointless to even try, so that we could sit back and relax. All the stories which are told about the wind are undoubtedly true. It is quite impossible to stand up on the glacier on many occasions, and the awesome clouds of glacier debris thrown up by the wind can be compared to desert storms. On the mountain, climbing becomes impossible, not just because of the force of the wind, but also because of its continual gusting. It is this gusting which destroyed our box tent [an early precursor to the portaledge, but with more steel, weighing fifty pounds], literally hammering it until the frame fractured, and driving water straight through waterproofed material."

On the day after Christmas, Bragg went off to try to solo Poincenot (he didn't get far), while Donini joined the Brits on a foray up-glacier toward Standhardt. "You wouldn't fucking believe what we found!" someone blurted when Bragg returned to camp.

On the glacier below Cerro Torre earlier in the day, they saw a fox, which looked to be feeding on something. As they approached, the fox ran off. "There's a boot!" From the cuff of old leather protruded the lower half of a human leg, mostly bone but with some intact flesh—preserved from nearly sixteen years in the ice.

"There is no doubt that Maestri's story of the avalanche is true since the exposed remains were accompanied by a large quantity of rock which could only have come from either rockfall or a snow and ice avalanche," Campbell-Kelly wrote soon after. "Amongst the remnants was a doubled cable-laid nylon rope—what used to be called No: 2—one end of which was frayed and could have been snapped during the fall."

How could they be sure it was Egger? Well, back then few people ventured to the Torres. It was well known who went and, certainly, who never returned. Furthermore, Doinini reported, "There can be no doubt that it was Toni's body because of its position and the equipment, the boots made in Kitzbühel."

Standing on the glacier with Cerro Torre towering a mile overhead, their awe grew. "We have no doubt that Egger and Maestri could have climbed Cerro Torre, and studying the line they took, we paid respect to two very brave men," Campbell-Kelly continued. "They had done what we were trying to do—a major climb, alpine style. But with a great difference: They had none of our modern equipment. No ice hammers or axes with those ice-biting picks. No drive-in ice screws or chrome-molybdenum pegs. No superb waterproofs, Dacron duvets, or box tents."

Nearby they uncovered some other remnants of Egger's body, pieces of his shredded rucksack, clothing, a piton hammer, a broken ice ax. They scoured a vast area for the team's camera—Maestri claims Egger had it when he perished. Summit photos would irrefutably prove their ascent. Each time the Americans and Brits passed by, on their multiple forays to Standhardt, they searched again but never found it.

The Brits took the ax and hammer home to Europe for identification and got blasted as "grave robbers." As for the rest, "We took his remains, moved them over and buried them under some rocks," Donini remembers. "We got a lot of criticism for that, because Egger was from Catholic Austria and the Austrian press, I guess, was like, 'Why didn't you bring him out for a proper burial?' Anyway, I took a carabiner from the remains and that's where the idea started germinating about climbing Torre Egger."

IN 1974 THE ONLY SIGNIFICANT BODY PARTS found were Egger's right lower leg and foot. Then, in 2003, his left lower leg and foot emerged at the bottom of the upper Torre Glacier. The flesh on his left was perfectly intact, from mid-shin through the foot—naked, no boot. A few other remnants were with it: a small chunk of his spine, a piece of a sweater that matched the one Egger wore, part of a 1959 crampon, and a section of matching rope.

Weird. What about the rest of Toni Egger? Buried under the ice, and only his lower legs and smaller remnants ever came out? Odd,

I suppose, but not impossible. I couldn't help but wonder about the location of the 1974 remains. Where did they emerge? Nobody I talked with seemed certain or able to remember the spot.

I'd been emailing with Campbell-Kelly, and asked if he had any photos from the day they found Egger's remains. He sent me scans of slides that he hadn't looked at in over thirty years. The images were shocking. In one, sticking out from under some old tattered clothes was a rib cage and other bones—it was most of Toni Egger's torso and arms.

They had to have noticed the rib cage then, but memories can fade over the years. "At that time, the body parts were a sad bunch of sodden rags and just confirmation of Egger's death," Campbell-Kelly said. And intrigued as they were by the remains, they'd been focused on their own climbing.

Beyond the torso, Campbell-Kelly's photos revealed something more telling: location. Landmarks in the background of his photos showed that Egger's 1974 remains were found near the junction of

More remains, partially hidden under Egger's sweater, which had been largely forgotten over the years.
Photo: Ben Campbell-Kelly

the upper and main Torre Glacier, near a distinct rock outcrop about 1.1 linear miles from the base of the wall and 2,300 vertical feet lower.

The other leg, the one found in 2003, emerged from the glacier only about 330 feet down-glacier from the 1974 remains.

How could that be? This would mean that over the course of almost sixteen years, from the base of the wall, where Egger died—his body could have tumbled a little ways down—the glacier had moved his body over a mile. Then, in the ensuing twenty-nine years, where his other leg emerged from the ice in 2003, he'd traveled only an additional 330 feet.

Then again, glacier speeds are known to vary dramatically, even at different areas within the same glacier. I learned this when studying rates of glacial flow and talking with some climbing rangers who work in glaciated mountains in different parts of the world. A well-known glaciologist who specializes in the Andes—he has published peer-reviewed research on Patagonian glaciers and has climbed in Patagonia—confirmed that it was impossible to draw authoritative conclusions about flow rates without specifically studying the glacier in question.

More telling, yet still confusing, was the rope (they were double ropes, but used together, parallel, as if they're a single cord) found with Egger's remains. The Brits made a sketch of the rope configuration in 1974. The sketch had made the rounds, and those who saw it always found it puzzling. At the end of the ropes was a main loop, estimated at two meters in circumference—about six and a half feet—and closed with a reef knot (a.k.a. square knot). Far too big to be a waist loop, and tied with the wrong knot. The standard tie-in knot in 1959 was a bowline around the waist (back then they didn't have harnesses). Coming out of that main loop was a long stretch of double rope, fifty to eighty feet, which then returned to a carabiner on the main loop, where it was clipped with a clove hitch. Coming from the other side of the clove hitch was about eight feet of the double rope, with its ends severed and frayed. To climbers, it made no sense.

The old slide scans that Campbell-Kelly dug up for me included images of the rope. The total length looked right—there was a lot of

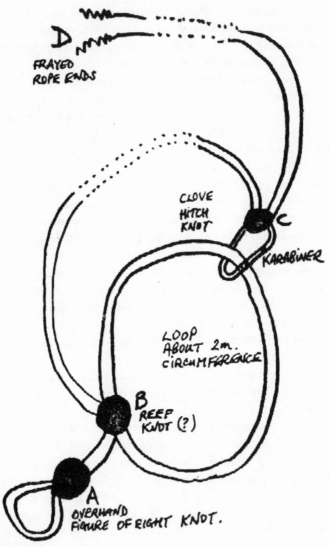

D
FRAYED
ROPE ENDS

CLOVE
HITCH
KNOT

C

KARABINER

LOOP
ABOUT 2m.
CIRCUMFERENCE

B
REEF
KNOT (?)

A
OVERHAND
FIGURE OF EIGHT KNOT.

DISTANCES :-
A-B ∿ 0.2 m.
B-C ∿ 15 to 25m.
C-D ∿ 2.5 m

Arrangement of Egger's Rope

The initial diagram depicting the rope configuration found with Egger's remains, and a photo of the actual configuration. Diagram and photo: Ben Campbell-Kelly

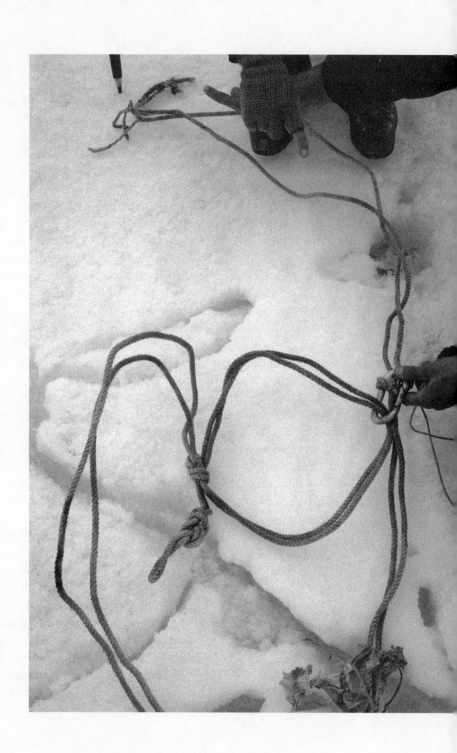

rope. One image showed a close-up of the main loop, spread out for display, with a sense of scale given by a human hand holding the carabiner. Although the sketch labeled the loop as two meters circumference, it was about half that. Clearly in the ballpark of a human waist, especially if thickly clothed. The sketch had another error in it: The knot wasn't a reef knot. The loop was closed with a bowline. The tie-in knot.

Still, what could the configuration mean? The main loop of double rope being Egger's tie-in made sense. But the inexplicable fifty- to eighty-foot loop coming back to him, clipped with a clove hitch? And the other ends, coming off of the clove hitch, severed? The huge mystery loop is exponentially bigger than what you could throw around a boulder and clip back to yourself for a belay anchor. In discussion with elite guides as well as old-timers who tied in with bowlines, nobody could make sense of it.

Only one thing is clear: It is not a configuration used to lower a person. Which is what Maestri has long maintained he was doing when the avalanche came, snapped the rope, and took Toni Egger's life.

Two of the earliest accounts, however, told of a different death scenario. The first source, printed in a Río Gallegos newspaper less than four weeks after Egger's death, reports with a first-person passage from Maestri. The second, printed in the 1959 *American Alpine Journal*, cites a report received from Argentina and signed by all surviving expedition members.

Both accounts state that Maestri was rappelling, with Egger waiting at the anchor above, when the avalanche came. Maestri heard the sound, went back up the ropes, but Egger was gone, swept from the wall. If true, however, Egger would not have been tied to the ropes, and certainly not with the large loop of slack found with his remains, because Maestri was using them.

How did Toni Egger die?

Was it rockfall or an avalanche or a crevasse on the glacier? Could the mystery loop be from a failed crevasse rescue attempt? Maybe the frayed ends are from the double ropes actually breaking. Maybe Egger fell while climbing, and they wanted to bring him home for a proper burial. The mystery loop could have been added for greater control while trying to drag him down, but maybe they had to leave him due to fatigue or storm.

Toni Egger on Jirishanca, in Peru, in 1957,
ascending fixed lines with the prevailing method
of the day: climbing hand-over-hand, while
belayed on the rope tied around his waist.
Photo: Alpenraute—Lienz, Austria

Could Egger have actually been alone, rope soloing when he
died? If so, the mystery loop might not be so mysterious. He could
have been using the double ropes as a backup while climbing hand-
over-hand (as was common then, insecure as it is) up their fixed
lines, or as a self-belay to recon the climbing above.

A common and fairly simple system for rope soloing—although
I was unable to determine if it was prevalent back then—uses a
clove hitch to adjust the slack as you go. One end of the rope is tied
to an anchor. The other end is tied to you (these days, you tie into
your harness). In between, the rope is also clipped to you with a
clove hitch. The clove hitch, since it's strong and easy to adjust,
serves as a temporary, moving tie-in point between the two ends of
the rope. Since you don't want the entire length of rope out in case
you fall, when you start up the pitch you allow only a small amount
of rope between your clove hitch and the anchor below. Of course
this means there is a huge loop of slack coming out the other side of
your clove hitch, between the clove hitch and you. The farther up

the pitch you climb, adjusting the clove hitch to pay out more rope, your slack loop gets smaller. If you fall, the section of rope between the anchor and your clove hitch—which, again, is clipped to you—arrests your fall.

Or, if your luck is bad and you're climbing on 1959 ropes, maybe the ropes break. If that happened, the rest of the double ropes would be somewhere up on the route. They would be securely anchored to the rock at one end, and broken on their other ends.

Good theory, but only a theory. Nobody knows, except for two people who always stuck to an impossible story. And over the years, as more questions than answers arose, Cesarino Fava (now dead) and Cesare Maestri remained defiant to detractors and silent to legitimate inquisitors.

But the truth matters.

I asked Tom Dauer if, during his extensive research for his book, *Mythos Patagonien* (German, 2004), he knew whether Toni Egger's family or close friends questioned Fava and Maestri's story of how Toni died. I wondered if maybe it was easier to accept the official account, to just accept that Toni died in the mountains, however it happened. Dauer comes from a climbing family in Germany and has many connections to the Austrian climbing scene, and to Egger's family.

Toni Egger's sister, Stefanie, was the only one who outwardly expressed doubt. "If three men started traveling and only two came back, what would you think?" she told Dauer. Blame is not implicit in her question; just a demand for honesty.

Stefanie asked Fava and Maestri about her brother's diaries—Toni Egger always wrote in his diary, which should have been with his belongings in base camp—but neither Fava nor Maestri gave her anything. Neither diaries nor answers.

Stefanie Egger remembered when Maestri visited the Egger family after the trip. Dauer recalls discussing the occasion with her: "Stefanie was pretty young then, and there certainly must have been an aura of grief and silence, so she was left alone with her questions and her hate. That's what she said, she 'hated' Maestri at that time."

Toni Egger's family never again heard from Cesarino Fava or Cesare Maestri.

THE NEXT SEASON, IN NOVEMBER 1975, Bragg and Donini returned with a third climber, Jay Wilson, and a handful of non-climbing friends and girlfriends.

Learning from their previous season's travel trials, this time they had the idea to ship Donini's VW van, loaded with their climbing gear, ahead of them on a boat to Buenos Aires. Problem was, when they got to Buenos Aires they didn't know whom in customs to bribe, and so the van collected dust. Argentina was chaos. The country was in social and economic shambles, amid a succession of political upheavals and military coups.

After two or three weeks of partying in Buenos Aires, they ran into an expat Brit, a hustler type, who, Bragg recalls, "knew who to talk to, and how much to bribe him."

Donini, with his new Argentine girlfriend, and Wilson drove the van while the others—Bragg, Wilson's sister, and another woman climber friend—flew to Río Gallegos, from where they hitched a ride with a road crew. The crew was widening and grading the road, early steps toward the eventual paving thirty years later. The road workers thought the blonde, long-haired, handsome Bragg was a pimp and these were his two hookers. To ward away the offerings of pesos, they came up with the story that one woman was Bragg's wife and the other was his sister.

When they finally connected with Donini and his van, they had to shuttle gear and people. These things took time on a yet-ungraded road, and Bragg remembers a couple of days waiting at the road camp. The weather was clear and the road crew had made a soccer pitch. Bragg didn't know how to play, so he spectated as goalkeeper. He remembers standing at the end of the field watching Wilson, a former collegiate soccer star, and the dusty road workers darting about the gravel pitch as the sun set, an illuminated Fitz Roy jutting above a distant horizon.

By the first of December, they reached the mountains and stayed through March.

AT FIRST GLANCE Torre Egger appears considerably smaller than Cerro Torre—its summit is eight hundred feet lower—but its walls begin a similar distance below on the glacier, and are equally daunting. For decades many top climbers have called it the most difficult summit in the Western Hemisphere.

Along their north–south axes, Torre Egger and Cerro Torre share a col—the Col of Conquest. Leading up to this col is the east-facing terrain that Fava and Maestri claimed to have climbed with Toni Egger in 1959. From the col, Egger and Maestri allegedly continued up the north face to the summit of Cerro Torre.

Torre Egger had seen one serious attempt, two seasons before, by the battered remnants of a predominantly British climbing team. Seven Brits, two Americans, and one Argentine started out, but their numbers dwindled due to several illnesses, some loss of interest, and one death—Argentine Rafael Juárez disappeared early on while attempting Cerro Adela, likely victim of a crevasse fall. As the remaining members of the team tried to fix ropes up a large gash that forms an apparent weakness, the mushroom atop the spire shed layers in the heat.

One of the many paradoxes of climbing in the Torre group is that when storms wrack the mountains, you run for shelter; once the weather clears, the sun loosens the precarious rime, and chunks shed from the mountain: You can't win for losing. While on their attempted route, a piece of ice the size of a tennis ball broke an arm of one of the Brits. Their gully, a natural funnel for all things falling, took on the character of a bombing range.

Bragg, Donini, and Wilson's plan seemed logical enough. They'd repeat the Egger-Maestri line to the Col of Conquest and then, where Egger and Maestri went left up Cerro Torre, they'd fork right and try to surmount the final thousand feet of Torre Egger's shaded south face.

Though doubt had mounted in some circles about the 1959 climb, the Americans went to Patagonia fully believing Maestri's story. "I thought, Jesus, a guy like Maestri you gotta take his word for it," Donini said, even if he wasn't a fan of some of his statements. "I'd heard some things about Maestri, like when he named the Col of Conquest and took a dig at Bonatti (with their naming of the Col of Hope), 'there is only the will to conquer, hope is the weapon of the weak,' I mean, what the fuck?"

Bragg and Donini were two of the top American climbers of their day. Wilson was the best athlete of the team, though not as seasoned in the mountains. Donini had honed his rock craft over years in Yosemite—the world's preeminent big-wall climbing destination. The south face of Torre Egger appeared to be a smaller, alpine version of the walls where he'd cut his teeth.

I talked to Donini in 2013. He's seventy years old, razor sharp, and extraordinarily fit. I've climbed with him over the years, and have never been able to keep up. He's lanky and strong and a former Green Beret. He never slows down and rarely shies away from offering up his thoughts.

"At this time, Bragg and I had both done big walls in Yosemite, so we thought that our rock climbing skills and our wall skills were probably superior to [Egger and Maestri's], given their techniques and their equipment in 1959. There's an obvious line going to the triangular snowfield about a thousand feet up, really steep to there, and above the snowfield it kinda kicked back and you got to a corner, and from the corner you have to turn and then it's about a four-hundred-foot traverse into the col. From below you're looking up and the traverse looks really hard, it looks like a vertical, blankish wall, and we thought, well, man, that's gonna be the hard part. But we thought, those guys did it in '59, and we've climbed the Salathé Wall and The Nose. We should be able to do it."

Whenever the wind allowed, they humped climbing gear and supplies from their base camp in the forest to an advanced camp—a snow cave below the wall—and then to the route. In short spurts spread over weeks they worked upward, fixing ropes in the obvious dihedral leading to the prominent but small triangular snowfield.

"It was like a trip through history," Donini said. Remnants from the Egger-Maestri 1959 climb hung in the lower dihedral. Old fixed ropes rotted away. Yank on them and they'd break. Old wooden wedges remained, too, but they placed their own gear, fixed ropes as they went, and retreated when they had to. The climbing was technically difficult, as Maestri had described. Indeed, this section seemed to stretch thin the 1959 climbers; Maestri fell ill for several days immediately following their fourth and final day of fixing ropes.

Atrocious weather raked the mountains for the next six weeks, allowing only tiny openings for climbing but plenty of time to marvel at the remnants they had seen from 1959. They were the first climbers to travel that terrain since Egger and Maestri's historic climb.

They had plenty of time, too, for card games, reading, conversation, and quiet, peaceful moments in the forest. "In those days they were raising sheep up in the forest, and every once in awhile one of those sheep would disappear and... uh... we ate pretty well," Donini recounted with a sly grin.

Clouds, wind, and rain passed in a blur as the weeks stretched through December and January. Finally the sky cleared and the rime-plastered spires again emerged. In a frenzy, they headed up. The rope they had fixed from the base of the route down to their snow cave was the only thing that marked its location—the cave was buried under thirty feet of snow. Two days of digging and they got to their equipment, then started climbing again. The iced-over rock yielded slow progress. A warm sun released sheets of ice and avalanches that peeled from the walls, echoing throughout the cirque.

They pushed the route higher, and as they neared the top of the lower dihedral—about a thousand feet up the route—in a relatively sheltered nook, they came upon an equipment cache left by Egger, Fava, and Maestri. At the time, they saw no reason to look inside. Later climbers reported two coiled, cable-laid nylon half-ropes, a bunch of big wooden wedges and steel pitons, and a rucksack.

Another storm rolled in, sending them back to base camp. Again and again, days then weeks dragged on with wind scouring the spires. Finally, mid-February, they got a break, ascended their ropes, and pushed higher.

At the Col of Conquest they huddled together behind a make-shift snow wall, thinking they were only the second team to see the world from this particular place. But they'd seen peculiar things below that left them wondering.

Come morning they climbed and fixed ropes higher up the shaded, sheer south face of Torre Egger. Free, aid, blank granite, pendulums, overhanging seams, three-hour leads. A lasso move unlocked the upper part of the wall. Clouds began drifting through the spires, coating them in a mist, but the wind held off. Rock yielded to ever-thickening ice; cirrus tails streaked the sky; darkness shrouded the bulbous maze of confusing summit mushrooms overhead. Back to the col. Rain spit intermittently throughout the night. They hunkered down for another day at the col, while rime grew on their ropes like frosted worms. Darkness fell again but the wind remained calm. Up again come morning, they ascended their ropes and wove through the mushrooms, catching apparition-like glimpses of adjacent snow-capped spires seemingly floating in the clouds. On the evening of February 22, 1976, they climbed to the summit. They laughed, talked, snapped pictures, and left the carabiner Donini had taken from Toni Egger's remains.

THEY HAD MADE a groundbreaking ascent. While multiple routes might ascend a mountain over the decades, there is only one first ascent. Along the way, they had been the first party to repeat the famed Egger-Maestri line to the Col of Conquest.

left The upper Torre Glacier, showing where, according to Maestri's account, Toni Egger presumably died after being swept from the wall in 1959, and the locations of Egger's remains found in 1974 and 2003. In early 2014, slightly up-glacier from the 2003 site, Rolando Garibotti found several pieces of Egger's sweater melting out of the ice. Photo: Rolando Garibotti

right Looking down on the hidden traverse ramp leading to the Col of Conquest, as seen during the first ascent of Torre Egger. The Col of Conquest is off-photo just to the right, while the triangular snowfield is visible below and left. Photo: Jim Donini

What they found, and what they didn't, was the most significant evidence concerning the ascent claimed by Cesare Maestri and faithfully backed by Cesarino Fava.

Things got perplexing only a thousand feet up—just halfway to the Col of Conquest.

"Immediately [upon starting up] we started seeing artifacts. It was like, 'Oh, my god,' because we were young climbers and in those days most climbers read all about the history. I had read books by Gervasutti, Bonatti, Hermann Buhl, Lionel Terray, and all the Europeans, and they were supermen, and we were climbing through history and we found a piece of rope hanging, and a wooden wedge, and some old bolts, and some pitons," Donini told me.

In the lower dihedral—the first thousand feet to the equipment dump, just below the triangular snowfield—artifacts were every-where. Fifty, a hundred pieces of gear, they lost count.

On the last pitch to the equipment dump, the final section of the old fixed rope was peculiar. For the entire pitch the gear was spaced surprisingly close together, every two feet or so. And the rope was clove-hitched to approximately every other piece. Nobody could explain it then or now; it serves no conceivable pur-pose. This was the only pitch fixed in such a manner.

Alongside that final section of the 1959 fixed rope, sixty feet below the equipment dump, a pronounced block of rock protrudes from the wall. A pair of thin, nylon climbing ropes was anchored to the wall a short distance below the protrusion. The double ropes then ran up and over the block, and then down the other side. About twenty feet down, their ends were broken and frayed. Just like the rope ends found with Egger's remains. The ropes appeared to be identical. "I wasn't sure," Donini told me. "I'm still not sure—but they were just hanging there."

ABOVE, EVERYTHING FLIPPED like a switch.

"We had read the accounts where Maestri said the first part was difficult, vertical. Then he said the part from there to the corner, before you made the traverse into the col, was easy, lower angle. Then he said the traverse was very difficult. Now, this is exactly how it looks as you're looking at it from below."

Then two things happened: "One, from that equipment dump to the Col of Conquest—and we went back up and down it a few times—we found zero artifacts. Now, that is not completely damning, although it's pretty damning. You know how it is, you're on a route and there's natural lines, and also rappel lines, and you always run into stuff if people have been there—especially after we've seen fifty to a hundred pieces below. But none, zero, and not even any rappel points. And we're really looking around, looking for rappel pieces, and just nothing. I'm going, well, this doesn't make any sense."

As they climbed farther above the last traces of the purported 1959 climb, their doubts mounted. "The other thing was that the route description turned out to be different from the way it looked. The climbing from the equipment dump to the traverse was harder than it looked—it was lower angle overall, but you'd get a little head-wall here and there—it was real climbing. But all of a sudden you get to the corner, and you turn around the corner and there's a ledge."

This is the section that looked so daunting from below, where Maestri reported the most difficult climbing of the route. "You couldn't see it from below because of the angle. The only place you can see that ledge from as you're going up is when you get right on it and you turn the corner and it's ten feet from you. There's a couple of fifth-class moves to get to it, and then it was fourth class—scrambling—to the col. It was by far the easiest terrain on the entire climb."

The terrain above the last traces ever found of the 1959 team was the opposite of how it looks from below, completely different from what Maestri described. The Americans hadn't even finished their climb by the time the evidence was undeniable. "I knew right then and there that Maestri had not only *not* climbed Cerro Torre in 1959, but he didn't get to the Col of Conquest. I think his high point was the goddamned equipment dump," Donini said, still incredulous. "Only a thousand feet up."

The trail into the Torre Valley. Photo: Kelly Cordes

chapter 10

ORIGINS OF BELIEF

Historian Mirella Tenderini is one of Italy's most respected authors and editors on adventure and exploration. She is in her seventies and lives most of the year in the same house where she and her husband raised their two children. It's up a road of hairpin switchbacks three thousand feet above the village of Ballabio, at the base of the Grigna Spires, where the famous Ragni di Lecco climbing club honed their craft. The house, built into a hillside, has a stone foundation that supports beautiful old wooden framing. Inside, Mirella's library contains thousands of books in a multitude of languages that date back centuries. Photos of mountains, deserts, cities, old climbers, friends, and family line the walls.

I'd come to Italy to explore the Italian perspective on the controversies surrounding Cerro Torre. Never has a technical peak, especially so far from any population centers and mainstream hype, drawn such unmitigated and even unhinged passion. And never has a mountain been so influenced by one person, as Cerro Torre is by Cesare Maestri.

Mirella greeted me at the door and welcomed me warmly. The sparkle in her eyes and her engagement in the world projected an unexpected agelessness. Our mutual friend, John Harlin III (my boss during my years working as an editor for the *American Alpine Journal*) put us in touch over email. He wrote fondly of her, her work, and her knowledge; "She knows everybody."

When I wrote to Mirella, expressing my hope of spending an afternoon talking about Cesare Maestri, Cerro Torre, and the controversy over the Compressor Route de-bolting, she replied:

"The recent discussions… of Maestri's route on Cerro Torre have revived the everlasting controversies around Cerro Torre. I think that matter has never been handled with the necessary detachment and fairness and would be very happy if someone went deeply into it. You'll have all my support and collaboration. I am so old as to know personally all the people involved in that story."

The afternoon of our interview expanded into four days of conversations. She invited me to stay in her house, and I explored the trails and spires of the spectacular Grigna Spires. Mirella arranged several interviews for me with people knowledgeable about the Cerro Torre affair.

Mirella listened intently, intensely, yet had an ease and warmth about her. She was thoughtful and kind, though I suspect she is not easily manipulated. Her entire face illuminated when she talked about her work, which has entailed a lifetime devoted to the study of history. Casual conversation led to stories about Algeria and tales of travels to the Royal Geographic Society in London, where she read journals of early explorers who traveled the Alps hundreds of years before. She read original letters from the Duke of Abruzzi and Ernest Shackleton while researching her various books. During her years as an art curator, she discovered previously unnoticed works stored in boxes in the basement of the Louvre, as well as da Vinci originals in the Hermitage.

Regarding Maestri's Cerro Torre expeditions, Mirella knew the people and knew the time. I listened in silence as she told of growing up in nearby Milan during World War II. She talked of her love of the Americans when the Allied tanks and troops came through the city, signaling that Italy was free. She and her friends ran into the streets among bomb-riddled buildings, tears streaming down their faces; they sang and danced, filled with feelings of hope and renewal.

Mirella Tenderini. Photo: Kelly Cordes

When she was twenty-four she met a climber and mountain guide named Luciano. After a few months they piled all of their possessions onto a motor scooter (with a set of chains for winter) and for the next twelve years became year-round custodians of a series of mountain huts in the Alps. During that time they had their first child and eventually settled down in the house where we were talking.

Mirella never climbed seriously herself, but she was connected to the climbing world. As she recalled those early days, she seemed to travel to another time, to days of youth, love, and possibilities. Her friends included some of the greatest climbers in history—Bonatti, Cassin, Mauri, Maestri.

She and her husband (who died in 2007) had been good friends with Cesarino Fava. Mirella edited and published Fava's 1999 autobiography. She retains a palpable fondness for him—the memory of him—and described him as generous and simple, a kindhearted man with a sort of "ancient wisdom."

Mirella still remembers her first day climbing. She was in the Grigna Spires, and climbing nearby was Cesare Maestri, the great Spider of the Dolomites. It was the first time they met.

Over the years they've kept in touch, but she hadn't seen him in a few years. From time to time they talk on the phone, but he seems different now. Maestri was always the type of celebrity that some love and others hate. He was flamboyant and outspoken, perhaps outsized for his tiny village of Madonna di Campiglio, yet he was also one of their own. Maestri made his living as a guide and a sponsored climber, and he always handled criticism and controversy with a strength and defiance that embodied a spirit many wanted to identify with. When, later in life, he got cancer, "It was a battle, a real battle. It was a battle to win," she said. He defeated cancer, but now, Mirella said, in his eighties his voice sounds faded.

"Being called a liar devastates him," Mirella said. "It's taken its toll over time. He's bitter. He's very bitter." She prefers the memories of the way he was.

"We believe Cesare. It is like a faith for me, for us. I, we, believe him.... Coming from our time, it was impossible to question someone's word," she said.

After our first night of conversations, when I headed to my room I wrote in my journal about Italy's rich and complicated culture. Mirella struck me as a person clearly able to see the advantages and drawbacks inherent in most things, like those embedded in every culture on earth, including her own. It made me wonder about my influences and the limitations in my own thinking.

Before putting my pen down and hitting the light, I scribbled notes about a part of our conversation when we were talking about the past, and I mentioned how young my country and culture is—a blink of the eye compared to hers. Her eyes seemed fixed in the distance for a moment, as if she were thinking about something. Then she returned to the present and said, "We also have the burden of history. Sometimes it is very heavy."

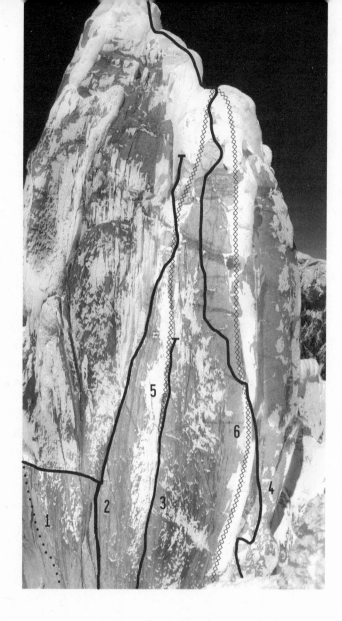

The north face of Cerro Torre, with lines indicating actual climbing and the diamond lines noting two of Maestri's various claimed routes.

Lines from left
1   Burke-Proctor 1981 attempt (dots for hidden portion on east face).
2   Aguiló-Benedetti 2013 attempt (high point at intersection of 1981 attempt).
3   Niederegger-Ponholzer 1999 attempt.
4   El Arca de los Vientos (Beltrami-Garibotti-Salvaterra, 2005).

Diamond lines from left
5   Maestri's route marked on a photo in *La Montagne* in April 1960 (lower half of line is obscured by 1999 attempt).
6   Maestri's route he marked for *L'Europeo* in April 1959.
    In a 1961 article in *Club Alpino Italiano Rivista Mensile*, he described yet a different line that begins between the 1999 attempt and the 2005 route before crossing the ridge (*L'Europeo* line) onto the northwest face midway up.

Photo: Rolando Garibotti

chapter 11

POSEIDON AND ZEUS

In his calm and rational demeanor, Patagonia hardman Elio Orlandi, veteran of countless adventures, told me in no uncertain terms that he didn't want to go down as being a Maestri defender. I'd begun to detect a pattern, a frequent traditionalist reaction to the 1959 story. An insistence that Maestri *could have* done it. Elio's fundamental point boils down to the premise that you can't prove a negative—that you can't *dis*-prove Maestri's claim. The mountain of evidence doesn't seem to matter.

At times it's like talking with people who believe in Poseidon, god of the seas, and Zeus, god of the sky. Many of Maestri's defenders are so earnest and often so likable. You'd love to agree with them. But the strength of both arguments—Poseidon-Zeus and Egger-Maestri—remains essentially the same: You cannot absolutely prove that Maestri did *not* climb Cerro Torre, just as you cannot absolutely prove that Poseidon and Zeus did not rule the water and the sky.

One difference is that if you expect to be taken seriously in the world, you can't go around making the Greek gods argument.

"Damn, sea levels are rising. Science points to climate change."

"Nah, dude. It's Poseidon. He's pissed off."

"Come again?"

Emotion and faith are powerful forces. People believe all kinds of crazy shit. Evidence or not, people often believe what they want to believe.

It was fall 2012 when Elio and I talked at Mirella's house in Italy, not long before the Lance Armstrong scandal finally blew up. Until his confession, tons of Americans *believed*. Lance was our hero. His cancer recovery made for a damned compelling story, too. Granted, once the evidence became overwhelming, most fantasies subsided; when he confessed, even the true believers had to give in. The guy's human, thus flawed. He cheated. He lied.

ELIO ORLANDI DROVE THREE HOURS to meet with me.

He's well known among Italy's mountaineers for his devotion to Patagonia, where he's established several difficult new routes and made multiple attempts on unclimbed lines on Cerro Torre. He's also—so I had thought—one of Maestri's biggest defenders. I gathered that he had read some of the things I wrote after the 2012 de-bolting controversy. Before our meeting he sent me a strongly worded statement that he had also written on the issue. Our opinions, it seemed, couldn't have been further apart.

He has thick, black, curly hair and stands well over six feet tall, with sausage fingers from decades of climbing. The son of a peasant, he was born and raised in the Brenta Dolomites, in the mountainous Trentino region, where he still lives. Everyday life back then involved what could be considered training for climbing, with time spent outdoors, scrambling up hillsides and rock outcrops, tending to the family's farm and livestock, gathering firewood, the daily tasks of living in the mountains.

Elio's a humble man of few words. There's a warmth about him, though at first he seemed guarded. I wondered if what looked like sadness in his eyes was real or if I was projecting; I knew what happened on his last trip to Patagonia.

On January 1, 2010, he and his friend Fabio Giacomelli were descending from another attempt at an extremely difficult, new big-wall route up the center of the east face of Cerro Torre. It was their fourth season trying the line, and they'd fixed ropes high on the face. They'd been going up and down their ropes, working the line, and had brought with them the ashes of Cesarino Fava. "He was like a father to me," Elio said.

Up on the wall, as snow fell in buckets for the second straight day, Elio organized their gear while Giacomelli readied to descend— he would prepare water and food for when Elio joined him in their snow cave on the glacier. It was after dark when Elio arrived at the cave, but Giacomelli wasn't there. Elio went back into the night, searching by headlamp until he found Giacomelli's footprints in the snow. The tracks disappeared above a crevasse that was covered by avalanche debris. Elio dug through the debris and rappelled into the crevasse. He searched for three days, alone. Finally, he found his friend's body.

Elio is an artist. He sculpts, draws, and paints gorgeous mountain scenes, and writes romantically of his journeys and of the mountains. He recently published a book about his mountain adventures, including those in his beloved Patagonia.

In 1982 he took his first trip to Patagonia. He loved the absence of rules, the sense of total freedom in an almost untouched landscape. He's returned something like thirty times, and has a house in El Chaltén.

On that first trip in 1982, he went with Ermanno Salvaterra, a living legend of Cerro Torre. Salvaterra lives nearby in Trentino. Within about a twenty-five-mile radius in the Trentino province live or lived many of the greats: Maurizio Giarolli, Cesarino Fava, Cesare Maestri, Elio Orlandi, and Ermanno Salvaterra.

Elio and Salvaterra had plans for Cerro Torre, and Elio wanted to chop Maestri's bolts on the Compressor Route. He considered the excessive bolts a violation of the spirit of mountaineering. But Salvaterra, who lives less than ten miles from Maestri, admired and was friends with the great Spider of the Dolomites. At the time, Salvaterra wholly believed that Maestri climbed Cerro Torre in 1959. He convinced Elio not to remove the Compressor Route's bolts. He saw them as history; what's done is done.

We're all entitled to change our minds. Growth forces us to examine our beliefs. Thirty years later, Elio, once ready to remove the bolts himself, published a scathing letter criticizing Kennedy and Kruk for doing just that.

ELIO, MIRELLA, AND I talked about Cerro Torre and the bolts.

The common topic of how the mountains should be available for everyone to enjoy arose. As with so many things, the question seems to be: Where do we draw the line? Before they were removed, the bolts greatly enabled access to the mountain.

I asked the rhetorical question, "If the argument for having left the Compressor Route intact is that the mountains are for everyone to enjoy, why not also an elevator to the top of Cerro Torre?"

Mirella laughed, and then translated. Elio laughed.

But I was serious. The capability certainly exists. It'd be a slow version of the helicopter ride that Terray was offered to the top of Fitz Roy in 1952. If the mountains are truly for everybody at every level, why can't my grandma take an elevator up Cerro Torre?

"Or a teleferique or an escalator," I added, and waited for a reply.

"Maybe sooner or later somebody will do that, in spite of all the climbers," Mirella said. Elio paused and gave a slight nod.

Over the years Elio and Cesare Maestri have become friends, though it wasn't always that way. For twenty years Elio was at odds with Maestri—and he still disagrees with him on some things. But once he got to know the man, Elio developed true admiration for Maestri.

After food and, of course, wine, Mirella asked, "May I tell Elio the things I like very much about you, and how you live?" She told him about the way I pieced together a living with a part-time editorial job at the *American Alpine Journal* for a dozen years, at first while living in a sixty-five-dollar-a-month shack, then upgrading to a seven-by-eleven-foot shack we all called "The Chicken Coop." (I now have a cabin that's several times larger than the coop.) I heard something about my beater car, the way I try to devote my life to climbing. I heard the word *frugale*. When she finished, Elio clapped his hands and nodded in approval. We've both structured our lives around the mountains.

"This is a demonstration that although you live in different countries with different history, education, everything, and you also might disagree about several things," Mirella said, "there is also something so near, that makes you absolutely people who understand each other." We raised our glasses for a toast.

Elio was sure to restate that he didn't necessarily believe Maestri, but he stopped well short of discounting the '59 claim entirely.

I asked him about the 1999 symposium he helped organize in Malè, Italy (Fava and Giarolli's hometown), to commemorate the fortieth anniversary of Maestri's great climb of Cerro Torre. For the event, Elio made a beautiful sculpture of Cerro Torre. Two meters tall, intricately detailed, a remarkable replica. When called onstage to talk about his climb, Maestri was unable to identify not only his supposed line of ascent, but even which aspect of the mountain he claimed to have climbed. (He wasn't thought to be ill or in decline.) Elio and Giarolli came on stage to remind Maestri of where he had gone.

Elio laughed it off, telling me how Maestri was often confused about the routes that he'd climbed, and generally messy with details. "It doesn't mean anything," he said.

I paused for a moment to consider how, indeed, we all forget sometimes. But if you'd done the greatest ascent in history, don't you think you'd at least come close? One time years ago, Elio said, Maestri visited a friend's house and upon seeing a photo of the Dru on the wall, he exclaimed, "How beautiful, Fitz Roy!" Elio and Mirella had a good, long laugh and said again how Maestri was often confused and forgetful. "It doesn't mean anything," Elio repeated.

"So," I asked, "do you believe 1959?"

He took a long pause, started to smile, took a deep breath, exhaled, and laughed.

"I would never say 'I'm sure Maestri went to the top,'" he said. But, having been on the face, he said he was sure that they could have done it in the conditions that Maestri described at the time; it was within their ability.

I mentioned how Maestri claims to have left seventy bolts on the route—sixty above the col—and yet above the triangular snowfield, nothing has been found. A piton a few hundred feet higher than the triangular snowfield, but still well below the col, that was rumored to be Maestri's was confirmed as belonging to a British team. Zero trace of Egger and Maestri has emerged in the upper three thousand feet. Most of the climbing world, at this point, considers it one of the biggest fakes of all time.

"Three hundred meters [one thousand feet] above the col have never been climbed by anybody," he said. "So, first, nobody can claim to have climbed that route. And, second, but most important, nobody can affirm that there are no bolts. This is a fact. This is not a personal opinion."

Internally, I sighed. I didn't think to ask, "Which route?" The route line Maestri drew for *L'Europeo* right after his return in 1959? Or the fully different one published in *La Montagne* a year later? Or the one he described in a 1961 article? They're drastically different. The general areas of these three contradictory lines have been scoured on dozens of attempts over the decades.

Sure, theoretically, there's the possibility that no climber has retraced every part of Egger and Maestri's supposed route. But no trace of Maestri's passage has emerged anywhere above the snowfield, despite the subsequent traffic. And there are contradictions and impossibilities too numerous to mention.

Elio borrowed my notebook and sketched the upper face, noting that the specific area where Maestri claimed (one of them) hasn't been repeated (in fact, it has been descended, on rappel). Elio even acknowledged his own multiple attempts, as well as those by the Austrians. A wealthy friend of Toni Egger's financed several trips by Tommy Bonapace and Toni Ponholzer, in hopes they would find proof of the 1959 ascent above the Col—to no avail.

One would think that Maestri's vagueness and inconsistencies would undermine his claim. But, in actuality, the ever-shifting target of his supposed line of ascent has had the opposite effect: Wherever someone went on the north face, when they found no trace of 1959, that only meant that they were in the wrong place.

Next Elio told me that a possible reason for no traces above the triangular snowfield is that the bolts they used in 1959 were unreliable, nothing like modern bolts. True. He was sure to emphasize that this is only his opinion and not a fact, but he suggested that such old bolts in exposed areas could have all been stripped away by the forces of the mountain—the avalanches that crash down Cerro Torre's flanks. Only in protected areas might some of the bolts remain—places, he says, like the initial thousand feet to the triangular snowfield. A virtual yard sale of fixed pitons and bolts from 1959 have been found in that first thousand feet—much of which, actually, gets hammered by avalanches shedding from the triangular snowfield.

Elio himself has climbed many previously untraveled pitches on his attempts at the north and northwest faces and has never found the slightest trace of Egger and Maestri.

On one of his attempts, with Maurizio Giarolli and Odoardo Ravizza in late 1994, they retreated high on the face, blocked by "overhanging snow patches and unstable ice," at a place where Maestri described fifty- to sixty-degree ice. But they considered it a new route and gave it a name: Cristalli nell Vento (Crystals in the Wind). The reason: They had intersected the 1959 Egger-Maestri route.

IN TRENTINO they hold conferences about Cerro Torre and have celebrations of Maestri and the supposed first ascent of Cerro Torre on every ten-year anniversary of 1959.

I said, "It seems that in Italy, versus other parts of the world, people are much more likely to believe in 1959. We all have different cultures, we all have different heroes. Is it possible that the role of belief is a big part of Italy's..."

"Is it being Italian, a sort of national sentiment?" Mirella asked.

"Not just that," I said, "but because Maestri is a hero in Italy, people want to believe more. So belief, faith, plays a much stronger role."

She translated for Elio, and out came a warm-sounding laugh, followed by his reply.

"In my opinion it is not a matter of national belonging. Personally, Maestri has never been a hero, but we are friends. I don't want to be considered a defender of Maestri, because I have always been opposed to Maestri's way of doing things. It's something completely separate. I think that he might have done the '59 route for the reasons I just told you, but not for sentiment of friendship or nationality."

"What I'd like to add," Mirella said, "is that it's not true that in Italy everybody is on Maestri's side. Maestri has an incredible amount of enemies, because of his ways—he is much too flamboyant, which most people do not like—we do not like. So you must be aware that not all Italians are on Maestri's side."

A member of the Ragni di Lecco team works upward on the 1974
first ascent. Photo: Mario Conti

chapter 12

COLD REALITY

Sometimes people perform beyond their expectations, beyond themselves, and shatter the collective notions of possibility. We love the idea that on the right day, given just the right conditions, something magical might happen. We are drawn to stories of records being broken, of once-in-a-lifetime performances.

Toni Egger was known as a great ice climber and alpinist—among the best of his time, some say—and Fava and Maestri insisted that the north face of Cerro Torre was covered in a sheet of ice. Nobody has ever again seen those same conditions, but ice by its very nature is ephemeral. Some of Maestri's various claims were that the sheet was more like crusted snow. If so, given the near-vertical angle of the face and its absence of thick snow and rime buildup, it would have had to be firm enough to climb as if it were ice. Sometimes the face appears covered in white, at least in part, but it's always a transient coating of barely adhered rime, the sort utterly worthless for climbing. It peels off to the touch and isn't thick or solid enough to climb. A day or so later, it's gone.

Still, even knowledgeable climbers sometimes say: *Yeah, they probably didn't climb it. But IF that ice sheet really did form....*

After all, only a hundred feet away, immediately across the Col of Conquest, is a virtual mirror image example. The western edge of the south face of Torre Egger is shorter and a few degrees steeper than the north face of Cerro Torre, but it holds an intimidating line of vertical-to-overhanging ice. The ice is visible in historical photos, although it wasn't until December 2011 that the incredible line, named Venas Azules, was finally climbed—it's by far the hardest ice route in the range.

American climber Colin Haley knows the area and conditions well. He first visited the Chaltén Massif when he was nineteen years old, and has returned ten times and counting (as of November 2013). About half of those visits he spent the entire austral summer in El Chaltén. He's been to the Col of Conquest twice and is familiar with the terrain:

"In the past three decades that people have been taking pictures of the north face of Cerro Torre, it's clear that it has never had blue ice on it, like Venas Azules does. It only has rime, which probably has to do with the fact that it's north facing and not south facing. But regardless, even if the north face of Cerro Torre back in '59 was so iced up all the time that the ice was just as good as Venas Azules, it wouldn't make any difference, because then it would be Alpine Ice 6 [an ice climbing grade near the top of the difficulty scale], and in 1959 they wouldn't have had the slightest chance in hell."

Why not? Isn't anything possible when it comes to human performance? Particularly when that performance involves a climber as ahead of his time as Toni Egger was?

What if that ice sheet really did form?

ICE CLIMBING DEPENDS ON EQUIPMENT for ascent, far

more so than rock climbing does. While the protective gear for rock climbing has certainly evolved, the actual climbing remains very much the same as always: Your fingers and toes (toes with special shoes, granted) are the interface with the rock. Theoretically, starting up a rock climb stark naked wouldn't hinder a skilled climber as long as he or she didn't fall. Do the same on ice and one couldn't get an inch off the ground. Bare fingers and even shoes or boots are utterly useless. Without crampons and ice tools, an ice climber goes nowhere. And those tools have changed dramatically over the years.

IN BEN NEVIS: BRITAIN'S HIGHEST MOUNTAIN,

the book by Ken Crocket and Simon Richardson, a history of one of the world's standard-bearing ice climbing areas, the chapter titled "Revolutions" opens: "Until 1970, winter routes were climbed in virtually the same style as they had been climbed at the turn of the century, a single, cumber-some, wooden ice axe laboriously wielded by the leader who hewed a line of hand and footholds."

Before what became known as the "Ice Climbing Revolution," around 1970, most of the mountains in the greater ranges were still climbed in slow style via lesser angled snow routes, rather than steep ice routes. Free climbing (with tools) vertical ice was a distant fantasy, and sustained steep ice (in modern terms) was rarely, if ever, climbed. What was often called "ice" was usually firm snow or névé, into which climbers would chop handholds and steps. Hard ice faces were generally avoided, considered out of condition. Long stretches of unavoidable steep ice required aid climbing, fixed ropes, and large parties. And for one primary reason: Modern ice tools had yet to be invented.

What's considered steep varies with time. In both the 1959 and 1970 editions of Gaston Rébuffat's book *On Ice and Snow and Rock*, he defined "steep slopes" as between forty and fifty degrees, and the "very steep slopes" as over fifty degrees. Rébuffat, a famous French mountain guide and author, knew his craft well. He was a member of the French team that made the first ascent of Annapurna in 1950 (the highest peak climbed in the world at the time), and he was the first to climb all six of the great north faces of the Alps.

On slopes steeper than about sixty-five degrees, climbers of old aided directly off of their ice pitons (unreliable metal spikes, akin to tent stakes) and, on the steepest climbs, sometimes used portable ladders. The bold and talented sometimes steadied themselves with one hand holding an ice piton or a crude, tiny ice dagger—its pick resembled a sturdy awl—for balance while resetting the long ax.

Members of the Ragni di Lecco team working their way up ropes
and ladders fixed on the 1974 first true ascent of Cerro Torre.
Photo: Mario Conti

Rébuffat described the technique: "Ice-dagger (U-section piton with hand-grip): This is a point or hand-pick which is held in the free hand (the one not occupied with the ice-axe) and which helps to maintain balance when using the toe-spikes of crampons to climb a very steep ice slope."

The skills of ice and alpine climbers from that era, before modern gear, boggle the mind. These climbers mastered precision, balance, and, unquestionably, toughness. Longer, sustained climbs—many of which we can romp up with modern ice gear—required the use of fixed ropes and multiple uncomfortable bivies. German author Tom Dauer interviewed many climbers from the era for his book on Cerro Torre. He told me, with a bit of humor: "Bivouacking was part of the game, and the guys were strong—or dumb—enough to sit out major storms for a few nights."

In Kendal, England, in 2013, I spoke with some older climbers, including the venerable Dennis Gray. We got talking about Cerro Torre and Maestri's original story. "Correct me if I'm wrong," I said, "but nobody was climbing vertical ice then."

"I'll correct ya!" Dennis said. "Zero Gully on Ben Nevis," he stated. Having climbed at the Ben, I'd heard of the route.

"Dennis," I said, slightly intimidated, "I'm pretty certain that the route was nothing like the sustained vertical that would form on the north face of the Torre. Short sections back then were one thing— Cerro Torre is another."

He pondered for a moment, then exclaimed, "You're right!" And without missing a beat, he continued, "Maestri was a damned good climber, though—he was a terrific singer, too. Opera." Dennis then launched into a brilliant operatic impression.

That's the thing—sure, short, steep sections of ice were climbed before modern tools. A few aid moves or various creative tactics (Rébuffat described the shoulder stand in his book—with care while wearing crampons, one presumes) could get you past small sections without substantial delay.

But don't the multiple steep ice routes climbed before modern tools contradict my argument? Not when you examine the details.

The three-thousand-foot Couloir Lagarde, on the northeast face of Les Droites in the Mount Blanc Massif, was first climbed in 1930 in a twelve-hour dash. It has two pitches of ice about seventy-five degrees, and had seen seventeen failed attempts. But the first ascent was at the end of July, and they went around the melted-out ice steps by climbing rock off to the sides. The rest of the couloir is mostly snow. The seventy-five-degree ice is how we climb it today, with modern tools.

In 1956, Kurt Diemberger established a new route on the north face of Königsspitze, a glaciated peak along the Italian-Swiss border, climbing a substantial overhang to finish the route; but the overhanging cornice (which has subsequently melted away) entailed one pitch of aiding off of ice pitons and ladders. The rest of the face is about fifty to sixty degrees.

In Patagonia in 1965, Argentine climbers Carlos Comesaña and José Luis Fonrouge made the second ascent of Fitz Roy via a new route, the Supercanaleta, in alpine style in a bold three-day round-trip. It was a remarkable achievement. The route, while mostly mixed climbing and technically the easiest on the mountain, is five thousand feet long, has 5.9 rock climbing and ice to eighty degrees. But most of the ice in the Supercanaleta is less than sixty degrees, and the few steps of near-vertical are short—only a body length or two.

Countless examples stand testament to the skill and resourcefulness of the old-school climbers. But they weren't climbing anything near sustained, vertical ice. Nobody was, at least not swiftly. The tools simply did not allow it.

"WHAT WE DID BACK THEN," Gottfried Mayr said to Tom Dauer in 2003, "has nothing to do with present-day ice climbing. Vertical ice was impossible."

Toni Egger and Mayr were close friends and climbing partners, and they climbed many impressive alpine routes together in the Alps, including the Cassin Route on Cima Ovest in 1952 and a one-day linkup of the north faces of Cima Ovest and Cima Grande in 1954.

When Dauer was talking with Mayr and some of Egger's old climbing partners, and studying the gear used in Egger's era, he saw that the ice axes Egger and his partners used were standard for the era. The ax found with Egger's remains was indeed a standard long-shafted wooden ax with a straight pick. A piton hammer was also found with the body, but no other ice tool. It's possible that he used another tool, though, as sometimes climbers experimented with shorter tools. I asked Dauer for his thoughts, given his communications with Egger's partners and his knowledge of the tools of that era: "There is some speculation on this, but I would guess that Egger climbed with a long ax in one hand and a so-called 'Stichel' in the other hand. This was an iron shaft without curve, maybe fifteen centimeters long, similar to an ice piton, which the climbers just stabbed horizontally into the ice."

YVON CHOUINARD DESCRIBED A TIME in late 1965 on an

iron-hard ice couloir in the Alps that rose to over sixty degrees. He was using the standard technique of the day—swinging a long ax for purchase, placing a "wretched dagger" with the other hand for balance, and working upward with his crampons. His legs were fatiguing and cramping under the strain of the flexible boots and crampons climbers wore then. "The thing that kept me going," he wrote, "was thinking about how I was going to go back to the shop and forge a hammer with a long, thin pick with teeth on it for climbing ice. No more of this ice dagger bullshit for me."

On a glacier in the Alps in the summer of 1966, Chouinard tested every ice ax he could find. Afterward, he convinced a climbing equipment factory in Chamonix to make him a fifty-five-centimeter ax (much shorter than the norm, thus easier to swing overhead), with a curved pick. His idea with the curved pick was to match the natural arc of the climber's swing, hypothesizing that this shape, along with deep teeth carved into the pick, would keep it from popping out the way straight picks invariably did when pulling on them. The ice ax worked and other climbers soon took note.

Around the same time, climbers in Scotland had been experimenting with similar refinements in their tools. Hamish MacInnes invented the similarly revolutionary Terrordactyl tool, a short ax that had a steeply downward pointing pick. Both types of tools were catching on in their respective circles and making an impact.

left Ice climbing gear typical of what Toni Egger took to Cerro Torre (from his friend Gottfried Mayr's collection.) Photo: Tom Dauer

right Post-revolutionary ice climbing gear: an early Chouinard ax. Although the difference may appear minor, the curved pick changed ice climbing. Photo: Jim Surette

The resultant effect on ice climbing proficiency cannot be overstated. "A climber could support his entire weight on the ax and it wouldn't come popping out," Chouinard wrote in *Climbing Ice*. "This meant that, armed with one of these tools in each hand, the ice climber could attack vertical or even overhanging ice without chopping steps or using artificial aid. This strenuous technique was first done in the winter of 1967 in California and was later named *piolet traction* by the French."

It was as if the covered wagon had instantaneously been replaced by the automobile. Ice was no longer deliberately avoided and climbers weren't slowed to a crawl upon encountering steep ice. With a shorter, curved-pick tool in each hand—like extensions of the arms—climbers could realize a new realm of potential. Standards exploded, with climbers in North America, Scotland, and the French Alps leading the way.

YET ON THE GLOBAL SCALE, in those days, innovations sometimes spread slowly. In most of Italy, for example, the newly invented ice tools and techniques didn't arrive until several years after the frontrunners. When the 1974 Ragni di Lecco team began their month-long ascent of Cerro Torre, fixing thirty-seven ropes along the way, they weren't well versed in modern ice techniques.

Though highly skilled rock climbers, on ice they still mostly relied on a single long ice ax, as Mario Conti told me in our 2012 interview. Photos from the expedition—including the 250 I studied—confirm the climbers' unfamiliarity with the new tools and techniques. Conti said the shorter, curved-pick Chouinard ice tool had just been introduced in Italy. Though they used it, they were unpracticed in its application, and they climbed most of the ice with the leader using the old-school technique: one long ax, occasionally employing a shorter ice tool for balance while re-setting the longer ax, and directly aiding off of the axes and ice pitons when the ice and rime approached vertical. Of the steep ice pitches Conti led in the dihedral and on the ice headwall—grade 5 ice—he told me, "Of course I did it artificially [aid climbing]."

The old tools and techniques necessitated expedition-style climbing tactics. "In our opinion we didn't have enough material to climb as only a team of two," Conti explained to me, recalling the era. "The idea of alpine style on something like that was impossible.... *Piolet traction* arrived and changed the possibilities."

Meanwhile, in New Hampshire in 1973, a talented young climber named John Bragg—the same Bragg who would go on to make the 1976 first ascent of Torre Egger with Jim Donini and Jay Wilson—led every pitch on the first ascent of a vertical ice climb called Repentance (WI5).

Bragg had spent his first ice season, the winter of 1970–71, chopping steps with a seventy-centimeter ax. Then he got the new tools: Chouinard rigid crampons, two fifty-five-centimeter Chouinard axes and the then-obligatory third tool to be used for leverage to turn the ice screws.

On Repentance, after the first pitch, Bragg's partner, veteran climber Rick Wilcox, remembers thinking, "This is the new world of ice climbing. This is something that I thought never would happen, that you could climb pitch after pitch of really steep ice."

Bragg returned to Patagonia in January 1977, with partners Dave Carman and Jay Wilson, intent on climbing Cerro Torre's west face, the Ragni Route. By that time, they'd been practicing modern ice climbing technique—unfamiliar to the Italians in 1974—on their backyard icefalls for over half a decade.

When I spoke with Bragg in 2013, I asked why they didn't go to the Compressor Route. He didn't hesitate: "Because I thought it was an abomination. And we'd been to that side [the eastern side of the Torre group], so our reasons weren't totally moral; we were after an adventure. The west face was unknown." All they knew was that the Ragni team had climbed it in 1974.

Compared to Bragg's previous Patagonia travels, this one went smoothly. They flew from the U.S., caught some rides, and eventually got dropped at the end of the road, from where they headed along the Río Túnel valley, over Paso del Viento onto the ice cap. Carman and Wilson sorted their pile of equipment while Bragg went ahead to the only estancia. The family invited him in for maté, and Bragg asked if they could horse-pack them further. Bragg recalls asking the old gaucho if he knew where they were going. "Yes," the man told him, "I packed Walter Bonatti and Carlo Mauri into there in 1958." And so it was—after an asado, they were on their way to Paso del Viento.

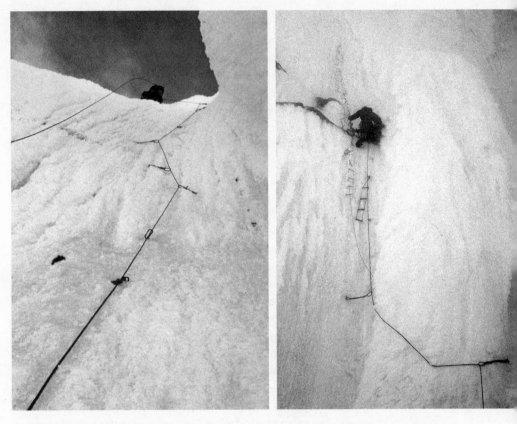

John Bragg leading the headwall, past remnants from the extended 1974 siege, during the American team's rapid 1977 repeat of the Ragni Route. Photos: Bragg collection

On the edge of the ice cap they rigged a makeshift sled salvaged from gear the 1974 team had abandoned, and for two days dragged their supplies through snow and ice to set up camp below Cerro Torre. On their second day in base camp, the weather cleared. Bragg knew better than to waste good weather in Patagonia.

They started climbing, bringing food and equipment for ten days. They reached the top of the Helmet and bivied atop the mushroom. They lay on their insulated pads, inside sleeping bags, looking off to the ice cap. Throughout the night, clouds crept across the sky.

The next day Carman dug a snow cave while Bragg and Wilson climbed above, fixing their four ropes to the base of the ice headwall. When they returned, the weather had fully shut down, and for two days they holed up in the snow cave. The storm relented and they ascended their ropes. Bragg finished leading to the top of the head-wall, where they found a natural ice cave, carved by the wind into the mushrooms of the upper ridge. Inside was a twenty-foot-wide room, with ice columns and platforms and flat spots of blue ice that formed a floor. The wind chimed and howled throughout the room, a brief and audible detour on its eternal circles around the globe.

Clouds swelled again by morning. They looked out of the cave and decided to keep going until forced to retreat. In a sea of clouds below the upper mushrooms, they traversed far to the right as had the Ragni, and they found a passage, two pitches of half-tubes, like water slides carved by the wind. The rime gave little purchase, collapsing and disintegrating as they tried to climb. "It felt like swimming upstream, wallowing up," Bragg recalls. Just below the top, the weather broke and like magic the clouds vanished. From the summit they could almost see to the Pacific Ocean, the white and blue of ice and water to the west and south, the mountains rising in the distant north, and the brown and yellow grasslands to the east.

Under still-perfect skies they descended to their snow cave atop the Helmet, and celebrated by eating all of their remaining food. Come morning, they woke to another raging storm. In a whiteout Bragg rappelled off the wrong side of a bulge, and dropped into a world of icicles dangling from the underside of the mushroom. He slammed into the rime wall, knocking off one of his crampons.

As he saw it disappear below, he recalled the book *Annapurna* and Maurice Herzog's costly mistake of losing his gloves just below the summit. "I remember thinking this is the beginning of this incredible epic and we're all gonna die!" he says now, with a slight laugh. Bragg composed himself and prusiked back up the ropes. They navigated down the other side and followed their noses and what markers remained in the ice and rime of their ascent, Bragg with only one crampon, continuing down to their camp on the glacier.

They had been on the mountain for less than a week, including storm days. The Ragni team had spent a month sieging the route just three years earlier. What started as a simple quest for adventure became an unintended Cerro Torre case study of the monumental shift in ice and alpine climbing standards.

That shift, as exemplified by these two ascents, provides eloquent commentary on Maestri's 1959 claims. If you try, you can rationalize away many of his contradictions. You can even believe in a once-in-a-millennium sheet of ice on the north face of Cerro Torre. But you can't claim to have raced-up thousands of feet of nearly vertical ice when the tools to do so didn't exist.

Jim Bridwell in 1976, after one of his many first ascents in Yosemite.
Photo: Mike Graham

chapter 13

BLESSED BY BRIDWELL

Jim Bridwell had planned and saved for a year to make it happen. But when he and his two partners arrived, they got a glimpse of the improbable Cerro Torre and a taste of the unrelenting storms. His partners bailed. Turned around and went home.

"The line dividing a climber's boldness from a climber's stupidity is razor thin," Bridwell wrote. "In Patagonia, perhaps, there is no distinction. I questioned from the beginning whether we weren't playing a form of Russian roulette with four chambers loaded. But I had become obsessed with climbing the beautiful tower called Cerro Torre and was prepared to succeed at almost any cost."

Bridwell stayed. The Yosemite big-wall ace is one of the most prolific climbers in history. In the 1970s and '80s he embodied the counter-culture rebel persona of American climbers. He'd already climbed eight new routes on El Capitan and Half Dome, and was well on his way to becoming an American climbing institution. He was highly regarded in Europe, and a year earlier he'd made his first Patagonia trip.

It was December 1978 and he was without a partner. He wanted to climb the Compressor Route and considered trying to solo it. Then, on Christmas eve, he bumped into Steve Brewer—a young American climber who had hitchhiked alone to the area. Brewer had spent a good season climbing in Peru, then Bolivia, where he contracted hepatitis and spent a month in a hospital. He recovered and now, in Argentine Patagonia, he was looking to climb. Bridwell quickly convinced Brewer to join him for what would be only the fifteenth attempt at Cerro Torre.

They forded the river on December 26 and hiked to base camp in the Torre Valley. Through drifting clouds they caught glimpses of the Torre before blankets of gray overtook the valley and hid the mountain. The wind broke branches from the trees in camp, and one of Bridwell's tents blew away. They passed the time baking bread, reading, swilling rum by the campfire, chasing sheep and—when they were successful—gorging on mutton stew.

They studied the barometer, as climbers did then. But one had to be wary of barometer paralysis, as it could make you miss a window. The endless micro-cycles of barometer fluctuations would drive climbers nuts. If the stars were out, you had to go. This time, the barometer rose sharply, the weather cleared, and Bridwell and Brewer set off toward the southeast ridge, home to the Compressor Route, with light packs.

They broke trail through deep snow on the upper glacier toward the snow cave where Bridwell, early in his trip, had cached all the climbing gear needed for the ascent. The snow and wind of the previous couple of weeks had buried any sign of his two-foot-high marking stakes and any sign of the cave. Rocks and ice crashed down from thousands of feet above as the temperatures rose. They dug for hours in the area where Bridwell had made the cave. Nothing. They returned the next morning and dug some more. Again, nothing.

They descended and scrounged gear from the handful of other climbers in the area, putting together enough for an attempt. At 3:30 a.m. on January 3, 1979, with scant supplies—food, twenty-five pitons, wired nuts, some cams, twenty-five carabiners, six ice screws, a small bolt kit, and two ropes—they started back up.

"If you're not scared, you're not having fun," Bridwell wrote. "If that's true, Cerro Torre is worth a couple of years at Disneyland.

Treading close to the edge elevates the fear factor, but it also focuses the mind...."

By 5:30 a.m. they'd already gained the Col of Patience, where Bridwell took over. They made fast time, the pitches passing in a blur, Bridwell leading the rock and Brewer leading the ice. They slowed only when Bridwell had to use his Yosemite-honed technique on an offwidth that was coated with ice.

Brewer wore traditional clothing layers. Bridwell remembered being soaked the previous season—despite his high-tech climbing clothes—and climbed in a one-piece neoprene diving suit.

A few pitches higher, while resting below a small roof, in the rising warmth of the day chunks of ice roared past and they huddled closer to the wall—they weren't wearing helmets. "Ice crystals floated through the brilliant blue sky like tiny winged diamonds, all the richness and wealth we needed at that moment," Bridwell wrote.

As with many climbers, Bridwell had raised an eyebrow to Maestri's insult to his countrymen, the one about hope being a vain word and a weapon of the weak. Every alpine climber relies on hope, a requisite component to the fantasy of launching into crazy, hostile terrain.

In his account, Bridwell inserted an adjective before the *h*-word. "Everything was going according to my plan.... Let us rephrase the great Maestri's words, 'Irrational hope is a vain word in the mountains.'"

They motored through brilliant free climbing mixed with occasional aid, snow, and ice, along with sections of fourth class. "Where was the huge number of bolts the British had accused Maestri of placing! Instead, we encountered five or six clusters of hardware: clogs, pitons, rurps, cliffhangers, fifi hooks, ice screws, even clog ascenders, and carabiners—so many carabiners we couldn't use them all. Fixed ropes trailed from the anchors, broken, and shredded. They also were presumably left by the British team which had failed here in 1972," Brewer wrote, in reference to one of the route's prior attempts.

By noon they stopped and rested on a small ledge, while the sun sent more chunks of ice plummeting past. Several more pitches brought them to the first of Maestri's bolt ladders—the monumental traverse across blank rock that bypassed the aid seam above, which was led by the Anglo-Argentine team in 1968. It is here, where the bolt ladders begin, that the Compressor Route's name becomes apparent. Brewer and Bridwell simulclimbed across the bolt ladder, continued up a chimney, another bolt ladder, and another chimney. Soon, the vertical headwall loomed overhead. More abandoned gear littered the wall, and an old rope lay frozen in the ice. The sun set and they spent an hour and a half chopping a ledge. Just before midnight they cooked a sparse dinner.

Wisps of wind rose through the night, but, come morning, the weather held. They finished off the ice and mixed pitches, ascended more bolt ladders, and were finally at the base of the five-hundred-foot final headwall.

On the headwall, Bridwell reported having to clean six to twelve inches of rime ice to find each bolt. Clouds gathered in the sky. Rime grew from the air like shards on a magnet, forming ice worms on their clothes and frozen feathers on the rock. In urgency, they started simulclimbing the bolt ladders.

They climbed over the compressor, lashed to the wall a hundred and fifty feet below the summit, as the sky grew darker. "If you're worried, this is the time to go down," Bridwell told Brewer over the increasing wind. They continued up. Near the top, suddenly, the bolts ended. Bridwell knew from Maestri's account that he'd smashed some of his own bolts on his descent in a twisted effort to prove to other climbers that his bolts were necessary.

But Bridwell saw something even more shocking: "Looking up, I saw seven broken bolts leading up and slightly right, but eighty feet of blank granite stretched between the last bolt and the summit snow. My God, I thought, Maestri must have nailed [with pitons] eighty feet of ice tenuously bound to smooth rock. It was a bad joke and inconsistent with the magazine articles."

A bad joke indeed, and one presumes Bridwell's words facetious. Maestri, who said they'd forgotten their pitons below, hence the abundant bolt ladders, hadn't even finished the headwall. Despite his initial descriptions of standing on the icy summit, he later admitted that he'd foregone the summit mushroom, claiming it was "Just a lump of ice and not really part of the mountain. It will blow away one day." Not only that, but he never even touched the summit ice slopes. The evidence was crystal clear: Maestri retreated on dead-vertical terrain.

All traces of his passage had, once again, disappeared below the summit. As with 1959, his path had been unmistakably clear. Then, nothing. In a day where even the best in the world left slight scars from their passage while climbing hard aid pitches, there was no trace from Maestri.

Bridwell reached into his Yosemite bag of tricks—Yosemite climbers represented the global state of the art for big-wall climbing, and Bridwell was king. He used his bolt kit to drill tiny holes in the rock from which he could aid, and delicately tapped in pitons and copperheads. He pieced together tenuous A3 (aid) climbing. At one point he yelled down to Brewer that there wasn't enough time to continue—the storm was coming too hard. Brewer shouted up encouragement. Bridwell kept climbing.

He eventually excavated an ice-filled crack, placed a cam, switched to free climbing for some moves. Then, with feet smearing on rock and an ax planted in the ice leading to the summit cone he lashed crampons to his feet and romped up the lower-angled ice. (Over the ensuing decades and repeat ascents, this "Bridwell pitch," to top out the headwall, was often completely fixed with pitons and other gear; it sometimes required at least one hook move and/or a few free moves between fixed pieces.) Brewer came up and continued leading atop the final summit mushroom, battling through a six-foot overhang of unconsolidated snow, and crawled onto the summit. Sixty mile per hour winds hammered them from the west, rendering their shouted comments inaudible. They embraced, snapped a few photos, and got the hell out of there.

For all the controversy and complexity Maestri had brought to the line over two extended siege sessions, and for all of his bolt ladders and the influence they would have for decades to come, Brewer and Bridwell had made the true first ascent of the route. While Maestri's bolt ladders would be forever synonymous with the Compressor Route, he still hadn't reached the top of the mountain for which he was most famous.

"Storm dragons darted across the maroon and slate-colored sky," Bridwell wrote of their descent. "The wind is the stalker on Cerro Torre, and the climber is a very tiny prey."

They rappelled back to their bivy and dozed off. Come morning, still halfway up the tower, snow blanketed everything, spindrift shed down the walls, and fog obscured both the summit and the valley below. Their ropes were frozen cables. Avalanches roared through the cirque below, and their ropes got stuck more than once. They kept at it.

On the monumental bolt traverse, Bridwell led short rappels for logistical ease. Once, after mistakenly clipping in with the low-strength keeper sling on his hammer, he found himself airborne. His mind disengaged from reality, "assuming the viewpoint of spectator." He slammed onto the end of the rope—he hadn't yet removed the ropes from his rappel device—and smashed into the rock. He'd fallen more than a hundred feet, broken some ribs, smashed his elbow and hip, and "rearranged my mind. No serious damage.... Pain is the main thing I remember about the rest of the descent."

Their rappel devices squeegeed water down their legs, the snow further soaked them, and the wind froze their ropes between rappels. Bridwell shouted in pain.

Down on the glacier, they stumbled upon an Italian party who'd been attempting Torre Egger, camped in a snow cave. The Italians brought them in with a warm welcome, gave them soup, tea, and rum, and wrapped them in warm, dry sleeping bags. The Italians were astonished by Bridwell and Brewer's speed. "I told them we moved so fast because we were so scared," Bridwell said. He added that he was only half joking.

The "Bridwell pitch," above the last trace of Maestri's passage, en route to the summit of Cerro Torre via the Compressor Route. This location corresponds with the arrow atop the route line on page 78. Photo: Paul Gagner

Cerro Torre in its usual state: blasted by storm. Photo: Leo Dickinson

chapter 14

THE GRANDFATHER CLAUSE

In 1970, after Maestri and his compressor treated Cerro Torre like a construction project and reported reaching the summit, he returned home to terrific fanfare. The greater climbing world was less impressed. Most climbers considered Maestri's tactics an affront to the spirit of alpinism and to long-held notions of fair play. The September 1972 issue of *Mountain* magazine, the most influential English language periodical in the world at the time, had Cerro Torre on its cover and featured a now-famous article entitled "Cerro Torre: A Mountain Desecrated."

Despite the initial outrage, something curious followed: The Compressor Route became the most popular route on Cerro Torre.

After Bridwell's 1979 ascent, the Compressor Route had the blessing of climbing royalty. To stand on Cerro Torre's summit was a dazzling prize. And most who climbed the route reported it to be damned good, regardless of the bolt ladders. By anybody's definition, the route included plenty of superb "real" climbing. To top it off, you still had the final, notoriously variable, summit mushroom. Many a climber finished the headwall and romped up the short ice slopes, only to then be denied the true summit, heartbreakingly close, by overhanging rime.

Few climbers even attempted other routes on Cerro Torre. Until the mid-2000s the Ragni Route—practically an expedition in itself just to get there—was summitted only four times. Out on the ice cap, climbers could look forward to waiting for a weather window while festering inside a snow cave, as the full fury of the incoming storms blasted across the ice, rather than camping in the pleasant lenga forests to the east.

From the late 1970s onward, climbers made over a dozen attempts at the tower's northern aspect, home to the mythical Egger-Maestri 1959 route. Those attempts covered most of the various, conflicting lines claimed by Maestri, but until 2005 none reached the top. And none found even the slightest trace of Maestri's claimed passage above the triangular snowfield.

Meanwhile, on the massive south and east faces, Slovenian and Italian teams established difficult new routes. None of them, however, finished on previously unclimbed terrain. Each route veered off to join the Compressor Route below the headwall. All three of the south face routes—cold, loose, vicious big-wall climbing—ended and descended upon intersecting the Compressor Route. Both of the east face routes—better rock but still incredibly difficult—continued to the summit courtesy of Maestri's bolt ladders.

As testament to Cerro Torre's inherent difficulty, aside from the four complete ascents of the Ragni Route, until 2005 every other climb to the summit (around a hundred) depended upon using the bolts of the Compressor Route to get there.

Even as the allure of Cerro Torre grew and more climbers came and tried, multiple years would pass, often consecutively, without a single ascent. Each summitless season, each nightmarish attempt that ended in a hellacious storm, and each rare success further embedded the Compressor Route as part of Cerro Torre's lore. The moral affront of Maestri's prolific bolt ladders became easier to overlook for many climbers.

The storied attempts enhanced the route's mystique. In 1980 Kiwi climber Bill Denz made thirteen attempts to solo the route. He endured a seven-day bivouac trapped on a tiny ledge a thousand feet below the top on one attempt. Another time, his best attempt, Denz retreated only two hundred feet below the summit.

Tales of terror were omnipresent. Since storms race in from the west, if you were high on the Compressor Route, you wouldn't know you were in trouble until it was too late. Eyelids froze shut. The wind would send ropes sailing horizontally into space before shifting and launching them back into the wall like wild, slithering snakes, twisting them irretrievably around flakes and forcing climbers to cut their ropes and make ever shorter rappels with what remained. Climbers would stagger down to the safety of the forest looking like battle-worn soldiers, their eyes fixed in thousand-yard stares.

American climber Gregory Crouch, author of *Enduring Patagonia* (2001), climbed regularly in the Chaltén Massif in the mid-1990s. Every time he started up a route, he told me, he climbed with a sense of panic over the impending epic. In the 1995–96 season, Crouch threw himself at the Compressor Route fourteen times before succeeding. "The Compressor Route was one of the best statements of my character, because I kept going back to it. I had a great time on that climb. Yes, it's a completely compromised route with its construction, and no way would I have done a first ascent like that. I wouldn't have chopped it, either. Climbing doesn't matter, not in the grand scheme—what matters is what it means to us as individuals. And climbing that route meant a lot to me. Still does."

IN THE DAYS of Old Patagonia, the influence of Cesare Maestri, the most famous Cerro Torre climber to never stand on its summit, remained inseparable from the mountain—in spite of his transgressions. Or, actually, because of them.

Reinhold Messner. Photo: Kelly Cordes

chapter 15

INSIGHT FROM REINHOLD

I had emailed Reinhold Messner to request an interview, and his assistants basically replied, "No way, too busy." He'd recently written a book, *Grido di Pietra: Cerro Torre, la montagna impossibile*. (It's published in Italian and German. The English translation of the title is Scream of Stone: Cerro Torre, the impossible mountain). Not only is Messner universally regarded as the greatest mountaineer in history, he's also a climbing historian and a defender of mountain environments and the alpine-style ethos. Everybody tries to interview Messner, I figured, so after a couple more pleas that went nowhere, I'd given up.

But, as it turns out, Mirella Tenderini's friend Sandro was tight with Messner. Sandro hooked me up.

I was to meet him at the Messner Mountain Museum near the city of Bolzano in Northern Italy's South Tyrol province. Messner officially resides within Italy's borders. The greater Italian public loves to claim him as one of their own. But everybody told me that Messner's not Italian. He's South Tyrolean. Just as Trentino is an autonomous province and very much old-school Italy, the bordering South Tyrol is an autonomous province primarily comprising German-speaking people from Austro-Bavarian heritage that's technically located in Northern Italy. South Tyrol is like a part of Austria inside Italy's border.

I arrived fifteen minutes early, found Sandro, and introduced myself. He was friendly and relaxed and told me to come back in an hour—Reinhold Messner, of course, was quite busy. So I checked out the museum, an immaculate combination of art and history laid out within a giant castle that dates to the year 945. The theme of the displays is "man's encounter with the mountains."

I returned and patiently waited for Messner. After a while, from a doorway across the outdoor patio emerged the man himself, his wookie-like bushel of hair a dead giveaway. Fellow tourists in the castle's outdoor cafe whispered and stared. I intercepted him and introduced myself and tried to start a conversation.

He was polite but had no time. "You can find everything in my papers, I wrote fifty books," he told me. I persisted, trying to ask about the notion of conquest alpinism and the values people place on the summit versus the process. He walked briskly and bluntly told me he doesn't know why people would still engage in conquest alpinism, and that for him the Compressor Route never held interest. I was like a pesky reporter, and I tried again to mention the human desire to dominate nature and what it means in climbing. Again, he was curt, "Nobody can dominate nature."

Yes, I said, but on Cerro Torre they have tried, Cesare Maestri tried, and... I fumbled along, hoping to trigger his interest. I was failing, and he was blowing me off. I couldn't blame him. He doesn't have time to talk to everyone. I followed him and Sandro down some stairs into a room where he sat down with a newspaper reporter. Sandro made brief eye contact. Messner first ignored me, then glanced at me and said, "Five minutes for her, five minutes for you," and began talking to the reporter.

After about five minutes the woman thanked him and began packing. Sandro leaned over to Messner and whispered something in his ear. His expression changed. He said, "You have climbed Cerro Torre?" Our interview began.

He asked which route, "The Maestri route?" meaning the Compressor Route. I tried to describe where we had climbed.

He asked, "So you do not know the Maestri route?"

"I have rappelled it," I replied. I explained that I had seen this example of what Messner has called "conquest alpinism."

"Yes, but conquest alpinism was the alpinism for a hundred years, and generally the climbers went only to conquest the mountain. It was all. They did not go for enjoyment. And Cerro Torre, the conquest of Cesare Maestri was very late, in '70, but it's a conquest. But in reality, the motivation for Maestri to go there was to show that he went up the time before, in '59. He didn't show this."

I tried to ask another question, but Messner was in a hurry and he cut me off.

"Maestri showed that he did not go up in '59. If you really want to go in on the scandal of Cerro Torre, it is proved that Cerro Torre was not possible for *anyone* in '59. Nobody could climb it.

"If you know the whole history, why Cesare went there, it's because he was in competition with Bonatti. He was taken out of K2 [Maestri had hoped to be selected for the 1954 Italian K2 expedition that made the first ascent of K2], it's understandable that he tried to do something crazy, and he was not able to do it.

"And especially the other one, this terrible Fava. Fava is the liar. And he was able to tell to Cesare, after the tragedy—nobody knows how the tragedy went, but—he went to Cesare and said, 'You and I went to the Col de la Conquista and you did the whole thing and afterwards....' This is an invention surely from Fava. No doubt. And Cesare is trapped."

Thoughts flashed through my mind: *Fava? Why does he think Fava? The charming, hardworking, immigrant Fava? The man who lost his feet selflessly trying to rescue a climber on Aconcagua whose guide abandoned him, the Fava everybody loved? Maybe it was something in Messner's research on Egger....* We kept rolling.

"Once you tell it you have to keep telling it," I replied. "I wonder if he convinced himself?"

"No. No, he was sure that nobody will go to Cerro Torre. It was *so* difficult in '59 to go there... so they were thinking, nobody will go and we tell this story and nobody will care about it."

Messner is best known for being the first to climb all of the world's fourteen 8,000-meter peaks, and to do so without supplementary oxygen. Given his outspoken stance against the siege-style expeditions in the Himalaya, I asked if he saw any similarities between the Compressor Route and the style in which people are climbing 8,000-meter peaks these days? (Tactics often involve large commercial operations set up for high-paying clients, operations that employ scads of fixed rope, high-altitude Sherpa support, and bottled oxygen.) It may have been the first thing I'd said that grabbed his attention.

"Yeah, there is." He paused for a moment, then said, "What they are doing is exactly what's happening now in the Alps. Especially in Germany. Also in Austria but not so bad. Less in Italy. Now, tourism organizations are asking climbers to prepare the classical routes for big masses. So they make these via ferratas. Spitting [bolting] the routes. Now they are putting every ten meters belay stations so nobody can fall down. The first people to have this philosophy... was the German Alpine Club. They said, 'We are responsible to make the mountains secure. Safe.' And I answered to them, 'You are the killers of mountaineering.' And they answered that I should go in jail because people are all dying when they fall."

"It's your fault, right?"

Finally, he laughed. "It's my fault, yes."

He said that the German tourism boards want visitors, and visitors want safe mountain experiences. Just bolt everything, and the people will come.

"They say, we need tourists. It's very simple. Our hotels are only full if the mountains are spitted. If no spit, no one is coming."

I asked why so many people, especially in the Trentino region, despite all of the facts about 1959, still believe Maestri's story.

"For '59, Cesare is a very famous man. He's known, people like him, he speaks a lot [public presentations]. The old climbers, I think they know it, but they are from a... how you say?"

"Protective?"

"Yeah, protective, but it's a special word. More than protective— there is a solidarity."

He then told me about the 2009 Trento Film Festival: the golden jubilee of the supposed first ascent of Cerro Torre. Messner was a featured guest, his Cerro Torre book had just been released. To have Reinhold Messner at your mountain film festival is like having the Rolling Stones play your birthday party. Anybody in the world would put him front and center. Well, almost anybody.

Messner proposed a discussion. "I said, 'I think that fifty years after 1959, it is time to discuss it.'" They told him he could present his book, but no discussion.

During his presentation, sprinkled throughout the audience, including in the front row reserved seats, many people wore match- ing T-shirts with a photo of the cover of Messner's book, and across it, in red capital letters: "BASTA! LA POLEMICA VENALE UCCIDE L'ALPINISMO"—"Stop! The venal controversy kills alpinism."

"In the evening they make *huge* festival, five hundred or a thou- sand people, around Cesare Maestri, cheering, clapping, 'You did this!'" Messner shook his head. "It's incredible."

GEAR CACHE

Cerro Torre from the east, with the white triangle marking the gear cache which represents the highest certain traces of the 1959 expedition. Artifacts too numerous to count have been found below. Just above is the obvious triangular snowfield. An old piton found at its upper margin in 1978 might have been from the '59 attempt. Nothing from 1959 has ever been found higher on the mountain.
Photo: Rolando Garibotti

chapter 16

EXAMINATION OF A MYTH

"If someone told you he had just run a ten-minute mile you would shrug your shoulders and say, 'So what?' If someone said he had just run a three-minute mile you would be amazed and skeptical, and a reasonable response would be to ask for evidence." Those are the opening lines of a manuscript we received from Rolando Garibotti at the *American Alpine Journal* in 2004.

When climbers do new routes, they generally provide reports that include some form of evidence showing that they actually did what they claimed. A plausible description of the terrain usually suffices. Summit photos, route photos, corroboration of others who were there—all support a claim. But the burden of proof in climbing is so low, surely every so often a climber lies about a new route. Some claims are so outrageous that they demand our attention.

I worked directly with Garibotti during my dozen years at the *AAJ*, as he was our regional correspondent for the Chaltén Massif. He's the world's foremost expert on climbing there, and his unsolicited manuscript dissected the claimed 1959 Egger-Maestri ascent. It was far and away the most thorough examination of the famed controversy ever compiled, in part due to Garibotti's multilingual fluency, which allowed him a depth of understanding absent from prior articles: He studied original documents, interviews, and photographs published in English, Italian, French, and Spanish.

Garibotti's idea for the manuscript germinated in 1999, while he was researching his guidebook, *Patagonia Vertical*, which was published in 2012. At the time, he says, "I had an opinion that was completely uninformed." But while studying historical accounts of the 1959 climb, he couldn't ignore the numerous contradictions and implausibilities. Intrigued, he continued to read and analyze all of the details and eventually "put two and two together."

So exhaustive was his research that when we printed the manuscript in the *AAJ*, we couldn't fit the complete bibliography (it went to the web). Every subsequent informed analysis of the 1959 climb, including my own, relies heavily on Garibotti's meticulous research, which uncovered everything from obscure Trentino journals to diaries archived in Buenos Aires. His 7,800-word thesis, "A Mountain Unveiled: A Revealing Analysis of Cerro Torre's Tallest Tale," reached readers late summer 2004. It was such a thorough, evidence-based dismantling of Maestri's ascent claim that it destroyed any rational notion that Egger and Maestri climbed Cerro Torre in 1959.

But you can't force people to read. Some Maestri defenders certainly didn't know about the article. Some averted their eyes, while others clung to elements of delusion. It makes you wonder: How much evidence does it take to convince people who want to hold onto their version of the truth?

The article, in various forms, was widely available outside of the printed *AAJ*. We posted it for free on the *AAJ* website, a version was published in Dauer's Cerro Torre book, Ermanno Salvaterra did a rough translation into Italian that made its rounds online, a shortened version was published in Slovak, and, recently, it was translated into Turkish. It's also available free under the "knowledge" section of Garibotti's website, pataclimb.com.

Nobody has ever mounted a viable rebuttal of "A Mountain Unveiled."

"I would have definitely welcomed a fact-based rebuttal," Garibotti says. "Would have loved it. Would still welcome it today. The questioning of 'A Mountain Unveiled' was all focused on shooting the messenger and in faith-based rhetoric that has no factual basis."

Despite the mountain of evidence in Garibotti's article, some argued that until somebody succeeded in climbing Cerro Torre from the north and could confirm the presence or absence of the anchors Maestri claimed to have left, we could not be certain. But that, too, would soon happen. And, in the minds of the true believers, it wouldn't change a thing.

PART THREE

previous spread Hayden Kennedy high on the headwall during
the first fair-means ascent of Cerro Torre's southeast ridge.
Photo: Jason Kruk

above Bean Bowers in El Chaltén. Photo: Kelly Cordes

PART THREE

chapter 17

NEW PATAGONIA

The single biggest change in the history of climbing in Patagonia arrived in the 2004–05 season. It happened far from the mountains, and it wasn't the bridge over the Río Fitz Roy, or the airport in El Calafate, or the paved roads, or even the evolution of modern climbing gear.

It was weather forecasts.

Weather station data and Internet connectivity arrived together, which was essential because one without the other meant Old Patagonia. The two combined equaled New Patagonia.

In Old Patagonia, you'd be camped in the woods, maybe just back from an attempt where a sucker-window of weather had slammed shut when you were three thousand feet up your climb. It was as if the fury of the gods had suddenly descended upon you, but somehow you'd survived. Your body went numb, the wind slammed you into the wall, and you couldn't hear your partner yelling at you from three feet away. Every second of every hour for the next twelve was laced with a primal fear. Then, you staggered back to camp and crashed out, deep into a dreamless sleep. You hadn't slept in thirty-some hours and as the storm raged, you hoped for only one thing:

that it would continue, so you wouldn't even have to think about going back out there. But in the middle of the night you had to piss. You'd rolled over and mumbled, unzipped the tent door, and staggered outside. Through bleary eyes your gaze strayed to the gaps between the lenga trees, and you'd seen stars shining bright. *Fuck*.

In 1975, following one of his many expeditions to the area, Ben Campbell-Kelly wrote: "An expedition should be prepared to be spending a minimum of three months in the mountains, particularly if they have chosen a difficult objective."

When I was in El Chaltén in 2013, a friend had been monitoring the forecasts from the U.S. He saw a window coming, took advantage of today's increased accessibility, hopped a plane and a few days later climbed the Ragni Route on Cerro Torre. Around the same time, a pair of young Slovenians arrived, dropped their bags at their hostel—the forecast was perfect—and, without sleep, ran up the trail to Fitz Roy and established a hard new route.

Within a few years of that 2004–05 season, the forecasts had become so accurate that climbers could confidently leave behind most of the storm gear they used to carry, making for lighter loads and faster climbing. Remove the crippling fear of being caught in one of those legendary storms, and the change in Patagonian climbing is impossible to overstate.

Nowadays climbers in town (nobody camps in the woods anymore) can be heard saying things like, "Yeah, looks like sixes and eights tomorrow, then dropping to twos on Wednesday." They are talking knots of wind speed at the lower, forecast elevation, which translates into nay or yay for climbing at the higher mountain elevations.

WEATHER BALLOONS had probably been going up around

Patagonia long before anyone made forecasts, Jim Woodmencey told me. He's a climber, skier, and former Grand Teton National Park ranger who owns a forecasting company called MountainWeather. He says each country has weather service stations, and they launch balloons that gather data at various points in the atmosphere. There are other ways to gather data as well, like surface observation stations, ocean buoys, and satellite photos of clouds at different elevations

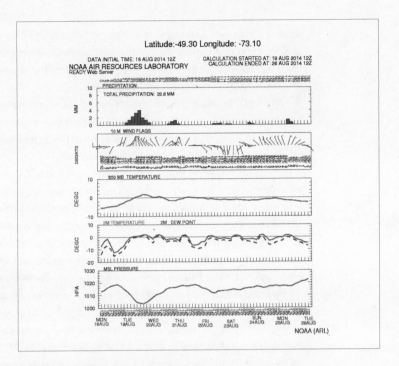

Screenshot of weather forecast for the massif. Courtesy of noaa.gov

and time intervals, which indicate things like wind speed and atmospheric moisture concentration. Even though data is comparatively sparse in less-populated places like Patagonia, virtually nothing stands between the storms brewing in the ocean and the Chaltén Massif. Thus, the data collected allows for accurate forecasts.

Data alone means nothing, though. It's computer models that actually analyze the data and make predictions—forecasts—and they've improved tremendously over the years. Data transformed into a forecast answers the key question: *Is it climbing weather or not?*

In the 2004–05 season, German climber Thomas Huber decided to see if his weather guru, Karl Gabl, could provide forecasts from afar. Forecasts for the Chaltén Massif were unprecedented. "We had no idea if it would work for Patagonia," Thomas told me. "But it worked, so everybody was looking at me to see if I'd go or stay, because the climbers thought I knew via Innsbruck the secret about the weather. I had a great first season. Not only for Patagonia but everywhere, weather reports changed a lot in alpinism."

As Gabl's forecasts have shown over time, accurate mountain forecasts require specific knowledge. Even if you could teach yourself how to do it, you'd need the ability to access the information, which requires functional Internet access.

The Internet didn't come to El Chaltén until 2003. Even then, it was scarce, and it barely worked. The first *locutorio* (Internet cafe) arrived in 2004; climbers would come to check the weather on NOAA, but they'd struggle because the connection was so bad.

Local resident Adriana Estol recalls, "I came here in 2006 and it was almost impossible to have Internet at the house, but some houses were lucky." One of the lucky houses belonged to Bean Bowers.

Bowers, a tough-as-nails alpinist and full-on lifestyle climber from the U.S., was always the do-it-yourself sort. For several consecutive years, he'd lived the entire season in El Chaltén, and he'd scraped together enough money to buy a small house there. In 2011, at age thirty-eight, Bean died of cancer, but several of his friends remember how he figured out the weather. He guided in the Tetons in the summers, where, one season, Climbing Ranger Ron Johnson showed him how to read weather models.

Doug Chabot, an accomplished alpinist and avalanche forecaster, also helped out. "I gave Bean the weather basics on forecasting in 2004 since he was keen to learn. In fact, during his first trip there [to El Chaltén], he would call me to check on a few weather models. I was avalanche forecasting; I'm used to looking at weather models every day." He added, "Most importantly, I had a real job and was reachable by phone."

Bowers also took a course from Woodmencey on mountain weather forecasting.

Climber Josh Wharton remembers well the first season of forecasts, as he and the late Jonny Copp were climbing together in the massif. Many climbers expressed gratitude to Huber for sharing his forecasts that season, and soon the gratitude would shift to Bowers. "Bean was reading the navy maps a friend had showed him, but he was still pretty new to it, so it wasn't always that spot-on. Thomas Huber was using a satellite phone to call his Austrian meteorologist, and between the two I remember growing increasingly confident throughout the trip. In fact, when Jonny and I started down Poincenot [the final tower in their fifty-two-hour linkup of Agujas Saint-Exupéry, Rafael, and Poincenot], the wind came up harshly right on queue, almost to the hour Thomas's guy had predicted three days earlier. It was an 'ah ha' moment!"

As he was learning, Bowers kept his dirtbag forecasting knowledge close to his chest, mostly sharing it with friends. In 2006 he taught it to Rolando Garibotti, and soon climbers were knocking on their doors asking for forecasts and how-to instructions. After all, knowing the weather in Patagonia was like having a golden ticket— and it was especially good because it was free.

Climbers literally lined up at Garibotti's house wanting to learn, so he typed up a how-to email (now he has a weather forecasting section on his pataclimb.com website). Before long, everyone could get a spot forecast for the massif—just follow the steps, punch in the data on the right websites and you get frighteningly accurate projections for precipitation, temperature, and, most importantly, wind speed.

The most horrifying and brutal component of Patagonia climbing could now be avoided while you rested and went bouldering off the mountain. The place would never be the same.

Rolando Garibotti. Photo: Hans Johnstone

chapter 18

EL ARCA DE LOS VIENTOS

Maybe it was like the avalanche Maestri described in 1959, roaring down Cerro Torre. The one he said killed Toni Egger. It surely happens several times each season, a cloud like this one, thundering a hundred miles per hour down the four-thousand-foot wall toward Alessandro Beltrami, Rolando Garibotti, and Ermanno Salvaterra.

It was early November 2005, and the white wave came from a snow mushroom shedding off the upper ridge. The mushrooms grow outward, rime layer by rime layer, until their weight bows to gravity and their frozen bonds break. House-sized blocks come barreling down the mountain.

Garibotti had been resting by their snow cave when he heard the sound. He thought only of other times when he'd seen avalanches roaring down a mountain. Barefooted and lounging in the sun, he instinctively sprinted down-glacier, trying to outrun the torrent. Beltrami escaped farther into the cave. Salvaterra stood calm, grabbed his camera, grinned, and started shooting. During its thousands of feet of travels

down the wall, the low-density mushroom broke apart and disintegrated into crystals. The wind lifted and carried it away like dust before it even hit the glacier.

Salvaterra, then fifty, had made more than twenty expeditions to Patagonia, had already established two new routes on Cerro Torre—both so hard they've never been repeated—made its first winter ascent, and climbed a host of other difficult routes in the region. Many Patagonia regulars call him "Mr. Cerro Torre."

Of the many climbers interested in uncovering the truth about the first ascent, Salvaterra had tried the purported 1959 line three times, but had never gotten beyond the Col of Conquest. He was in good company, as dozens of the world's top alpinists had tried to climb Cerro Torre from the north over the years, but nobody had succeeded. And none had found the slightest trace of the 1959 expedition above the triangular snowfield.

Salvaterra's initial plans were with fellow Italian climber Alessandro Beltrami. Beltrami, only twenty-four years old at the time, is an accomplished climber and former Nordic ski racer. He works as a mountain guide and had climbed in Patagonia only once before: In 2004 he, Salvaterra, and fellow Italian Giacomo Rossetti established a new route on Cerro Torre's imposing east face.

Salvaterra had long believed Maestri and for years had been a loyal supporter. But over time, as he learned more, he changed his mind and found himself at odds with many pro-Maestri climbers—which in Trentino meant quite a few. Finding any trace of Egger and Maestri's passage above the Col of Conquest would be enough to vindicate Maestri. Before leaving, Salvaterra said, "If I find one of their pegs [pitons], I'll fling it in the world's face, but first and foremost in mine."

As for the quiet Beltrami, who worked in the same guide's office in Madonna di Campiglio that employed Maestri (who is still a celebrity in his old age and was guiding easy treks), he went to Patagonia believing Maestri. "Here, Maestri is a very known alpinist, an icon for some people, and a respected and important person. It's quite normal to believe him without question."

Garibotti, a longtime friend of Salvaterra's, was obviously convinced that Maestri had lied. Fiercely passionate and immensely

El Arca de los Vientos (dots for hidden portions).
Photo: Rolando Garibotti

Looking down at the belayer, high on Cerro Torre's north face, with the summit of Torre Egger below. Photo: Rolando Garibotti

talented, the enigmatic then-thirty-four-year-old had long been known among serious alpinists for his incredible ascents and his disdain for hype.

Born in Italy, Rolando Garibotti grew up in Bariloche, Argentina, in northern Patagonia. He climbed his first technical route in the Chaltén Massif at age fifteen. When he was seventeen, he and a high school classmate got within five pitches of Cerro Torre's summit via the Compressor Route. In 1993 he moved to the U.S., but his heart remained in Patagonia, where he has made mind-bogglingly fast ascents of big, technically difficult objectives in perfect style without fanfare.

His prolific record isn't limited to Patagonia. In 2000, Garibotti free soloed the Grand Traverse—an epic, technical enchainment of ten peaks in the Tetons, in less than seven hours. At that time most climbers took several days. In 2001, Garibotti and American alpinist Steve House climbed the Infinite Spur, a nine-thousand-foot techni-cal route in Alaska that had been considered the most committing in the Denali region, in twenty-five hours. Of the route's few ascents, the next fastest had been eight days. Despite his avoidance of the limelight, Garibotti is a phenom.

Gregory Crouch described Garibotti in his 2001 memoir, *Enduring Patagonia*:

> He has the good characteristics of the Latin stereotype on abun-dant display. Rolo is warm, friendly and open, tall, dark, handsome, and hard-core, but utterly without a macho peacock's attitude. He's quietly competent and tough, or perhaps he's just so god-damned good that he has no need to display it. Rolo praises the people he admires, gets psyched for the accomplishments of his friends, and doesn't seem to have an envious bone in his six-foot-one-inch frame. I believe Rolo is megacompetitive—nobody that good isn't—but his competitiveness isn't rooted in a desire to see other people fail. Rolo uses his competitive fire to put the whip to himself, probably too much…. The alpine compliment I covet most in the world is Rolo's terse 'Good effort.' It's not lightly given.

Surprising as it may seem, given his interest in the Egger-Maestri story, Garibotti had no desire for the peak: "Cerro Torre was never a dream of mine. I never thought it would be the kind of mountain that would allow me to climb it in a style I would be pleased with." Cerro Torre, quite simply, is so desperately steep and endures such sudden and violent storms, that establishing a new route in good, minimalist style seemed unlikely.

When Garibotti asked Salvaterra to join him for one of his Patagonia projects, the veteran saw an opportunity and made a proposition. He'd join Garibotti for his project later if Garibotti would join theirs first—the mythical Egger-Maestri route. Deal.

"I thought we would arrive to the base, 'meow' a couple of times, then find something else to do," Garibotti admitted afterward. "My interest in this affair was not to climb along the lines of Maestri's fantasy, it was to climb a new route on Cerro Torre, alpine style, along a line that was independent of the bolted travesty. The history thing is a side show. I went there as an eager alpinist and not as a historian."

THE "MEOW" NEVER HAPPENED. "As it turns out, after

we dug a snow cave and spent a few days at the base, I started warming up to the idea. Then I got to climb a few pitches and liked the thing, so I felt motivated enough for a good try," Garibotti said. Salvaterra and Beltrami felt it, too. But their first attempt ended in failure three thousand feet up with an incoming storm.

Upon retreat, they were immediately fired up for another go. "The transformation happened at the bottom, the morning after the first attempt. No pill involved. In this I can speak only for myself," said Garibotti. "But that next morning I realized that this was not only well within our reach, but that it was a good, fun objective; so, all of a sudden the torch got lit, and there was energy available to no end."

Within three days the weather cleared. They trimmed even more weight from their packs and, though still slightly weary from the first attempt, set off again for the tower and the journey through history.

THEY STARTED CLIMBING by headlamp at 4:45 a.m. on November 12, 2005, and they made fantastic time. They were already familiar with the terrain from their first attempt, and with Garibotti's technical expertise, Salvaterra's experience, and Beltrami's strength, they were fully in synch as a team. They raced up the initial thousand feet, where fixed gear from 1959 abounds. Like the others who'd climbed there in the previous forty-seven years, the trio saw nothing more from 1959 as they continued toward the col and found the terrain starkly different from what Maestri described. They followed the one clear line, the blatantly obvious line of least resistance, like climbers do. Especially like climbers would have done in 1959, on an unclimbed peak.

Beltrami, Garibotti, and Salvaterra reached the Col of Conquest by noon. Actually, they were somewhat higher—if targeting Cerro Torre's northern aspects, the obvious line angles up a rock pillar that finishes a hundred feet above the col. Maestri, despite pains-taking detail in his descriptions of the climbing to the triangular snowfield, never mentioned this unmistakable and important feature. Garibotti continued leading and short-fixing, starting up each pitch with a huge loop of slack and no real belay. "This saved hours. It is a bit of a dangerous maneuver, but we were not too concerned about safety to be honest," Garibotti told me soon after.

"As for the dangers, since having health problems a few years back, I have a different perception of longevity and its usefulness. I am very aware that there are no certainties, and that it is worth try-ing to rip as much juice as possible from every opportunity that arises," Garibotti explained.

Garibotti climbed like never before. Above the col lie another two thousand feet of harder climbing to the summit.

Following the only logical line, they dipped around the corner onto the northwest face for several pitches before crossing the north ridge, onto the north face, and back again to the north ridge. They found no signs of Egger and Maestri's passage; at all of the ledges they could see, ledges on which Maestri claims to have placed anchor bolts, they saw only unmarred granite.

"Rolo climbs with missile-like speed. Every time we get to the belay he's already many meters beyond [short-fixing]. Incredibly, at four-thirty in the afternoon we're at the comfortable ledge that last

left Rolando Garibotti, leading below the col on El Arca de
Los Vientos. Photo: Ermanno Salvaterra

right Rolando Garibotti leading on the north face of Cerro Torre.
Photo: Alessandro Beltrami

time took us two days to reach," reported Salvaterra. Several more pitches and they found a barely manageable bivy spot. Beltrami and Garibotti lay on a faint snow and ice rib, while Salvaterra passed the night sitting upright on a tiny step. "The place is utterly out of this world," Salvaterra wrote. "Torre Egger is facing us, Mount Fitz Roy is to the right and Hielo Continental to the left. The cold is pretty biting, the sky unbelievably starry. The night passes quickly and we manage to get some sleep."

They started climbing at eight the next morning—not yet thawed but it didn't take long once the southern sun hit the north face. The climbing remained difficult, as Salvaterra described: "Rolo climbs two vertical pitches showing us once again his utter expertise. The cracks are clogged with ice and so he's got to clear them with the ax." By noon they'd joined the overhanging rime mushrooms along the summit ridge on the Ragni di Lecco Route, now indisputably the true line of Cerro Torre's first ascent.

Despite being close, they couldn't see Cerro Torre's summit: only the bulging rime formations shaped by the brutal wind. The climbing got desperate; they took turns, all trying a single pitch before it succumbed—four hours for one mushroom pitch. Clouds filled the sky and the wind roared. Day became night and they climbed through the seemingly endless mushrooms. Then, suddenly, atop their thirty-seventh pitch since leaving the glacier the previous morning, at 11:15 p.m. they shined their headlamps in all directions. There was no higher point on Cerro Torre.

They named the route El Arca de los Vientos—The Ark of Winds.

Alessandro Beltrami (left) and Ermanno Salvaterra, on Cerro Torre's
summit after the first ascent of El Arca de los Vientos. Photo:
Rolando Garibotti

Ermanno Salvaterra points to the gear cache and the likely
1959 high point. Photo: Leo Dickinson

chapter 19

AFTERMATH
2005

Beltrami, Garibotti, and Salvaterra were nominated for the Piolet d'Or, a prestigious French award for the best climb of the year. They declined the nomination. In an odd move, the committee refused their refusal. Maestri's lawyer then wrote a letter protesting the team's nomination and distributed it to the world's climbing media. The lawyer said that since the route was a repeat of the 1959 Egger-Maestri, and not a new route, it was ineligible. The letter contained sworn affidavits from Fava and Maestri.

"Maestri should be called by the courts to testify regarding what really happened with Egger, since there was a death involved," said Garibotti. "There is no gear of his and the terrain has nothing to do with his descriptions.... One thing is clear: They climbed three hundred meters on Cerro Torre and nothing more. That is it."

Back in Italy, where the Beltrami-Garibotti-Salvaterra ascent made front-page headlines, Salvaterra was direct about their findings. It wasn't what he wanted—he'd grown up believing the 1959 story, and he and Maestri had become friends. But unlike most in Trentino, he eventually decided to examine the evidence, and the evidence didn't support Maestri's claim. He'd hoped maybe the on-mountain reality would prove different. "Had I found something— not necessarily close to the summit, but even just beyond the first snowfield—it would have been enough for me and for the mountaineering skeptics."

Cesarino Fava, always fiercely defensive of Maestri, wrote a mock confession of their lie, published in several newspapers. Maestri still refused to address any of the crucial problems with his claim. "If you doubt me, you doubt the history of mountaineering," Maestri repeated. It was his only form of defense.

When Salvaterra returned home, many called *him* a liar. Maestri threatened to sue him for libel.

Beltrami returned to work at the guide's office in Maestri's hometown. "I don't want to judge his version or his reasons. But I believe only in what I saw: a magnificent cathedral of pure rock, ice, and snow, sometimes very difficult to 'paying court' [climbing in a respectful manner] even with our modern equipment," he told me. "I think that the Torre is a mountain which tells its history by itself.... Personally, I'm honored to be part of its history."

Beltrami is from a different generation; or maybe he's just more pragmatic. When I visited him, he'd sometimes smile wide as we talked and look at my recorder and make a face that said, "Before I answer, are you recording this?" I'd offer to turn off the recorder, and he'd laugh and say, "It's OK." He was generous and kind—and careful.

A few months after the ascent, a conference was held on Cerro Torre in Lugano, Switzerland, an Italian-speaking city near Lecco, just over Italy's northern border. With such overwhelming evidence presented, one might wonder why the time and effort was being wasted.

When Cesarino Fava spoke (Maestri, as expected, did not attend), he exuded his trademark charm, telling stories of passion with emotion and humor. He seemed completely unmoved by the final nail in the coffin of the 1959 myth.

Leo Dickinson, a documentary filmmaker and journalist from the U.K., wrote about the conference. Dickinson approached Fava and said, "I completely disagree with everything you say, but I think you are very courageous coming here tonight."

"Do you believe Mallory and Irvine reached the summit of Everest?" Fava fired back, regarding the British pair's famed, and fatal, 1924

Josh Wharton on the southeast ridge, battling through rime on the fair-means variation to Maestri's infamous ninety-meter bolt traverse. Photo: Zack Smith

Cesare Maestri in an interview at his home in Italy in 1972. During the interview, he was pointedly disinterested in discussing the great climb of 1959. When Ken Wilson, the primary interviewer and one of the most scrupulous early examiners of the Maestri affair, pressed for details, Maestri grew increasingly agitated. Wilson then asked him to draw his 1959 route line. Maestri marked a sheet of paper and handed it back—it was a map, with directions for leaving town. The interview was over.
Photos: Leo Dickinson

Hayden Kennedy in early morning light on the first fair-means ascent of Cerro Torre's southeast ridge. Photo: Jason Kruk

left Colin Haley below the west face headwall, during the first linkup of Los Tiempos Perdidos and the Ragni Route, 2007. Photo: Kelly Cordes

right top Rolando Garibotti on the upper north face of Cerro Torre, on the first ascent of El Arca de los Vientos. Photo: Ermanno Salvaterra

right bottom Alessandro Beltrami and Ermanno Salvaterra (in blue) on El Arca de los Vientos, the first route to climb Cerro Torre's northern aspect, nearly 47 years and dozens of attempts after Maestri's 1959 claim. Torre Egger is in the background. Photo: Rolando Garibotti

Colin Haley hiking up the Torre Glacier before the first linkup of Los Tiempos Perdidos and the Ragni Route. Photo: Kelly Cordes

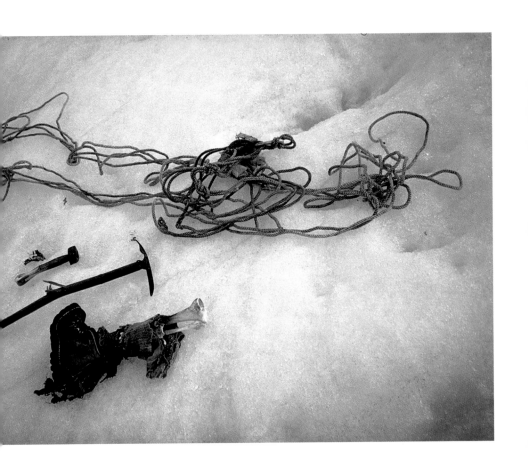

left Some of Toni Egger's remains, found in 1974. Photo: Jim Donini

right Members of Italy's Ragni di Lecco team pulling loads to base camp on the ice cap, 1974. Photo: Mario Conti

David Lama belaying high on the headwell during his 2012
fair-means first free ascent of Cerro Torre's southeast ridge.
The compressor is visible to the right. Photo: Lincoln Else-
Red Bull Content Pool

Jason Kruk following a pitch at dawn on the first fair-means ascent of Cerro Torre's southeast ridge. Photo: Hayden Kennedy

EL CHALTÉN 1986

EL CHALTÉN 2013

Top El Chaltén in January 1986, less than one-year-old, when the town had only one building. Photo: Sebastián Letemendia

Bottom El Chaltén in January 2013. Photo: Kelly Cordes

attempt (it is generally thought that they did not reach the top).

Dickinson smiled and said, "As an Englishman there is nothing I would like to believe more, but on the evidence that exists it's improbable that they climbed past the second step."

"Ah, Dickinson, that is where we differ. I believe they did reach the summit. My heart has a good feeling for their success. You are negative and do not believe."

Dickinson then asked Fava to point out on a model of Cerro Torre the highest position he personally had attained. He locked eyes with Fava, studying his face, dissecting his composure. Nothing. Without flinching, exuding utter belief, Fava pointed to the Col of Conquest. Dickinson has interviewed the greatest of the greats, heard the stories, picked up on the exaggerations, and noted the spin. But, he wrote, he'd "never seen anything remotely like Fava's blankness."

"All this would have been funny if it wasn't so completely ridiculous," Dickinson wrote. "Back in the U.K. I discussed it with a psychologist. She reckons the 1959 team are displaying clear signs of a syndrome known as 'dissonance,' as are some of their supporters. Here, people's well-entrenched views lead them to distort ambiguous evidence so that their original attitudes are supported. It could explain how Fava wobbled me when he pointed to the Col of Conquest, believing 100 percent that he was there. It was no longer a lie. It's conditioning. In his mind I am the one who is wrong."

Soon after the Beltrami-Garibotti-Salvaterra ascent, respected French journalist Charlie Buffet, who is fluent in Italian, secured a rare interview with Maestri. It's thought to be the last interview Maestri gave about his Cerro Torre claim, and it didn't last long. Buffet provided me with the complete transcript and original audio of the interview. Maestri was all over the place, growing increasingly agitated with Buffet's questions, then hurling personal attacks at Garibotti and Salvaterra. Throughout, his tone remained proud and defiant.

Some of his first words [translated]: "I don't want them to believe me. I don't ask them to believe me. I am fighting based on principle. If they don't believe me, if they question my climb, I'm questioning the whole of mountaineering."

Buffet asked multiple legitimate questions. Maestri flopped at every turn, deflecting details about his alleged climb.

Maestri	Who says that Messner reached the top of Everest? Understand?
Buffet	Messner had a photo...
Maestri	I don't give a fuck! You know well that photos can be faked! Photos mean nothing.
Buffet	How do you explain the controversy surrounding 1959?
Maestri	It is created by all those sons of bitches. I am not a son of a bitch. In my life, in my whole life, I never told a lie. Everyone knows I am sincere, I am loyal, I never tried to destroy someone in order to make headlines. I made headlines because I was the strongest solo climber in the world. Do you understand?
Maestri	Listen, pay attention. When we attacked in '59, the north face, south, sorry, the north face of the Torre, it was a sheet of ice and snow. We went up, Egger was the strongest ice climber in the world, we went up taking advantage of this, because it had been three weeks of bad weather, because the Torre was a sheet of ice, we went up the whole route as if it were a wall of ice, but I don't give a fuck about this, it's been covered, holy fuck, you can't...

	can't you understand?
Maestri	They can invent what they want, pitons, no pitons, I don't give a fuck. I don't have to teach... to explain anything to anyone... let me be clear... because I am... the one who did the most important endeavor in the world alone, but this does not mean that I... with this, that I made it to the top, understand? Do I make myself clear?
Buffet	No, I do not understand.
Maestri	I don't know how to explain it... I don't speak much French...
Buffet	Say it in Italian.
Maestri	If we question one climb, we must question all of mountaineering.

The interview continued much the same way, and toward the end Maestri repeated his only, desperate defense:

"I don't give a shit, either they believe me or they don't, I couldn't care less; it's the principle, after this I'm done, I base it on the principle that if I question one climb, not mine, any climb in mountain-eering, then we need to question the whole of mountaineering."

The Chaltén Massif. Photo: Kelly Cordes

chapter 20

STOP MAKING SENSE

We all want to believe. Our heroes help us shape our own identities. When they fail us, we sometimes choose to ignore it, delude ourselves; our belief can be even more important than the hero we've helped create.

I think of the horrors of my alma mater, Pennsylvania State University, when Head Football Coach Joe Paterno and other university officials covered up child molestations perpetrated by Assistant Coach Jerry Sandusky. It was pride over perversion. Lives were ruined to keep a football reputation intact. While I was working on this book, the Lance Armstrong doping scandal broke. Thing is, with those cases and countless others, once the evidence emerged, any emotional desire to defend the guilty swiftly succumbed to stark reality.

Not everybody accepts reality; there will always be irrational outliers and conspiracy theorists. Generally, though, when confronted with legitimate evidence, people re-examine their beliefs. Or at least that's how it tends to work in most societies.

In Italy, when discussing Maestri and Cerro Torre with thoughtful and smart people, I'd often notice them wavering, like blinders would occasionally drop over their eyes, like rational thought and blind faith were present then absent in turns. They would go out of their way to say they did not want to be called a Maestri supporter, while agreeing the lack of evidence for the 1959 claim was problematic. Some would even acknowledge he probably didn't climb Cerro Torre. But of all those people, I rarely found any willing to state that Cesarino Fava and Cesare Maestri lied. Those who would come out and say it—like Garibotti, Messner, Salvaterra—inevitably dealt with the backlash.

MIRELLA TENDERINI, one of my main contacts when I was in Italy for research, who generously welcomed me into her home, and who I came to admire for her perspicacity, her insatiable curiosity, and her intelligence, even she seemed to have an element of blind allegiance when it came to Maestri. She had never studied the evidence—or lack of evidence—from 1959. This from a woman who has been well aware of the ongoing controversy. This from a woman who edited Fava's autobiography and translated for all of the climbing greats who came to Italy, who studied Ernest Shackleton's original letters at the Royal Geographic Society in London while writing one of her seven books, who is a keen researcher and who clearly values the truth.

When I mentioned specific problems with Maestri's 1959 claim, it was as if she didn't want to hear it. "I'm not a climber, I don't understand the technical details," she said with a warm smile and a wave of her hand. We talked more, and she eventually acknowledged the possibility that Maestri might not have summitted, but she made excuses: Since he was found barely alive below Cerro Torre, surely he had hit his head and he was confused, mistaken. She said. "I am sure that he *thought* he was on the summit."

WHEN IT COMES to support for Maestri's story, I noticed distinct differences from generation to generation. The climbers of Maestri's generation—the World War II generation—are most likely to believe. Those of the next generation have probably at least glimpsed the evidence, and they struggle with their desire to believe and their awareness of objective reality. Most of the young climbers know that the 1959 ascent didn't happen, even if they won't speak up. I could see it in Alessandro Beltrami's face and his playfully pretending that he wouldn't talk when I pulled out my audio recorder. Who can blame him—who wants the trouble?

I asked Matteo Della Bordella about Maestri and belief. He's one of Italy's best young climbers, a world-class rock climber and alpinist with impressive new routes on Torre Egger and Uli Biaho (Pakistan) in 2013 alone. "For Maestri 1959 you're totally right. In Italy most of the people believe Maestri's ascent... myself and the younger generation of course don't believe Maestri's 1959 ascent and are in favor of having chopped the bolts on the Compressor Route; but that's unfortunately a minority of the climbing community. In Italy we have a dictum which I translate as 'the worst of the deaf is the one who doesn't want to listen.' So with many alpinists, not only the older but also the medium aged (thirty to forty), it is impossible to discuss because they are not open to any discussion. They believe in Maestri in the same way a Christian believes in God."

Given Della Bordella's prominence, and his experience in Patagonia, I was surprised when he told me that he'd never been publicly asked if he believed the 1959 story. But when he voiced his approval of the de-bolting of the Compressor Route, he was immediately seen as a "black sheep, the disrespectful youngster who is too young to be fair."

Della Bordella concluded, "Hopefully something will change in the future, but for sure not rapidly..."

Korra Pesce, a thirty-two-year-old alpinist in Chamonix, France, lived his first nineteen years in Italy. He's a cutting-edge climber with a critical eye and a unique insider-outsider viewpoint.

"I don't know if many people really believe the story of Cerro Torre's first ascent," Pesce told me. "Believers are an extremely small yet noisy minority. Most people actually think it is unlikely at best, yet they prefer to hide behind the fact that there is no proof that might discredit Maestri. In Italy, in particular in the Trentino region, the climbing community is like a family. A family with a storied past and some unpleasant secrets. Maestri is like a grandpa for all of the climbers, he's the one with the legendary past, the one who was always helpful and kind to younger, promising alpinists.

Fava also was extremely kind and helpful and really appreciated by the community. Now it happens that grandpa has a potentially embarrassing secret, but, hey, it's grandpa, so like it or not, if you are a member of the family, you have to defend him or at least shut up. Those who don't gather around him are not welcomed anymore by the family."

I came to realize support for Maestri was never about the facts—especially in tightly knit Trentino, and among those with ties to Fava or Maestri. That's why they'll hold anniversary celebrations of Maestri's 1959 endeavor, they'll reject attempts to discuss the inconvenient details, he'll receive an honorary doctorate degree, and they'll continue to feature him in documentaries and books.

I REMEMBER the way Mirella described the scars of the war and

their joy when the Allies came through Milan and liberated them. She was living in a bombed-out building and suddenly had hope and joy and a new life; she told of tears streaming down her face as she and her friends celebrated and sang and danced in the streets. And then the distant glimmer in her eyes when she recalled those early days in the Grigna Spires in the 1950s with Bonatti, Cassin, Mauri, Maestri, and her husband Luciano, when they were young and free and in love with life.

In the same vein, that defining time is why K2 was so important to Italy. When Italians made the first ascent of the world's then-highest-unclimbed peak in 1954, a crowd of forty thousand cheering countrymen and women greeted the team's return. The climbers were national heroes.

"The conquest of K2 gave the Italian nation a period of euphoria that is difficult to understand, until it is remembered that not many years had passed since the end of the Second World War. With this mountaineering triumph Italy was able, for the first time, to raise proudly its flag over the debris of humiliation and defeat," Giovanni Cenacchi wrote in his and Lino Lacedelli's 2004 book, *K2: The Price of Conquest*.

The official stories released by the K2 expedition's leader, however, were terribly flawed and dishonest. Furthermore, actions high on the mountain by at least one of the summit climbers had resulted in the team's young Pakistani climber/porter returning to his village permanently disabled. In the years and the decades following, the nasty details of what really happened emerged. But they seemed strangely unimportant. To the greater public the overriding point was simple: Italians made the first ascent of K2. The official account was the story Italy wanted—the story Italy needed.

Little could compare to the national pride of K2 in 1954 Italy. And while the post-war effect softened over time, it did so slowly. In 1959, after Egger died and Maestri returned home with the story of Cerro Torre's first ascent, he, too, was greeted by cheering crowds and celebrations. Cesare Maestri became another necessary hero.

Mirella told me that she worries that all of the controversy and questioning might have made Maestri begin to doubt himself. She reiterated that if he didn't summit, he only said he did because he was confused.

"He might have been wrong, but he didn't lie," Mirella told me. She paused and her eyes grew intense. Her voice rose and quavered slightly as she looked at me and said, "You cannot call him a liar."

Kelly Cordes on the thin-yet-moderate ice of Los Tiempos Perdidos.
Photo: Colin Haley

chapter 21

LOS TIEMPOS PERDIDOS

"C'mon, duder, you know you've got nothing better to do," the kid on the other end of the phone told me. It was fall 2006, and I wasn't in the mood.

I'd never been to Patagonia, but while cragging together a few weeks earlier I'd admitted my interest to twenty-two-year-old Colin Haley. We'd had a blast on a mini road trip in the Sierra. Haley, a serious up-and-comer, had had an incredible previous year of alpine climbing, catching the attention of climbers everywhere, myself included.

Colin would go on to be one of the most accomplished Patagonia alpinists. He had been there twice before and climbed several routes in the Fitz Roy group, but he'd always wanted to climb Cerro Torre. He'd had a picture of it on his wall since he was twelve years old. Colin's dad introduced him to climbing, and he was immediately hooked on the mountaineering adventures in his backyard range, the Washington Cascades. He slept on a plywood board in high school to prepare himself for alpine bivies. (Once he started meeting girls he compromised his plywood principles.)

Colin babbled over the phone about how we *needed* to go to Patagonia, and I offered vague excuses for why I couldn't. Then, a thought drifted through my mind.

The story goes that Jim Donini and Jack Tackle—both eminent American alpinists, both friends and heroes of mine—gave a clinic on how to plan a climbing expedition. They hadn't prepared, so a couple of hours beforehand they got together with a bottle of Scotch. Soon they came up with some rules. I never heard the full list, only the first and most important of their alpine climbing tutorial: "Buy the fucking ticket."

Once you do, you're committed. You're going. Everything else falls into place.

But I was tired. I'd just returned from seven weeks in Pakistan, I was broke, and I didn't have the energy. All I wanted to do was sit on my ass, go cragging, and drink margaritas for a while.

IN THE SUMMER OF 2006 Josh Wharton and I had traveled

halfway around the world to throw ourselves at the 5,000-vertical-foot north ridge of a peak named Shingu Charpa in Pakistan. The striking line, mostly rock but with a short bit of ice climbing to finish, had been getting attention as one of the great remaining unclimbed prizes in alpinism.

On our best attempt we climbed forty-five pitches in three days, all free on lead, to a couple hundred feet below the summit—we retreated on easy ice slopes, maybe fifty degrees, foiled by our ultralight plan that eschewed real ice climbing equipment. But "easy" without the right gear is hard—it was like we'd brought a knife to a gunfight. Planning is part of the game and we blew it.

We hadn't brought sleeping bags, either. We shivered through each night, only to get up and keep trying, only to retreat heartbreakingly close to the top.

Pakistan 2006 was a new experience for me. Not Pakistan itself, where in the northern villages I've met the kindest and most generous people anywhere in my travels. But new in that it was my first direct experience with climbing liars.

Only a few days before our attempt, a Ukranian trio returned to base camp. At the start of the trip we'd met them and said hello. Over seven days they climbed the north ridge to the top, they said, and when they arrived back in camp we offered hearty congratulations. So it goes, they got it first.

While sipping celebratory whisky in their cook tent, something seemed weird. The youngest guy, who we'd sensed was the team's rope gun, looked at the floor and said nothing. The team leader, an older guy, and apparently a respected climber back home, babbled in broken English about their climb. At one point he boasted "all free!" The third guy interrupted and said, "No, no, some aid, maybe fifty or a hundred meters." When we watched them through binoculars from camp, they clearly appeared to be aid climbing some sections; we chalked it up to the language barrier.

When they'd started, we'd watched them hike from camp up the side-glacier and join the route about one-third of the way up, where a gully slashes to the ridge. They'd climbed the initial part a week earlier and bailed down that same gully. On their final go, however, they took the shortcut. Fine, shortcut-out a third, as long as you're honest about it. But all of the published route line photos presented a continuous line from bottom to top, and made no mention of skipping the initial 1,500 feet on their actual ascent.

At the end of our trip, while hiking out, villagers in Kande told us that the Ukrainians had retreated below the top. Turns out, on the upper ridge, the route turns a corner; while not visible to us from camp, the line was visible from the village, and they'd been watching through binoculars. We shrugged it off and moved on.

Still, Josh and I are both sticklers for accuracy in climbing reports. Yes, it's "just climbing," but that's no excuse to lie—in fact, it's all the more reason not to lie. Facts are facts. They should be reported as such.

Afterward, online reports said the Ukranians had freed the route. But then we saw a photo on a Russian website showing a pitch with the leader standing in étriers.

Their ascent was widely hailed, then nominated for the Piolet d'Or award. We kept quiet. What could we say? They climbed it, we didn't. Nobody wants to sound like a whiner.

As the months went by and the Piolet d'Or ceremony approached, the younger climber on their team—the one who was silent in camp afterward—came forward. In a bold move, he told event organizers that he would not attend the ceremonies in France because his team "had not reached the summit and had no moral right to be among the nominees." He reported that, like us, they'd retreated about a hundred meters below the summit due to the ice climbing conditions.

Thinking of the blowhard team leader who'd done the reporting, I wrote in my *AAJ* report, "If you can't be honest about your climbing, what else in life do you lie about?"

All told, it took a good six months before the truth was known. A report in *Alpinist* magazine after the revelation read: "It is *Alpinist's* rule of thumb to abide by an established climbing tradition: a climber's word is generally accepted as the truth unless compelling evidence suggests otherwise."

If you doubt me, you doubt the history of mountaineering.

COLIN KEPT HASSLING ME about heading south. "Yeah, uh huh, maybe, let me check on some things," I kept telling him.

A couple of minutes into the call he dropped the line, "Ya know dude, you can keep talking about Patagonia your whole life, or you can actually step up and make it happen."

He was right. I bought the fucking ticket.

Colin and I arrived in El Chaltén in early December. We spent our first three weeks reading, talking, taking naps, and going for walks—in other words, waiting for a weather window. I even did yoga a few times. We also went bouldering, and stayed fit with time-trial trail sprints to town and back for more Doble V—the nine-peso bottles of whisky we plowed through while bullshitting around the campfire with friends every night.

Inside my tent I could hear the trees creaking above, moaning in the unrelenting wind. One day we helped a friend retrieve his gear cache on the Torre Glacier—his flight home was the next day. It was one of those days you hear about, where the wind can pick you up and slam you down. We battled like hell, leaning into the wind at forty-five-degree angles, each forward step feeling like a weightlifting exercise.

From home you say, *I can take it*. You think it's not that bad. From places of comfort you tell yourself it won't bother you. When you're there, the tough-guy facade falls away.

We did half an approach toward Fitz Roy during one sucker-window, before bailing. That's as close as we'd come to climbing. We had a tent in the yard of a hostel in town, but mostly we stayed in the woods at De Agostini camp. A handful of other tents were scattered among the trees—all climbers, most of whom we already knew.

Come the first of the year, 2007, our time was coming to an end. Another alpine climbing familiarity: an expensive camping trip. And then, just after the New Year, the weather map showed the mother of all high-pressure systems coming our way. The skies were clearing from there to Australia for four days.

NEITHER COLIN NOR I were interested in the Compressor Route. It wasn't how we wanted to get up Cerro Torre—but we didn't mind the idea of rappelling the route.

At the time, only two routes on Cerro Torre had been climbed to the summit without relying on Maestri's bolt ladders: the 1974 Ragni di Lecco Route and the 2005 route El Arca de los Vientos (which finishes on the Ragni Route).

Our plan would add a third line, though it was a far less impressive one. Technically, it covered no new ground; it would connect two existing routes in a linkup to the summit. Start on the southern edge of Cerro Torre and climb to the Col of Hope, continue along the upper west face, tag the summit and take the easy descent of the Compressor Route. It was an obvious objective; it made sense. It'd been talked about and tried over the years by climbers far better and far more experienced than we were, but nobody had pulled it off.

The lower route, Los Tiempos Perdidos, was first climbed by François Marsigny (France) and Andy Parkin (U.K.) in 1994. It approaches from the east and ascends more than 2,600 vertical feet of often thin and sustained yet relatively moderate ice to join

Colin Haley climbing the crux pitch, just below the summit, burrowing upward
and inward, digging his own tunnel for security and protection. Photos: Kelly Cordes

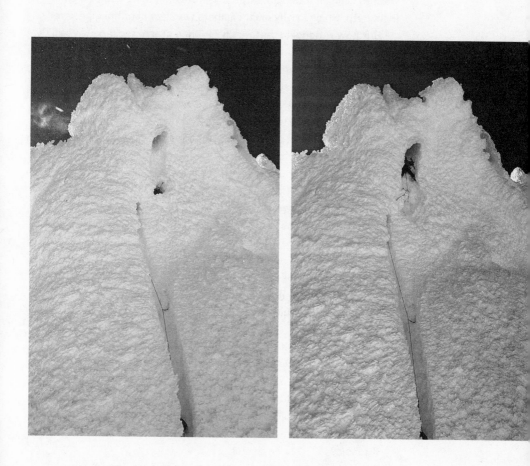

the Ragni Route at the Col of Hope. It's one of those independent alpine routes that ends at a prominent geographical landmark, and the intersection with an existing route, rather than the summit.

It had only been climbed a couple of times, partly because it's dangerous—three-quarters up, a sérac directly overhangs the ice you want to climb. If it cuts loose, it obliterates anything and everything in its path, which is why most climbers won't go near hanging séracs.

But how rational is that, really? Planes crash, too, and we still fly. Sure, séracs by nature are unpredictable. They seem to go in active-inactive phases. We asked around and nobody had seen this one rip in years. We studied the base and saw no evidence of sérac debris. Sure, we saw the usual wash of snow, avalanche runouts from storms, but we weren't climbing in a storm. There had been several days without major precipitation, and at least one full day of sunny weather in which the route shed itself of snow. The objective concern was the sérac ripping. What are the chances that we would be under the sérac if or when it let go?

Most of the time you don't even have to worry about it because the ice isn't there. Ice is ephemeral by nature, and on this particular route ice rarely formed. Sometimes yes, usually no, and you could never be certain unless you went up to have a look. That's the thing with alpine climbing—conditions and simple luck play a role. If you're fortunate enough to get good conditions, and you have the physical and psychological ability to pull it off, you might just be lucky enough to score big.

Regardless, the ultimate goal was clear: Climb Los Tiempos Perdidos and continue the remaining two thousand vertical feet to the summit of Cerro Torre via the meat of the 1974 Ragni di Lecco first ascent route. At that time, the Ragni had only five complete ascents; the upper mushrooms were notorious. But Rolando Garibotti offered key beta: Look for the tunnels.

Tunnels?

"Look for the tunnels, you might find one here," he told us one day in his cabin, pointing to a spot on a photo where bulges of white puff out from one another like stacked marshmallows. I interrupted.

"Wait, tunnels, you mean...?"

"Yes, tunnels." I looked at him puzzled and he stared back for a moment before continuing. "So this one should be slightly on the east side of the—how do you say," looking for the right word in English, "—of the arête? No, not arête—ridge, that is it. But it is more round than a ridge."

"OK, but Rolo, by tunnels do you mean like flutings?" I asked, carving out a shape with my hands, thinking that we had a slight misunderstanding of terms.

"No, Kelly. Tunnels! You find the fucking tunnels."

OK then. We would look for the fucking tunnels.

ON JANUARY 4 Colin and I hiked to Niponino, a bivy camp on the Torre Glacier, taking our time. Colin pulled out the binoculars and sat on a rock, studying the streaks of white coming from below the sérac.

"Kinda looks like snow-plastered rock to me," I said. "Maybe we should just go do the west face." The west face (Ragni Route) was farther away, meaning a delay in committing to anything. Colin, always keen, kept peering through the binoculars, before letting them drop onto the strap around his neck. He stared at me, his white-fro shooting up like Bozo the Clown, and said, "I don't think we'll ever get another chance for this route like we have now."

My mental cartwheels stopped. I glanced up at the route, then back at Colin. This is why I love climbing with younger partners: Their enthusiasm helps counter my laziness and fear. I paused for a moment. "OK. Sure, let's try." I said it out loud to convince myself.

A couple of hours into January 5, the alarm rang and I sat upright in the tent, the haze lingering until I shook my head from side to side. I never sleep before these things. I drift and doze for a few hours. It's never enough and the beep-beep-beep transitions me from dreariness to twinges of anxiety. It's always dark when you start, and that's a good thing, because that way it's easier to delude yourself about what you're about to do. We made coffee and instant oatmeal, ate some sausage and cheese.

Colin was out of the tent first, then I slipped out of my sleeping bag and into the biting air, my muscles tensing, breath freezing. We laced up our boots, adjusted our clothes, cinched our packs. "OK, dude, ready?" We weaved unroped from Niponino up the lateral moraine, onto the upper Adela Glacier, our headlamp beams fading

Kelly Cordes at the bergschrund, moments before
starting Los Tiempos Perdidos. Photo: Colin Haley

across depressions—*avoid that*—and ominous black slits disappearing into the glacier. We soloed together for two-plus hours and two thousand easy vertical feet to the junction of the ever-steepening glacier and the ice-glazed rock of Los Tiempos Perdidos.

At the bergschrund Colin flaked the rope and I racked the gear. For some reason I like to lead first, maybe because I'm always scared and I know that the sooner I start to climb, the sooner my mind will stop racing because it has to when you're on the sharp end. Our packs weighed barely more than ten pounds each—belay jacket, stove, emergency tarp, extra gloves, food, and water. Almost a vertical mile of climbing towered overhead as orange twilight flirted with the crest of the horizon. I shined my headlamp to the plastered white above. I still didn't know if it was unconsolidated snow that would shut me down within ten feet or perfect névé. Zoom back in, adjust gloves, quick mental double check of everything. Knot good. Crampons on. Deep breath.

"I on?"

"You're on, duder," Colin said.

I reached high on the body-length bulge that kicked me out onto my arms, worked my feet up, swung my axes again, and, without another word, began to climb.

Perfect, sticky ice. Thunk-thunk-thunk. I raced upward, aware that we needed to move, placing an ice screw to protect us maybe every fifty feet, sometimes less, and thinking of how that office-building-sized sérac loomed above. The one that nobody had seen rip in years, that had left no car-sized blocks on the glacier below, but that, if it did cut loose, would kill us swiftly and surely.

My heart rate pounded in my throat; I climbed as fast and as steadily as I could, finding a rhythm between force and touch, enough heft to sink my tools into the ten-inch-thick veneer of ice holding us to the mountain and light enough to conserve energy. Soon Colin's voice broke the silence.

"Ten feet!" he yelled.

I put a micro-ascender on the rope—a device that locks in one direction but feeds rope in the other, a nod toward safety while simulclimbing—and kept going.

Five long pitches of simulclimbing passed in a heart thumping, eight-hour blur, and at the Col of Hope, out of sérac danger, we took

a break to recover, relishing the immaculate surroundings and perfect weather. We knew it would be perfect: The forecasts are dead
accurate. Still, one day the forecast will be wrong and will catch a
ton of climbers—people like us—unprepared.

Colin and I rested and brewed up. We were done with our eight
hours of interval sprint training. Out of danger, so long as we could
climb everything above. If not, well... well, we never really talked
about that. In the back of my mind lingered Marsigny and Parkin's
epic. When they were here in '94, a decade before weather forecasts, they tried to continue above but were beaten back by storms.
Nobody wants to roll the dice on passing beneath a sérac twice, so
they retreated to the ice cap and marched south along the glacier,
through rain, fog, and low clouds. Finally, they came to a horrifying
impasse: the glacier calving into the deep blue waters of Lago
Viedma. In the whiteout they had missed the turnoff to Paso del
Viento. Eventually, they found a way off the glacier, climbed over a
rocky cliffband and into the forests and plains to the east, where
they staggered onward, crossing rivers, drinking from streams, and
surviving on dandelions. Nearly ten days after starting, depleted
and hallucinating, they stumbled upon an estancia.

In my pack I carried a postcard with an aerial photo of the west
face that I got at a shop in town. On back, Rolo had hand-drawn a
map with directions to Paso del Viento in case we got shut down.

Funny, now it's obvious. Just hike the glacier a bit north, head
over Paso Marconi and out the Río Eléctrico. Like everyone does for
the Ragni Route. But even in 2007, so few people had climbed the
route that the logistics weren't clear.

Colin and I slathered on sunscreen, ate more food, melted more
snow, and relaxed under a cloudless sky. True to forecast, nothing
but blue overhead in every direction. We gazed off, feeling as if we'd
been transported to a world beyond our imaginations—the endless
ice sheet to the west, twisted structures of blue and white jutting
at unfathomable angles above, and lazily rolling pampas to the east.

We wrapped up our three-hour break and started again. It was
Colin's block now—all I had to do was follow and cheerlead.

Rime the size of buildings bulged, with channels in their sides,
carved by the wind, a slice of a fantasyland unlike anything I'd seen
before or since.

Colin led brilliantly through the mushrooms, protecting the climbing when he could, confidently running it out when he couldn't, climbing with a wily ability that most climbers twice his age haven't yet mastered. We moved well, simulclimbing whenever possible.

He finished leading the ice headwall at sunset, some 4,500 vertical feet above our start. When I arrived at the belay, total darkness enshrouded us and the wind had kicked up. Maybe it was our location, perched on the very crest of where the west ridge turns north–south, only a few pitches below the summit. Desperate to escape the wind, we dug a tiny cave in the rime and crawled inside, shivering away the night without sleeping bags, drifting between rest and too much rest, between sleep and hypothermia.

In the morning, the air was calm as we crawled out of the cave. Like kids on an Easter-egg hunt we searched and found the fucking tunnels, crazy wind-formed tunnels. Blue ice inside, maybe three or four feet in diameter, carved by mini-whirlwinds tearing upward. If you're tired you just lean back, rest, and laugh uncontrollably. The tunnels lead to the top of the mushroom. You poke your head out and look around. It's like emerging from a secret passage into a world where you're certain to see goblins and hobbits playing banjos.

A couple of pitches later, our luck ran out. A hundred feet above, just at the point where an immense mushroom bulged and overhung, suspended in the rime was another tunnel. A heinous, vertical half-pipe of rime was the only weakness that might lead to its start. Thank god it was Colin's lead. It was the penultimate pitch and the crux of the route—if we could climb it, we were in there. If not, we were in for the mother of all epics, down to the ice cap without bivy gear or enough food or water and that postcard for a map.

"C'mon, Colin!" I yelled. He was doing battle, climbing—if you can call it that—using every known mushroom-climbing technique: pressing in with his knees, elbows, and shoulders, and punching his arms horizontally into the rime.

I'd dug a snow seat, buried my axes, and reclined. Wind raced between the channels forged by the wind itself, creating beautiful, haunting music, the organ pipes of the Torres. In every direction masses of aerated ice loomed like multi-ton sculptures pulled from a land of fairytales, otherworldly mazes rising, twisting, turning into the atmosphere. Cauliflowers, gargoyles, tunnels.

Colin inched upward, keeping it together on the most insecure type of climbing humanly known. Tiny rivulets of rime trickled below him like sand from an hourglass. He placed snow pickets horizontally in the vertical rime, but none of them would have held a fall.

Then, just as the mushroom began its overhang, young Colin disappeared. He dug *into* the mushroom, burrowing a tunnel of his own. He was hoping to create the only real protection on the pitch, like a vertical, human-sized version of the V-thread anchors that climbers make by inserting webbing through connecting holes in the ice made with ice screws.

"Lookin' good, man!" I cheered, though I couldn't see him and the rope hadn't moved in a long time.

I was gazing to the east when, out of the corner of my eye, I saw something come flying off. It was a chunk of rime from just below the natural tunnel. As the chunk shed off, it hovered in the air for a second, quivering in the wind, and then whoosh, gone, toward the valley a mile below. Colin's ax came flailing out of the hole left by the chunk of rime. His goggled head came next and jerked leftward, as if trying to figure out where he was, then darted back right. He looked up to the ice tunnel, our passage only a body length above. He paused and stared and I let out a huge whoop and started to cheer and shout because I knew we were in there. Colin didn't hear a thing; my voice disappeared into the wind, taken for another lap around the globe, carried away by the broom of God.

A final, short pitch of rime led to the top, and early afternoon on January 7, thirty-two hours after crossing the bergschrund, we spent a half hour on Cerro Torre's summit, without a breath of wind, talking little and staring off in every direction.

Our descent of the Compressor Route went like clockwork— Colin had memorized every pitch from a topo, and knew exactly how to do it. As we rappelled past bolt after bolt after bolt, many by absolutely perfect cracks, others seemingly intentionally avoiding natural features, I stared with amazement. Although I'd read about it, seeing it firsthand was altogether different. A strange sense of admiration for Maestri hit me, admiration for his determination, which could only be a byproduct of sheer lunacy. There is absolutely nothing rational about the way he blasted bolt after bolt after bolt into the rock, completely ignoring, even deliberately avoiding, what nature had provided.

"Kelly?!" Colin yelled. I snapped out of my reverie and continued rappelling.

By nightfall we wove through the upper Torre Glacier. Above, the tower's monstrous east wall blacked out the sky until I tilted my head and craned my neck to see the stars, outlining its silhouette. My mind had entered that weird semi-coherent state, where I just watch the floating images and sounds, let them drift, and consciously force concentration on the important things. It's a simple place, where rote memory and years of familiarity substitute for worry and fear. I remember insisting that we rope up—exhausted and bleary eyed, it was no time to take chances with the crevasses.

At 2:30 a.m. on January 7—exactly two days after we left—we stumbled back to Niponino. Everything was silent but for our clinking gear. Stars shimmered overhead. We barely spoke. No lights, no people, everyone asleep in their tents. We dropped our gear in a heap outside the front door of our tent, crawled inside and passed out. I woke only from weird electrical shocks when I rolled the wrong way onto my arms. Nearly five thousand feet of swinging ice tools left me with freaky, nervy zingers that zapped from my armpits to my fingertips.

Sometime midmorning someone shook our tent and gently yelled, "Yo, guys…" I half opened my eyes and suddenly a smiling face popped his head inside the door.

I sat up partway, still dazed, and the stench of ammonia swirled between the nylon walls of our tiny tent. Our friend said a few congratulatory words and told us that people had been watching us through binoculars, concerned about the sérac, and that the thin ice on Los Tiempos Perdidos had already melted away. It had been there two days before, but yesterday it was gone. They were reassured when they spotted two figures coming down the Compressor Route, and then someone heard clanging gear and a tent door opening in the night.

Colin turned to me inside the tent and said, "Dude, I'm a dirty hippie but you stink." Somehow I recalled an explanation from physiology class. It was a result of my body burning my own lean tissue for energy—our energy expenditure on route exponentially exceeded our energy intake (food). *Gluconeogenesis is where amino acid chains are* *broken down, the nitrogen component stripped away, and the remaining carbon chains converted in the liver to glucose. It's a survival mechanism, common in cases of starvation or extreme energy depletion, and the byproducts eventually become toxic. The nitrogen, which can't be metabolized, is excreted primarily in urine and in sweat, by binding with three hydrogens to form NH_3—ammonia. That's why I stunk.*

I staggered out of the tent and saw a happy crew of climbers in Niponino, all sharing enthusiastic words. Colin turned to me and said, "I've wanted to climb Cerro Torre since I was twelve years old."

WE GOT TO TOWN with a day to spare before catching our

flights home. After we grabbed showers, one of the first things we did was seek out Rolo and thank him for the crucial information—*the fucking tunnels.* In a mellow but sincere tone, Rolo said, "Good effort."

Early evening we joined a handful of friends for beers at La Senyera, one of the first buildings in El Chaltén. The festive mood was infectious, and I had that deep bone-tired feeling fused with deep-down satisfaction. When I went to pay for my beer, the woman said, "Your money is not good here—congratulations. Great climb."

"*Gracias*," I said, sheepishly.

We moved on to a rustic cabin, a bakery-restaurant called La Chocolatería. We'd already packed our bags, so we could stay out until our eyelids faded. Jim Donini, of all people, the old Patagonia legend who was down again for another round, had offered to drive us to the airport the next morning. As we walked across town, Patagonia's fabled winds raised dust devils in the dirt streets. Inside, the walls shook from the gusts as we sat comfortably, laughing, swilling beers, and eating pizza, as more and more people, all climbers, filtered in. The weather in the mountains was shutting down and everyone was congregating, some successful, others not, but everybody celebrating something.

left Colin Haley leads into a wind-carved tunnel of rime on the upper Ragni Route.

right View from inside one of the tunnels. Photos: Kelly Cordes

One of Maestri's major bolt ladders. Photo: Zack Smith

chapter 22

A NEW STORY

In the 1970s, Reinhold Messner, the greatest mountaineer in history, was asked if he would try to climb Mount Everest, the highest peak on earth.

At the time, it was thought impossible without supplemental oxygen. To Messner, theoretical impossibility did not imply that using "artificial" oxygen was fair. Not everything has to be climbed. The primary challenge of climbing Mount Everest is altitude, yet supplemental oxygen instantaneously—and usually dramatically—reduces the "physiological height" of the 29,028-foot (8,848-meter) summit.

Research shows that commonly used flow rates lower the summit oxygen pressure to the equivalent of a summit between about 20,000 and 23,000 feet. The actual on-mountain effect varies based on many factors, but typically reduces the physiological height to somewhere between 23,000 and 26,000 feet. Either way, the difference between that and the true summit altitude is enormous. Yet users unflinchingly claim to have climbed to the highest point on earth. It's a curious blind spot. At what point do external aids undermine the idea of fair play?

"By fair means, or not at all," Messner famously said. It has become one of alpinism's great refrains, and it dates back to Victorian mountaineer Albert Mummery, who rejected the norms in the Alps by climbing without guides, grappling hooks, and ladders.

Messner's implication was clear: Lower the peak by several thousand feet with supplemental oxygen, and you aren't *really* climbing Everest.

While not everyone agrees with all of Messner's principled stances (he also considered fixed ropes and fixed camps to be unfair aids), his emphasis on climbing style—on the process rather than only the summit—is inseparable from his greatest-ever status.

Messner never climbed in Patagonia, in part because in his earlier years, when he was a leading rock climber, aid climbing didn't interest him—he wanted to free climb. "I openly say I'd never have been capable to free climb a route on Cerro Torre. I didn't want to climb the Compressor Route, it's not my style," he said.

But in the high Himalaya, in 1978 Messner and Austrian Peter Habeler did the unthinkable: They climbed Mount Everest using their hands and their feet, their lungs and their vision. No artificial oxygen, no fixed ropes, no fixed camps. By fair means, or not at all.

Of course, in the ensuing decades, Messner's message on Everest would be buried by commercial interests and by an any-means-necessary thirst for the top. In turn, a majority of today's serious alpinists essentially ignore the mountain. Practically everywhere else climbing style remains the most defining factor in how alpinists rate the ascents of their peers.

Definitions change over time, so it's important to judge within the context of the day. That is why the early pioneering ascents of Everest, when they used supplemental oxygen, are still respected. Hornbein and Unsoeld's 1963 first ascent of the west ridge and first traverse of the mountain, far beyond the possibility of retreat, with their brutal open bivy at 28,000 feet, stands as one of the most committing ascents in the history of climbing.

On the remote Cerro Torre in 1970, however, Cesare Maestri's use of an internal combustion engine as a climbing implement, while deliberately ignoring natural features, was nowhere close to being "of the day." Not even when taking into account the early *direttissima* concept, once popular in the Alps (and which Maestri never suggested as his motivation, though some ill-informed climbers have tried to defend the route as such). With direttissimas, after a mountain's prominent natural features had been climbed, the idea was to attack the most direct line up the steepest wall, employing any means necessary. By the late '60s the climbing community had all but abandoned the style after some climbers treated the walls like construction projects. Direttissimas were the impetus for Messner's seminal article "The Murder of the Impossible," first published in 1968 and translated to English in 1971.

The question with Cerro Torre had long been whether somebody would climb the southeast ridge—home to the Compressor Route—by fair means, effectively a post-Maestri retro ascent. "Fair means," of course, entails subjectivity and change. Reasonable, sparing use of bolts on otherwise unprotectable rock has long been considered acceptable. Nobody complained, for example, about the few bolts that Ermanno Salvaterra added in his 1999 five-pitch variation to bypass Maestri's monumental bolt-ladder traverse (over a hundred bolts). Salvaterra's bolts are like a breeze compared to Maestri's hurricane. What remains clear is that Maestri's methods came nowhere close to fair play.

Many of the climbers capable of a fair-means ascent took their energy to other objectives. Those who went to the southeast ridge figured that since the bolts were there, they might as well clip 'em.

As a mountain, Cerro Torre is so vicious, especially with its storms, that it became easy to rationalize the Compressor Route. Each previous suitor validated the next, particularly when many were renowned figures—starting with Jim Bridwell's true first ascent of the route.

If someone did come along and climb the line by fair means, ignoring Maestri's unnecessary bolts, the question loomed: Would they remove them?

"As long as the bolts exist there will be always a debate about it. No doubt. But it's much more the question who is willing to take the shit on his back for chopping all the unnecessary bolts on the Compressor Route and when this will happen. Then, in my opinion, Cerro Torre would have back its high standard place in the mountaineering world—even today," German alpinist Alexander Huber said in 2004.

IN 2007 two climbers would make an attempt on Cerro Torre's southeast ridge. Though they would fail to reach the summit, and did not change the route, they would spark a firestorm that would affect the Compressor Route in the years that followed.

Americans Zack Smith and Josh Wharton, each in their twenties, arrived in El Chaltén a month after Colin and I left.

At the time, Wharton's growing record of major ascents was visible, though he remained low-key. He understood, if somewhat grudgingly, the way the game is played: With minimal effort, he could eke out a living as a full-time, sponsored climber.

Smith never had an interest in the sponsorship game, though not for a lack of talent. At the time of their trip, he was piecing together a meager living with guiding, rigging for adventure races and television productions, and working odd jobs, including digging a foundation on a house. "I literally—not metaphorically—dug ditches to buy my plane ticket," he told me. They had both made several trips to Patagonia, and though neither had climbed Cerro Torre, both had studied the history of the Compressor Route.

Smith and Wharton's hope was to climb the southeast ridge by fair means. They knew from research and discussions with other climbers that nearly all of Maestri's four-hundred-odd bolts were unnecessary, and the slew of unnecessary bolts on a beautiful line seemed wrong. They were eager to find out for themselves.

If they could succeed, they figured they'd remove the bolts— finally, after all those years of people talking about it, complaining about it, and... doing nothing about it.

"It wasn't some grand moment where we held our fists up and declared jihad on the Maestri route," Smith said. "It just seemed like the right thing to do. We recognized that the thing should be taken down by someone. We had the skill base to climb the thing without the bolts and then take them out—so why not us?"

ON A CLEAR MORNING in the long days of summer, on February 10, 2007, Smith and Wharton walked from De Agostini camp to the Torre Glacier, where they planned to nap until early morning at the Noruegos camp, just below the upper Torre Glacier.

They couldn't sleep, so at 8:00 p.m. they started hiking. After the glacial rubble, they labored through fresh snow on the steepening glacier, wove between crevasses, then simulclimbed easy mixed terrain to the start of the real climbing at the Col of Patience. By headlamp they continued, moving swiftly, short-fixing, hand-jamming crisp granite cracks, and switching back to ice tools for moderate pitches of mixed ice and rock. They found phenomenal climbing, the type that makes you wonder what all the Compressor Route complaining is about.

Then, at sunrise, they saw the stark delineation. Directly above, on the crest of the arête of the ridge, rose a razor-thin crack, though it was partially covered under a gravity-defying plaque of unstable ice. To the right, they saw a line of bolts splattered across a blank traverse as if sprayed by a machine gun: Maestri's infamous ninety-meter bolt traverse.

They weren't the first to try the natural line—the Anglo-Argentine team aid climbed the narrow crack in 1968, two years before Maestri came along. Nearly thirty years and dozens of Compressor Route ascents later, in October 1999, Mauro Mabboni and Ermanno Salvaterra aided the seam, then continued past the 1968 high point. They placed four bolts to protect dangerous runouts above (plus two anchor bolts), and in the end established a logical five-pitch variation to the Compressor Route, before retreating just shy of the top.

WHARTON STARTED UP some well-featured face holds just left of the prow, on the edge of the south face. When the holds dwindled, he placed a knifeblade piton in a seam. Using tension from the rope he traversed back right to the obvious crack, cleared away the plaque of unstable ice, and struggled upward. It took hours. But above, golden-brown granite held fantastic 5.10 free climbing, sprinkled with runouts, on the Mabboni-Salvaterra variation, before returning them to the vicinity of the Compressor Route.

The climbing wasn't trivial, but it was nothing cutting edge—barely harder than what Maestri allegedly free soloed, both up and down, in the Dolomites a half century earlier. They continued through terrific mixed pitches in the ice towers, ignoring the bolts, and climbed a wildly overhanging crack to the right before dead ending in a melting snow mushroom, about thirty feet below the headwall. They descended to their previous stance. It was only three in the afternoon—plenty of time to head for the top via the bolt ladders. Instead, they retreated.

"At one of the belays we stopped. Without moving my feet I could touch eight bolts. Many were next to hand cracks," Smith wrote in the 2007 *American Alpine Journal.* "We pulled a cat's claw [tool] from the pack and for the first time in our lives attempted to remove a bolt, to see if it would be possible to return Cerro Torre to its original state. After several minutes it barely budged. We returned to town."

Smith and Wharton descended to Noruegos on the afternoon of February 11, en route to the comforts of town. Word had leaked of their idea to remove the bolts, and on the glacier they were warned that another climber, who was there to attempt the Compressor Route, had heard of their plans and was "on the warpath, and to watch out."

They shrugged it off. After all, they hadn't removed a single bolt. Then another climber they passed told them that their base camp tent, at De Agostini camp, had been disassembled. Three hours later, with some relief, they found their tent had been taken down but left intact. They re-pitched the tent and went to sleep.

ON FEBRUARY 12 they hiked to their campsite on the edge of El Chaltén—the old Madsen camp (since removed), where they stayed when they were in town. Smith went for some food and Wharton sat outside their tent. He was approached by someone twitching with energy—it was the Warpath Guy. Behind him followed a small posse of climbers who were also set on the Compressor Route. "I felt like I was in junior high, and the bully and his buddies were coming after me. Only this time, the bully was crying," Wharton said. It was the man who took down their tent, an American climber accomplished in Torres del Paine, Yosemite, and other areas around the world, who had been obsessing over the Compressor Route. He'd failed on it multiple times.

Interesting thing is, the eventual fair-means ascent of the southeast ridge went at a standard easily within his abilities—in terms of objective difficulty, he didn't even need the bolts. Of course the weather and conditions are always a challenge, but that's alpine climbing.

Wharton described a bizarre scenario where the man was alternately sobbing and shouting threats, saying, "You're trying to destroy my dream!" He threatened to "crevasse" Smith and Wharton's bivy camp below the peak if they returned.

The minor fracas ended soon after, but the overall drama was enough to rekindle the long-simmering debate over whether or not the Compressor Route should go.

SOON A BRIEF WEATHER window arrived, and Smith and Wharton had another chance. On February 17 they left Noruegos at 4:45 a.m. and simulclimbed to the Col of Patience. Along the way, they passed Warpath Guy and his partner. They exchanged awkward small talk and told him that they weren't going to remove the bolts.

"I personally wasn't willing to offend that much of the community over some bolts," Wharton later told me. "We still thought it would be great to climb the route without the bolts, we still supported the idea of removing them, but we gave up on the idea ourselves because we didn't want to deal with the drama."

On the ridge, again they followed the natural line. Frigid gusts of wind toyed with them, like a cat battering a tiny mouse, forewarning the incoming storm—the window was already closing. They had to stop to warm their hands mid-pitch, balancing on their feet while alternately holding the rock with one hand and warming the other. Still, familiar with the terrain from their first attempt, they made good time. After the ice towers they again came upon the second major bolt ladder, where, on their first attempt, they dead ended to the right. This time they looked around the corner to the left: Fifty feet deep in the cleft of the ridge was a chimney, two hundred feet long and only three feet wide, choked with perfect blue ice. The pitch would be world class at any winter crag, and yielded fantastic climbing. Yet nobody had even *tried* it before—everyone who'd gotten this high on the southeast ridge had just followed the bolts instead.

From the start, ignoring the bolts felt natural and easy. They hadn't clipped any of Maestri's progression bolts (bolts used for advancement or protection when climbing a pitch, differentiated in usage from anchor bolts, which are used at belays and rappels), skipping a couple hundred of them by simply following the natural terrain systems. But the headwall was different. Options narrowed. Five hundred feet of vertical rock was capped by protruding ice mushrooms. They could tell that the rock was featured enough to probably go without the bolts, but not as easily as below. The sky turned gray, and wisps of clouds raced overhead like missiles.

Wind body-slammed them into the wall at the next belay. Thousands of feet below, they could see the other five or six teams on the route retreating. They kept climbing. On the first pitch of the headwall, Smith battled ice-choked cracks, requiring creative gear placements and delicate aid climbing. For a while, the bolt ladders were near the natural line. "The variations we made below the headwall felt natural and warranted, but here it felt ridiculous to be placing sketchy gear mere inches from bolts," Smith wrote. "I was doing hook moves in my aiders in gale force winds with a bolt unclipped next to me. But I tried. I think as far as mind control, it was the hardest seventy feet of climbing I've ever done. It's probably 5.9 jugs [big holds] in dry conditions."

Smith clipped one of the bolts, shrugged, and glanced down at Wharton with a look of disappointment. What the hell, the bolts were there, as so many others have argued. They aided upward by clipping a hundred bolts, each less than an arm's length apart. It didn't feel right—weather didn't justify ignoring the natural terrain—but they did it anyway.

"Occasionally, it was faster to free climb around them, even wearing boots and gloves," Smith wrote. "All around us were difficult yet climbable features. We arrived just below the fixed compressor, where the rock blanked out, and the bolts were finally justified."

Even then, Smith's statement calls into question what we see or don't see, and how our vision changes in the face of a storm.

top Looking down the phenomenal, two-hundred-foot, 2007 ice chimney variation.
Photo: Josh Wharton.

bottom Circles show a lower and higher bolt, with much of the 1970 bolt ladder
faintly visible in between. The arrow notes the location of the ice chimney, which
had been previously ignored. Photo: Zack Smith

They passed the hanging compressor motor, passed the metal studs left by Maestri when he began chopping them himself, climbed the Bridwell finish, switched into crampons and ice tools and scurried up the summit slopes to the final mushroom. Clouds gathered and hurricane-force winds increased by the second. Around to the side, an easy ramp wove to the top. At 7:30 p.m., only fourteen hours and forty-five minutes after leaving camp, they started up the ramp. But in the frigid wind, thirty feet below the true summit, they turned around and began their descent.

Afterward, everyone would ask, as climbers do with Cerro Torre, if they climbed the summit mushroom. It's not a bona fide ascent of Cerro Torre if you don't.

"It was funny to me when people said that we didn't climb Cerro Torre because we stopped about thirty feet from the summit. To me we didn't climb the last four hundred feet. As soon as we clipped the bolt ladders we stopped climbing," Wharton said.

"As soon as the route is called a bolt ladder route, or not legitimate, I think that a lot of the people who'd climbed it suddenly felt as if it somehow meant they never climbed Cerro Torre. I'm not going to say they didn't have their own valid experience on it, they did," Wharton later said. "But it seemed many couldn't divorce themselves from the experience that they had, and the reality of the route."

Twenty-four hours after leaving camp, on the morning of February 18, they returned, feeling a mix of emptiness and joy. Back at Noruegos camp, their tent and gear hadn't been crevassed.

Wharton's reflections, soon after, hinted at both the problematic nature of the Compressor Route and the difficulty of Cerro Torre: "I thought we did a great job struggling onward in horrendous weather. I'm disappointed, however, that in the end we took the easy way out, using the bolts in what would otherwise have been unclimb-able conditions. Human laziness and coveting the easy way to the top is a sad piece of the Compressor Route story, and, although Zack and I nearly avoided this path, in the end we fell just short."

As with the gradual acceptance of the Compressor Route among some alpinists, Smith and Wharton's experiences on the route would contribute to a building interest in its absence.

Who decides? Photo: Kelly Cordes

chapter 23

THE DEMOCRATIC REPUBLIC OF CERRO TORRE

"Patagonian Democracy" was the title of an article that appeared on the popular Italian website PlanetMountain.com. The reluctant author, an El Chaltén resident named Vicente Labate, is soft spoken and would rather have remained anonymous. But the website needed him to sign off on it.

On February 14, 2007, Labate found himself the impromptu organizer of a meeting about the Compressor Route at the Los Glaciares National Park visitor's center. Two Spanish climbers had just given a slide show of their adventures. As the audience—an international mix of climbers and non-climbers— filtered out, Labate approached ranger Carlos Duprez, who had originally suggested holding a meeting afterward to discuss the Compressor Route, given the recent incidents. Duprez had merely suggested the idea but wasn't interested in leading it. So Labate took the reins. They asked people to come back in.

A discussion about the route commenced among the forty attendees. The meeting, being spur of the moment, didn't include a panel of experts.

Who was qualified to decide the fate of the Compressor Route? Maybe the baker's opinion was as important as Ermanno Salvaterra's? (For the record, neither Salvaterra nor any Cerro Torre first ascensionists were in attendance, nor were Smith or Wharton. Rolando Garibotti, the world's expert on Chaltén Massif climbing, was out of town.)

Some accomplished international alpinists were at the meeting, though. Jon Walsh, of Canada, called the meeting "a joke."

Alexander Huber, one of the world's best climbers, was also there. "I voted for chopping the bolts as it is clear that Maestri's bolting practice was against the ethics. The people who had been participating in the meeting voted to leave the bolts in place. What I said after the voting is that I respect the result of the voting. Nevertheless, the community that had been participating on the vote was not representative. There were more people from the village than climbers," he told me. "Which people would form a representative community? Therefore I think any voting doesn't make much sense."

In what became an example of the chaos of misinformation surrounding the eventual de-bolting, several of the angriest in El Chaltén falsely claimed that Huber voted to leave the bolts in place. They used this false claim and his credibility as evidence of international support for the route.

The fact that they held such a vote was, as far as I know, unprecedented in the world of alpinism. Certainly a vote of forty random people after a slide show shouldn't be considered binding. Not in the global alpine world where the only people who "vote" are those voting with their actions on route. Yet, the impromptu meeting was later referenced repeatedly as a definitive statement that the Compressor Route should not have been removed.

When asked for a show of hands, thirty of the forty in attendance voted for the bolts to stay. It was intended as a suggestion, a consideration, Labate told me, acknowledging that alpinism is not a democracy. He didn't choose the title of his article. While it was provocative, perhaps a careful editor would have ended it with a question mark: "Patagonian Democracy?" Alpinism, in general, has no official rules or representation; it's an ill-defined mix of anarchy and meritocracy. It is definitely not a democracy.

Aside from the irrelevance of a vote on the Compressor Route bolts, it's an interesting thought experiment: Who would be allowed to vote?

Non-climbers were reportedly not allowed to vote at the gathering. The self-identified climbers who voted may have been boulderers, sport climbers, alpine climbers, or armchair mountaineers. They may have known everything or nothing about Cerro Torre and its complex history. None of this was ever established. Should that matter?

Need a person have climbed Cerro Torre to have a right to vote? Reached the summit or just an attempt? Would there be a threshold for how much time they actually spent on the mountain?

Maybe you'd need to be a "real climber" and pass some sort of knowledge test? You should at least be able to point out the Compressor Route on a photo of Cerro Torre.

Would nationality matter? Would it be locals only, climbers and non-climbers alike? Even the baker? The shopkeeper who couldn't identify the side of the mountain where the bolts exist? And who *is* local in an overwhelmingly seasonal town that was barely twenty years old at the time of the meeting? The Tehuelche roamed the region for around ten thousand years, which might give pause to any self-designated "local" proclaiming ownership.

Maybe it would be the Argentines in general, since it's their country. A national referendum?

International climbers were allowed to vote, though none of those who have played a significant part in Cerro Torre's history were present. At the time, foreign climbers had established 100 percent of the routes on Cerro Torre.

Some Argentine and Latin American climbers at the meeting thought that foreigners should not be allowed to vote. Understandable,

it belongs to Argentina... at least since they won it in the border dispute with Chile. (El Chaltén was established by the Argentine government in 1985 for the sole strategic purpose of claiming the land.)

Yet there are no restrictions placed on who's allowed to permanently alter their spectacular mountains. Climbers from everywhere install anchors or fixed protection at their own discretion. Not a single one of them has ever needed permission to do anything, beyond the free, recently instituted climber registration at park headquarters. Climbers from Argentina, Australia, Austria, Brazil, Canada, Chile, China, France, Germany, Italy, Japan, Korea, New Zealand, Norway, Russia, Slovenia, Spain, Sweden, the United Kingdom, the United States, Venezuela—to name a few—have come and done exactly as they pleased.

The freedom to do as we choose is essential to the nature and history of climbing—those who can, do. That involves the burden of personal responsibility, and is a tremendous part of what we love about climbing. Whether or not that freedom is sustainable in this day and age is another question.

Most interesting is how that freedom of action, coupled with the outward pointlessness of the endeavor, makes our climbing a definitively personal expression. This very expression is what we revere and celebrate. Which leaves us with a question: Since we are left to our own devices with the freedom of climbing, what do our actions say about us?

Tents in Madsen camp, 2007. Photo: Zack Smith

The Torre Traverse, from right to left: Cerro Standhardt,
Punta Herron, Torre Egger, Cerro Torre. Photo: Rolando Garibotti

chapter 24

DEMYSTIFICATION OF A MASSIF

Within a few years of weather forecasts arriving for the Chaltén Massif, a shift was underway. Sometimes the forecasts weren't perfect, but they always predicted the big systems. And they only got better over the years. Reliable forecasts and unprecedented spells of good weather—as well as more climbers around to take advantage of them—removed a huge portion of Cerro Torre's primary defense; it was a sort of lifting of the veil. The difficulty of climbing Cerro Torre was now based on a route's climbing challenges; the additional challenges of storms were largely removed from the equation.

Perhaps a telling episode came during a nearly two-week-long stretch of clear skies that hit the Chaltén Massif in late November and December 2008.

In his Chaltén Massif summary in the *American Alpine Journal*, Rolando Garibotti wrote: "The big news was that the Ragni di Lecco Route on the west face of Cerro Torre had six ascents (nineteen climbers), more than all previous ascents of the route combined. In contrast, the season saw only one ascent of the Compressor Route. It is as if overnight everyone stopped climbing Everest with oxygen, fixed rope, and Sherpa support. While Maestri's hundreds of bolts remain in place, the climbing community appears to have finally given them a cold shoulder. The list of non-Compressor Route ascents of Cerro Torre has now grown to fourteen."

At that time, the number of Compressor Route ascents had grown too many to count, but stood at well over one hundred.

It's impossible to know if the declining interest in the Compressor Route was genuine or a temporary coincidence. To Smith and Wharton, their attempt felt like a "psychological leap." Maybe the mentality extended into the community, bringing to the fore what most climbers knew: The Compressor Route was so compromised that it's hard to consider it a valid climbing route. Detractors of the route had long argued that having the entirety of difficult climbing covered in bolt ladders removed too much of climbing's innate natural challenge. When doing it in perfect weather, they were right.

Yet it's an interesting interaction, because weather and conditions are integral to alpine climbing. Climbing the Compressor Route in Old Patagonia meant something different than getting up it in New Patagonia. In the first couple of years after the forecasts arrived, many climbers still tried the route. Soon after, interest waned.

Comments from two Swiss climbers, both in their early twenties at the time, hinted at the shifting mindset. In early 2007 Cyrille Berthod and Simon Anthamatten did many impressive climbs in the massif. During their sending spree, they climbed the Compressor Route in just eleven hours from Niponino (including the approach). "We would have never summited on such a marginal weather day if not for all the bolts, but we did not get as much pleasure reaching the top of Cerro Torre as we did on other summits in the area," they reported.

Silvo Karo has climbed in both Old and New Patagonia. He endured vicious days while establishing difficult and dangerous new routes on the east face of Fitz Roy in 1983, the east face of Cerro Torre in 1986, and the south face of Cerro Torre in 1988; all three routes are unrepeated. By the time of his January 2005 trip, Internet weather forecasts had just arrived. He and fellow Slovene Andrej

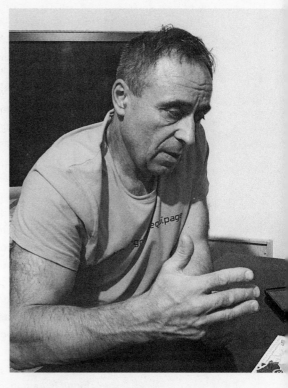

Silvo Karo describing Old Patagonia. Photo: Kelly Cordes

Grmovšek started at the base of a connecting formation three thousand feet of technical climbing below Cerro Torre and raced up to
the Compressor Route, which they took to the summit. It was as if
they were in a playground. Their linkup became known as the
Slovene Sit-Start, a half-joking reference to the world of bouldering,
where the emphasis is on pure difficulty on small rocks, and climbers often start seated in the dirt and pull onto the first holds.

One night at Karo's place in Osp, Slovenia, fall 2012, we were
talking after dinner and a day of cragging, and I asked about the old
days in Patagonia. Karo's hulking shoulders were slouched over his
plate and wine glass, and then he leaned back to talk. He's built like
a linebacker but climbs with ballerina grace. He recounted the late
'80s and early '90s, when Slovenian alpinists—this tiny country,

then a part of Yugoslavia—set standards in commitment and difficulty that have yet to be eclipsed. Karo was a core part of the crew. It came at a cost; a staggering proportion of his friends and partners died in the mountains.

He said, "I think the thing that has changed a lot in Patagonia, the weather forecast, no? In 2005 was the first weather forecast, or one year earlier. I remember at that time, we were all down—it was *so* nice, the weather forecast, uff. You could just go and climb. Before? Nobody know."

Continuing, he said, "I remember last time in Patagonia, they have a weather forecast that will be: tomorrow start period of good weather for three days. And man, it's just perfect. You just go to the wall at night, no problem, you sleep well, no shaking all the time with the weather, ooooooooh, it start snooooowing." For a second his eyes drifted, like he was back on a tiny bivy ledge thousands of feet up when a storm arrived. Then he gently returned and smiled. "It's *tooootally* different, no? Now to climb big climb in Patagonia it's much, much, much more easier. And you don't need to take anything just in case for protection, extra things, extra food. You know that next three days the weather will be good, and you will do it."

I suggested that maybe something has been lost.

"Other things is gained, of course. You need to go with the time," he said with a lighthearted laugh.

"IT HAS FREQUENTLY been noticed that all mountains appear doomed to pass through the three stages: An inaccessible peak, The most difficult ascent in the Alps, An easy day for a lady," wrote Victorian mountaineer Albert Mummery (of the original "fair means" term). Out of context, Mummery's comment appears sexist. In reality, he wrote it with intentional irony, as a compliment to his friend, pioneering climber Lily Bristow.

One of the surest ways to show that talent has outpaced terrain—or maybe vision has fallen behind—is when a mountain, or mountains, become home to refinement ascents. It happens everywhere, and it's part of the progression from by-any-means-necessary sieges of the easiest route on a mountain to seeking out harder routes to making speed ascents and solos and eliminating aid. They are ways of challenging ourselves. Of course we tend to tailor objectives to suit our strengths; there's always something harder you can do on any given peak.

Traverses and enchainments of multiple peaks in a single outing involves creativity, logistics, and endurance. For the superhuman, they're a way to further extend the conception of the possible. For the rest of us, they're a way to maximize the terrain in a particular area. You're at your local crag, and you linkup every formation in a day. As you get better, you linkup the best routes of a minimum grade on each formation. Or you climb the three biggest walls in the valley, or the five best local ice climbs in a day. Or, if you're good enough, visionary enough, maybe you look at not only Cerro Torre, but the Torres as a group connected by high cols, perfectly aligned from north to south, in ascending order: Cerro Standhardt, Torre Egger, Cerro Torre.

Critics sometimes half-deride such outings as contrived and low-commitment. Fair enough, as they typically have options for easy escape, and they often climb relatively easy routes for the climber and often on familiar, rehearsed terrain. Whether they are refinements proving that true adventure is dead, or that it's alive and well, we can debate forever. But the idea of enchaining the Torres in a single outing was so athletically outsized, to criticize it would be like criticizing a four-minute mile for being run on a track.

It's no surprise that Ermanno Salvaterra made its first attempts. In the late '80s and early '90s, Salvaterra tried it several times, joined by various partners including Adriano Cavallaro, Maurizio Giarolli, Elio Orlandi, Andrea Sarchi, and Ferruccio Vidi. The huge question mark had always been the north face of Cerro Torre, where Maestri's 1959 claim lay, which had been tried by the best alpinists of every genera-tion. To think of enchaining the Torres, with a desperate finale of that unclimbed north face of Cerro Torre, was testament to either crazi-ness or, as Salvaterra's unrelenting drive and ability had proven in Patagonia, the positive manifestation of fantasy.

Over time, a select handful of other top climbers joined the race, but after climbing El Arca de Los Vientos in November 2005,

Rolando Garibotti at a bivy on the Torre Traverse. Photo: Colin Haley

Beltrami, Garibotti, and Salvaterra held the remaining piece to unlocking the puzzle.

The trio had momentum and tried the traverse the following season, but bad weather shut them down. In the process, Garibotti and Salvaterra had a short-lived falling out, and then Garibotti suffered a back injury and had to sit out the remainder of the season.

The next season, 2007–08, each returned to try the traverse with different partners. Salvaterra's attempts failed, and he returned to Italy. Garibotti tried with three different partners—American climbers who came for set amounts of time before flying home. Colin Haley, twenty-three years old at the time, was nearing the end of his trip. He'd already skipped yet another semester of classes for

climbing, and he knew exactly how many days on the front-end of
the semester he could miss. He was out of time. But opportunities
like this don't come along every day, and college would always be
there (he would, with much prodding from his older climbing partners, eventually graduate).

Haley changed his ticket, and they started climbing on the blus-
tery morning of January 21, 2008. The weather window was forecast
to be short but good, so to get a jump start they dealt with wind and
clouds on Cerro Standhardt, climbing the line of the first ascent,
a primarily ice route called Exocet on the sheltered east face. Above,
rime plastered the rock on the north face of Punta Herron, the inter-
mediate peak between Torres Standhardt and Egger, spackling the
granite like electrified feathers of ice. As they climbed on the ridge-
line, wind threatened to rip Garibotti from the wall as he delicately
navigated ice-choked cracks and snow mushrooms.

Just below Punta Herron's summit mushrooms they dug a ledge
in the snow and rime and crawled inside their single, shared bivouac
sack to escape the ceaseless wind. They closed the zipper and
began melting snow to rehydrate. After awhile, the stove fizzled and
died. They lazily inserted a fresh fuel canister. It wouldn't light.
Neither would their lighters. "No oxygen!" Haley realized, and they
unzipped the bivy and fresh air slowly lifted their mental fog.

They were slow to shake the carbon monoxide poisoning in the
morning, but Haley led over Herron's summit, down to the col below
Torre Egger, and Garibotti took over, piecing together runout variations around the snow-blob-plastered rock in ferocious wind. As
predicted, the high pressure arrived in full force and the world
crashed down around them, the sun loosening tenuous sheets of
rime. But Garibotti knew the terrain, and in the realm of risk man-
agement he'd become a master.

The skies had cleared and just over the summit of Torre Egger
they studied their next objective, the final crux: the north face of
Cerro Torre. El Arca de los Vientos looked far from ideal, the rock
plastered with ice and snow. But, now, under the heat of the sun,
the rock began cleaning itself. They committed to the daunting
rappels down Torre Egger's south face, to the Col of Conquest.
Garibotti started leading, and wanted to try a different line he'd

seen, branching off of El Arca, but young Haley argued successfully otherwise: To launch into unknown terrain would surely lower their chances. Garibotti would later note that this decision, more than any other, was key to their success. Three pitches up they bivied again and watched the glowing sunset to the west disappearing behind the silhouette of the ice cap.

In the morning Garibotti continued, but ice-filled cracks and rime-ice mushrooms slowed progress, threatening to thwart their attempt. Midway up, Garibotti took two forty-foot sideways leader falls, nearly four thousand feet off the deck, trying to connect features. "Tired and drained, I hooked a few moves and at last, sinking in shame, pulled courage out of my pack and drilled Arca's solitary non-belay bolt. Since El Arca was my own route I felt I had the 'right' to drill, but I am less than proud of having done so," he wrote.

Garibotti continued leading to the end of the rock, where they joined the upper pitches of the Ragni Route, and Haley took over. "The evening sunshine made the rime shine like gold and warmed it into a spongy, humid mess," Garibotti wrote. "For nearly two hours Colin dug and dug, burrowing a forty-foot vertical half-pipe. Then, too wet and tired to continue, he decided to retreat. The last time I'd climbed this pitch I had promised I would never lead it again, and I didn't offer to now. It was Colin's lead block, I rationalized, but I also was scared. We decided to bivy. After carving a small ledge out of rime, we lay down in a fantastic setting: We were fifty meters from the summit of Cerro Torre, with the enormous Southern Patagonia Ice Cap at our feet, and mountains and glaciers extended as far as we could see, from San Lorenzo in the far north to the Paine group in the distant south."

The sun rose, and an uncharacteristically un-psyched Haley geared up for the overhanging rime. Only one pitch of hard climbing to the summit plateau, but one hell of a way to start the day. Haley drew upon his ingenuity a year earlier when he burrowed into the mushroom—something others, including Garibotti, hadn't thought to do—and dug into the rime, then back out to connect to the natural tunnel above. Three hours after starting the pitch, soaking wet and exhausted, they hit the summit plateau. Soon they were on the summit, where they embraced and gazed upon the expanse of the southern universe.

They were halfway there, as the saying goes. Methodically, carefully, they descended. By evening they butt-slid down the lower snow slopes of the Torre Glacier, like little kids playing in the backyard.

The ascent received all of the praise it was due, and added another piece to the demystification of the massif. If the Torres could be traversed alpine style in three days, what couldn't be done? Garibotti's reflections included a fair critique:

"The creative work behind the Torre Traverse had mostly ended before Colin and I even started; apart from a few variations forced by rime-covered rock, I'd climbed every meter of the traverse before. This time the greater challenges had been the complications of life itself: arranging enough free time, being injury-free and fit at the right moments, and finding a balance between desire and contentment.

"I truly felt and feel that some of the new styles we use and objectives we choose (traverses and linkups, more physical endurance and logistical than technical) are cop-outs to avoid climbing hard," Garibotti told me. "The Torre Traverse was not half the climb of what those climbs were [the Italian and Slovenian south and east face routes], in spite of the style they were put in, particularly Silvo's south face route. Simple fact, Silvo [Karo] could have done the Torre Traverse, but Colin or I could never do the south face. We are simply not capable enough, and that is a fact."

The Torre group. Photo: Kelly Cordes

chapter 25

A BRIEF COMMERCIAL INTERRUPTION

Commercialism is as old as climbing. Or at least as old as climbing in Patagonia.

Most of the early big expeditions to Cerro Torre were paid for by somebody other than the climbers themselves. Not all, of course, but state and local government sponsorship (do it for the flag) as well as commercial sponsorship (do it for the logo) funded many of the trips in the good old days. It's pure revisionism to pretend that back then everybody was pure and devoid of commercial influence, and now everyone's a sellout.

One need only look at the four hundred bolts that littered the Compressor Route, brought to you by Cesare Maestri and Atlas Copco. Maestri reported that his two 1970 Cerro Torre expeditions cost around thirty million Italian lire, which equals almost 300,000 U.S. dollars today. While multiple sponsors helped finance the trips, foremost was Atlas Copco, who paid him to take the unwieldy compressor.

A plate and a part from the compressor, as well as a bolt from each of Maestri's 1959 and 1970 outings, decorate Ermanno Salvaterra's mantelpiece. Photo: Kelly Cordes

To be clear, many climbers also do it the old fashioned way: They work a regular job, save money, and go climbing with zero outside obligations. A twist on the old-fashioned way (but with obligations), is that some climbers are good enough at climbing or good enough at telling their stories—or both—that climbing *is* their regular job. Or, at least, maybe they can get someone to pay for the trip.

Sponsors need a return on their investment. Nobody gives you money or plane tickets for nothing. In today's world, payback—a.k.a. return on investment—often comes in the form of usable media.

The backlash is understandable, especially as the new wave of instant look-at-me faceogram and selfies embody the collective worst of our traits: voyeurism and narcissism. Increasingly, commerce encroaches on every aspect of our lives. It would seem reasonable, as with all forms of change, to consider the role of restraint. How much is too much? Maybe it's like the difference between art and pornography: It's hard to define but you know it when you see it.

And everybody knew it when they saw it on the southeast ridge of Cerro Torre in 2010, home to Patagonia's biggest commercial fiasco since Maestri and his compressor bolted the bejesus out of the same place forty years earlier.

Sometimes it seems like everything changes, but nothing really does.

AUSTRIAN ENERGY DRINK GIANT Red Bull latched onto

a Cerro Torre project in November 2009, and they took the hype to new levels. Red Bull and its subsidiaries, Red Bull Media House and Red Bull Magazine, have an enormous budget (by outdoor adventure standards, at least) and typically produce adrenaline-pumping sports media. They sponsor a handful of climbers, including Austrian wunderkind David Lama.

Lama started climbing at age five when his parents enrolled him in a summer camp in Tyrol, Austria, run by their friend and climber Peter Habeler. Habeler told Lama's parents that their son had a "special feeling for rock." Young David took to climbing immediately, with full support from his parents, who drove him around Europe for climbing competitions (conducted on indoor, human-made walls with plastic climbing holds). Lama displayed prodigious talent from the start and soon was winning major competitions. At fifteen he became the youngest ever competitor in climbing's World Cup. He won the World Youth Championships in 2004 and 2005 and the European Championships in 2006 and 2007. By age eleven he was sponsored by the Swiss clothing and equipment company Mammut. A few years later, Red Bull jumped on board.

Over time, his appetite for adventure was whetted at home in the Alps, mostly on multi-pitch rock routes. "Right from the beginning, I was more interested in beautiful lines than in grades listed in guidebooks. But it was in the mountains that I began to view climbing as both an art and a sport," he wrote. "Just as an artist can only fulfill a limited part of his potential on a small sheet of paper, I could only realize a fragment of myself indoors. I longed for the big peaks and the walls outside."

In December 2008, on an expedition to Cochamó, Chile, a rock climbing area with walls up to three thousand feet tall in northern Patagonia, a friend showed him a photo in a magazine. Like so many climbers before him, the daunting symmetry, steepness, and shape of the mile-high spire immediately affected him. He was eighteen years old and it wasn't the first time he'd seen a photo of Cerro Torre, but this time was different.

"It was weird," Lama said, reflecting back one day in the fall of 2012 while we were cragging in the rain in Austria. "You know when you look at something, you can look at it ten or a hundred times, and you just look at it. And then at some point you just see something you've never seen before. I saw this line running through the headwall. I was like, OK, this is something I want to try."

By "try" he meant not only that he wanted to climb Cerro Torre, he wanted to free climb the southeast ridge. Mighty audacious words from a then-teenage sport climber. Few, if any, had even considered such a feat. Just getting up Cerro Torre by hook or by crook had extended many top climbers to their limits; fussing with free climbing would take it to another level.

Lama is small at a buck-thirty and five foot six. He's confident, self-assured, yet soft spoken. His Asian lineage emerges in his physical appearance, in his skin color and his features—his mother is Austrian, his father Nepalese.

"You know what attracted me?" he said. "Was probably that I knew that this would be a big challenge where I would have to develop myself, where I would have to step across personal borders."

WHILE NOBODY DISMISSED LAMA'S TALENT, few serious climbers did more than scoff when Red Bull posted a promo page in November 2009, just before Lama's initial Cerro Torre trip, dramatically entitled, "A Snowball's Chance in Hell." Quotes from Lama included:

"Back in the days of old-school mountaineering only conquering the peak was important—not so much how this goal was reached."

"Cesare Maestri, who made the first ascent in 1970, left an entire highway of bolts and pitons in the mountain's southeast face, which has nothing to do with today's climbing ethics."

David Lama. Photo: Martin Hanslmayr–Red Bull Content Pool

"Daniel [Steuerer, his climbing partner on the trip] and myself will be carrying all of our stuff into the park and out again. Transport flights are forbidden, but it's not in our interest to leave any traces anyway."

Later, Lama would reflect on his early follies, writing "In a burst of adolescent thoughtlessness and over-haste, I broadcast my free-climbing ambitions to the world."

Not only that, but he recalls his naiveté from a climbing perspective: "Someone who is able to repeat a multipitch 8c in the Alps in only one day should also be able to climb an 8a on Cerro Torre, I thought, as though pure rock-climbing skills were enough."

LAMA and the Red Bull filming team spent nearly three months in El Chaltén. Conditions were poor, and they made little progress on Cerro Torre, getting only to the start of the monumental bolt-ladder traverse—about ten pitches up. The easy part. He'd arrived in Patagonia "with dreams that were bigger than my rationality or experience. I had no idea about the scale."

For his part, Lama had to focus on the climbing. And so Red Bull hired a filming team, with an Austrian mountain guide overseeing a safety crew for the filmers. Word had gotten out that during their efforts the safety crew had added additional bolts and left fixed ropes hanging on the route. The overseeing guide responded that they added *only* twelve bolts; he justified the bolts and ropes as necessary for his film crew. Doing it without making a mess, or else not doing it at all, didn't seem to be considered.

Similar to old-style nationalistic siege climbs, which focused on reaching the summit by any means necessary (and almost always leaving a massive mess in their wake), large commercial operations often seem unconcerned about their impact. In both cases, the product typically comes first. Werner Herzog's 1991 film about Cerro Torre, *Scream of Stone*, employed helicopters, film crews, and thousands of feet of fixed ropes that they abandoned. By all accounts, they trashed the place. An interesting bit of Compressor Route trivia: Herzog's crew, while filming near the summit, used their helicopter to remove the compressor, but upon orders from the park service, after filming they re-installed it at its original location on the headwall.

Leaving a mess is far from a necessary evil to producing great work. In Fulvio Mariani's exceptional 1985 film, *Cumbre*, documenting Marco Pedrini's first solo ascent of Cerro Torre, via the Compressor Route, the team didn't fix ropes, and they left no fixed protection. When they were finished, the mountain was as clean as when they started.

In 2010, when the Red Bull team was due to leave, they hired local Argentine climbers and guides to retrieve what they'd left on the mountain. When the Argentines went up, they discovered far more than what the safety crew's guide had stated.

More than two thousand feet of fixed ropes and about sixty new bolts had been added to the southeast flanks of Cerro Torre— already the most overbolted alpine route in the world. The damage was all on the lower portions of the route, where abundant possibilities for natural protection abounded, where not even Maestri had yet gone wild with his bolting. (Early the next season, Rolando Garibotti, Dörte Pietron, and Colin Haley removed most of Red Bull's added bolts.)

Garibotti led the charge for accountability by notifying the park service as well as Red Bull. He exchanged dozens of emails with people involved in the production. After awhile, he said, it became apparent that Red Bull wasn't going to change course, and they were already planning their return. So he went public.

Garibotti broke the news on the popular climber's forum, Supertopo.com. The climbing world was outraged: Web forums were fired up, editorials were written, people wrote comments on Red Bull's site and letters to Lama's other sponsors. Though Lama didn't do the damage, the production was for his climb, so he bore responsibility. The pre-trip hype surely exacerbated the anger, and climbers felt violated—the iconic Cerro Torre was being trashed in the name of energy drink sales.

Amid the predictable mayhem of anonymous web forums, Lama became a target of personal attacks. Some posters, claiming to be Argentine, even threatened violence against Lama. Argentine climbers started a Facebook page that rapidly accrued members: "Red Bull, Clean Up The Mess Left By David Lama In Patagonia!"

Initially, Red Bull didn't budge. They responded with the familiar PR-department written no-apology apology. Lama also issued an unsatisfying statement. All emphasized that they hadn't broken any rules.

Public pressure mounted, and then the break came from an improbable source: Lama himself. The nineteen-year-old had been hammered with criticism. He's a real climber, and his peers were railing on him. "All at once," he later wrote, "I saw an image of myself that was completely different from the person I wanted to be. I'd come to free climb, and now more metal and trash had been strewn on the Holy Grail of alpinism. The critics have made me think, and above all, conversations with friendly alpinists have sharpened my views on these issues."

The project remained on, with Lama insisting on climbing with one climbing partner and no on-route film crew. Red Bull still wanted spectacular footage, so they hired a helicopter.

"I have without a doubt accepted the consequences from my critics and agreed with Red Bull that for the next attempt on this project other tactics will be used, and no additional bolts will be placed for the production. This decision will have consequences on the quality of the production, but I am happy that Red Bull is with me in this resolution. If it turns out that the film project is no longer possible and the production abandoned, I will not change my plan— to attempt to free Cerro Torre." Lama wrote.

Many observers remained skeptical. Talk is one thing, action another.

Cerro Torre's headwall, with remnants of Maestri's 1970 bolting spree.
Photo: Hayden Kennedy

Chris Geisler piecing together natural features high on the
headwall, while visible to his right, partially covered in snow,
is Maestri's rusting compressor. Photo: Jason Kruk

chapter 26

CONTRAST ON THE SOUTHEAST RIDGE

They were all attracted to the same thing.

"Its vertical relief, steep climbing, quality rock, stunning features, commanding posture, and outrageous ice formations drove us. That is what has drawn the people before and after us to be so goddamned motivated," Canadian alpinist Chris Geisler told me of his and Jason Kruk's 2011 attempt.

In the same season, David Lama was back, intent on free climbing the southeast ridge, and intent on not allowing a film-crew mess. Lama also, if unknowingly, ventured into the more nuanced world of climbing style and the unwritten mores of alpinism. He planned to summit Cerro Torre via the Compressor Route, rappel down, and, while hanging on his rappel ropes, inspect the upper headwall to see if it had enough features for a free ascent, and add any necessary bolts for a free climbing variation.

Yet on adventure climbs, the prevailing ethos has forever been to install protection, including reasonable and sparse use of bolts, from the ground up. Doing so protects the mountain from a proliferation of bolts, and requires the climber to solve the puzzle while dealing with the challenges of being on lead. Things change over time, but no climber had ever resorted to bolting on rappel in the peaks of the Chaltén Massif. To those concerned, it was like bringing roadside sport-climbing tactics to Cerro Torre.

Lama didn't yet understand the customs of alpinism and, in conversation in El Chaltén, he revealed his plans to inspect and possibly bolt the upper headwall of Cerro Torre while on rappel. As word got out of Lama's rap-bolting intentions the Internet went aflame. A petition even circulated, originating on Change.org— a well-established and powerful site (35 million users in 196 countries) primarily focused on social and humanitarian issues—urging Lama's sponsors to drop him and threatening to boycott the sponsoring companies.

If there's one thing climbers care about, it's climbing style. The petition made its rounds on the worldwide web and in less than a week had over a thousand signatures.

An update on January 31, 2011, closed the petition and read: "Thank you all for lending your signatures and voices to this effort. And thank you as well to David Lama for being willing to modify your plans—we genuinely wish you the best of luck (and weather) for your climb."

Initially, in El Chaltén, when Colin Haley and Zack Smith tried to explain to him why such tactics were considered anathema on Cerro Torre, he replied, "I can take it."

Youth can be brash, but it can also be flexible. Lama again listened and reconsidered his tactics. "It seemed hypocritical to rappel the headwall, hang on the rope, look around a little, and still call an ascent 'ground up,'" he wrote. "When many in the community opposed the idea of rap-bolting on Cerro Torre, their reaction made me realize the importance of small nuances."

He would refrain from bolting on rappel, and if he needed to place bolts in his attempts to free climb a variation to the Compressor Route, he would do so on lead. Also, his film team reported that they removed the seven remaining bolts they had placed the year before.

In a sense, it all seems silly, people nitpicking over two-inch-long metal studs that nobody can see until they're upon them. Isn't the point to get to the top?

No. Climbing style is everything in the mountains. Getting to the summit today means nothing. A helicopter can have you there in five minutes. The other extreme is free soloing naked. In between lie the nuances of the craft, and just like any game this one has rules. Only the rules are unwritten and the specifics forever shifting. But the fundamental principle remains: The mountains are not commodities. Silly as it might sound from the outside, these are our temples, places worthy of our respect. It's no sillier than anything else worshiped around the world.

CANADIAN CLIMBERS

Chris Geisler and Jason Kruk both hail from British Columbia. Geisler, thirty-seven at the time, is the classic, mild-mannered Canadian hardman. Kruk came from the climbing gym generation, and at the gym where he learned to climb, he saw a photo when he was ten years old. A photo of that same magnificent spire that hooked so many other climbers, that seems to speak to anyone drawn to climbing or to adventure. Over the years he evolved into a superb outdoor rock climber, with many routes rated 5.13 under his belt.

On February 9, 2011, Geisler and Kruk were hiking out of the Torre Valley. During their stay they'd tried and failed on various objectives between brief breaks in the weather. Their final outing came complete with a frigid open bivy—no bivouac gear, no stove, just shivering through the night on what they'd considered a "consolation prize" to Cerro Torre. They packed up. They were done. Geisler had to reach town that afternoon for his bus ride for his flight home.

They stumbled along the glacier as the sun beat down. They stopped, sat on their packs and drank from a glacial stream. As they sipped they stared up at the Torre. The sun seemed to vaporize enough of the rime that suddenly it didn't look so prohibitive, though maybe exhaustion was playing tricks on them.

"What exactly is stopping us from trying what we came all the way here to try?" Geisler asked.

Kruk took a long pause. "Well, you have to catch a plane to get home to your wife, daughter, and job."

But being polite Canadians, surely everyone would understand if he was late. "I dropped my pack—Kruk shuttled it back to camp—and ran to [El Chaltén] to change my flight," said Geisler.

At 3:30 a.m. an alarm, of sorts, sounded. "Yo, Kruk!" Geisler yelled. Kruk rolled out of the tent under the stars, took a pull off a bottle of whisky and they talked strategy. Geisler had run and power-hiked nearly twenty miles round-trip; he looked wrecked. But he'd changed his flight. They caught four hours of sleep, and, come morning, they brewed coffee and chowed what Geisler had brought from town: a huge steak and soggy French fries. Breakfast in the bag, they set off toward the southeast ridge of Cerro Torre—by fair means or not at all.

They bobbed and weaved through the crevasse-riddled upper Torre Glacier, around fresh-looking sérac debris, and climbed to the Col of Patience.

Kruk took the first section, cruising up moderate terrain using short-fixing speed tactics, and continued to where Maestri's ninety-meter bolt traverse branches to the right. There, they chopped a ledge in the ice and settled in for the night.

In the morning, Kruk led the fair-means variation, combining clean aid tactics in the seam with runout free climbing above. He crimped wafer-thin edges and smeared his feet on shallow scoops of amber granite along the crest of the southeast ridge as the vertigo-inducing south face dropped away to his left. Then Geisler took over the lead, the sharp end renewing his vigor on the heels of exhaustion.

Soon they were at the base of the headwall, where they climbed two more pitches with relative ease, placing natural protection and eschewing dozens more of Maestri's bolts. They reached a small, sloping ice ledge one pitch below the hanging engine block of the compressor itself. Time slowed. The line of bolts now seemed less senseless—as it had for Smith and Wharton before them—still unjustified, but through challenging granite that demanded either crafty skills or something Maestri lacked: the humility to retreat.

A helicopter hovered overhead. David Lama and Peter Ortner were climbing the Compressor Route at the same time—Lama had put his free climbing plans on pause, to gain familiarity with the mountain.

"The helicopter was basically buzzing us constantly for all daylight hours, two days straight (the entire time Lama was on the mountain). To say it was irritating would be charitable. It was like we were climbing in 'Nam. It was totally bullshit in my opinion," Kruk later told me.

On the headwall, as Geisler and Kruk slowed while avoiding the bolts, Lama and Ortner passed them. Nobody said much—Kruk describes the interaction as abridged and not particularly friendly. "I'm sure they sensed our displeasure."

In yet another layer of Cerro Torre irony, the bolt ladders of the Compressor Route were Lama's entry point; perhaps they were his gateway drug. On his and Ortner's ascent, he noticed something important: The much-feared headwall, ominous and improbable from afar, was more featured for free climbing than he, or anyone, had ever assumed.

The sun had set and Geisler launched upward, climbing by headlamp.

"I patiently belayed," Kruk wrote. "The hours ticked by and the cold darkness of a Patagonian night surrounded us. The rime ice bobbles whipped around the headwall carried by the Venturi effect and pummeled me constantly where I sat on the ice. Every couple minutes a softball would connect with my knee or my shoulder, awakening me from my half-sleep with sharp pain. I tied knots in the rope below my belay device, not really trusting myself to give an attentive belay. Suddenly, I heard a scream from above; Chris was airborne, the rope came tight. The edge he was hooking on had ripped, sending him for a massive whipper through the darkness."

Geisler headed back up. When his efforts proved fruitless, he drilled a single quarter-inch bolt and lowered to the belay. They had climbed all night, trying to finish the headwall without the bolt ladders. The sun rose and clouds blanketed the horizon, the infamous winds off the ice cap raced across the sky, blowing ice crystals horizontally until they collided with something—rock, ice, them. Rime grew on their faces. They couldn't see twenty feet below. Tantalizingly close to the coveted first fair-means ascent of the southeast ridge, less than two hundred feet from the summit and a mile above the valley floor, they began their retreat.

Geisler and Kruk had failed in the official sense, but it was the finest effort the southeast ridge of Cerro Torre had ever seen.

Darkness fell again by the time they stumbled to their camp on the Torre Glacier. Theirs was the only tent remaining. "We knew that I would be up at five to again march to town for my bus and flight," Geisler told me, "but I couldn't use my hands to unpack. Having opted earlier to put all options on the table, we did have Percocet and whisky. The combination meant that twenty minutes later I could move my fingers." After a few hours of sleep, at five they brewed Geisler a double espresso, and, exhausted, he shouldered his pack. He passed out twice on the six-hour hike, and ended up missing his bus.

"Wandering into town, I bumped into Colin [Haley] and Rolo [Garibotti], who kindly ran ahead and packed our camp, stuffed me in a taxi, and I made it to the airport with ten minutes to spare. The bartender mixed me two gin and tonics because my fingers were so sore. I landed in Buenos Aires on a holiday, with everything booked, but I found a cockroach-ridden hotel room. Lying on the dingy bed, too sore to move, I was thrilled. Having always dreamed of trying that hard at something and barely making it back, all the great epics, not the ones where people return with clean clothes and smiles, I was blown away, so thoroughly happy. I had felt that I had given all that I could, and I wouldn't be surprised if I don't see the right combination of circumstances again in my life. The next day, looking haggard and beaten, I made the series of flights home."

PART FOUR

previous spread Rolando Garibotti (left) and Kelly Cordes in El Chaltén.
Photo: Craig Scariot

above Cerro Torre, roiling in storm. Photo: Mikey Schaefer

chapter 27

SEVEN DAYS

On January 15, 2012, fifty-three years after Cesare Maestri's claimed first ascent of Cerro Torre, Hayden Kennedy and Jason Kruk cruised the crevassed approach to the southeast ridge—home to Maestri's infamous 1970 Compressor Route. Squalls had sputtered into a cloudless, windless sky.

The night before, Kennedy and Kruk, and Cian Brinker and Carlyle Norman, spent time together in a tent at the Niponino camp on the Torre Glacier, talking, laughing, and sharing excitement for their adventures to come.

Kennedy and Kruk had already climbed an incredible list of routes in the preceding weeks, and are among North America's top young climbers; Brinker and Norman were less experienced and hadn't climbed much together, but were eagerly aspiring toward their first Patagonia route. Brinker, Norman, and Kruk were already friends—they lived in western Canada and frequented the same climbing areas. Kennedy, easygoing and friendly, fit seamlessly into the mix.

Neither team had any idea of the controversy and the tragedy they were soon to know, each unfolding separately at the same time.

Cian Brinker had been to Patagonia the previous season without any objective climbing success, but was excited to be back. He was twenty-six years old at the time, an aspiring guide and a strong, ambitious climber. He'd been a high-level kayaker, but nearly died on back-to-back swims and started looking for something different. He'd gone to college, finished, and hated it; then he fell in love with climbing.

Carlyle Norman was twenty-nine years old and on her first trip to Patagonia. An only child, born in Calgary, Alberta, she was raised in the foothills of the Rockies on a ranch near the wild Ghost River. Her parents were both climbers and avid outdoor adventurers. When she was six, her mother died in a glissading accident near Lake Louise. Three years to the month later, her father was riding his bicycle in Calgary when he crashed, suffering head trauma that left him in a coma. A few days later, he died. .

Norman was only nine years old and had no living relatives, and was sent to a foster home in Ontario. But back east she struggled—not only had she lost both of her parents, but she was away from the community she'd already come to love, near the mountains of Alberta.

Family friends in Calgary initiated the legal process to bring young Norman back. One couple became her legal guardians, while their tightly knit community collectively, unofficially, adopted and raised her. Her love for the outdoors grew; she did solo trips abroad, then she returned and got a degree in philosophy from the University of Calgary.

Afterward she migrated just west to the mountain town of Canmore, where her passions for yoga, writing, and climbing merged. She came to embrace risk and the resultant growth, determined to live fully through the inescapable impact of losing both parents at an early age. But, according to her close friend Joshua Lavigne, beneath her broad smile and infectious energy lay her biggest fear: being left alone and abandoned.

A FEW HOURS AFTER LEAVING CAMP on January 15, Kennedy and Kruk gained Cerro Torre's Col of Patience. There, they pitched their bivy tent and lounged away the afternoon, resting up for their big plan: to climb the southeast ridge by fair means—without using Maestri's progression bolts. They set their alarm for 11:00 p.m., but snoozed through it.

left Hayden Kennedy (left) and Jason Kruk in El Chaltén, 2012. Photo: Rolando Garibotti

right Carlyle Norman at home in the Canadian Rockies. Photo: Joshua Lavigne

Brinker and Norman had headed the other direction, up the opposite side of the valley, toward a jagged set of spires of lesser, though far from trivial, commitment. It would be a good start to their trip. They planned to enchain Agujas Saint-Exupéry, Rafael Juárez, and Poincenot over two to three days, an ambitious but not unreasonable goal, with many possibilities for retreat along the way. They packed light, no sleeping bags, but with sufficient food, warm clothes, a tarp, and a bivy sack.

They hiked the rugged, rubble-strewn approach gully to their intended first route: a line called Last Gringos Standing, which joins the Austrian Route high along the southern buttress of Aguja Saint-Exupéry. They roped up and by sunset they'd climbed to a big ledge about 1,500 vertical feet from the base, near the crest of the ridge only a few hundred feet below the summit. Brinker and Norman were both exhausted from a big day and took a short break on the ledge. Only a few pitches remained to the summit. Both turned on their headlamps and Norman belayed as Brinker led.

Brinker climbed a perfect hand crack for fifty feet, then paused at a smaller ledge. A thin crack led upward, and he studied the line for a moment, shining his headlamp across the swath of rock. He paused, took a breath, and started climbing again. He made a couple of moves, then reached to the top of a horizontal ledge and grasped it with both hands. Suddenly the rock peeled away and a chunk of granite the size of a refrigerator door exploded from the wall. Brinker fell, landing on a small ledge just a body length below. The rock crashed into the big ledge where Norman sat, belaying. Brinker immediately shined his headlamp and called her name. Silence.

He quickly set an anchor and rappelled to the ledge, where he found her prone and motionless, crumpled under blocks of granite. Blood covered her face. He took her pulse and shined his headlamp into her eyes. There was no response, no change in her pupils. Nothing. Her helmet flopped loosely off her head, and above her right eye her skull felt soft and fractured. He called to her, spoke to her, shined his light, trying to get a response. He inspected her spine for visible damage. The only sound was her breathing, often wet and labored. He cleared blood and broken teeth from her mouth. Fluid oozed from her ears. After an hour, she made a random, sickening moan. His headlamp beam disappeared into vast darkness every time he looked up. Four thousand feet below to the west, he could see headlamps at Niponino like tiny pinpricks of light.

AN INTERNAL ALARM woke Kennedy and Kruk around 2:00 a.m. on January 16 at the Col of Patience. They brewed and gulped down coffee, and forty-five minutes later started climbing.

By midafternoon they were on the summit of Cerro Torre. They'd climbed the southeast ridge by fair means, without using any of Maestri's several hundred progression bolts. During their ascent, they used two of the fixed anchors and a handful of bolts from previously established fair-means attempts; reaching the top in this manner, they had transformed the southeast ridge from a description of a feature on the mountain to a proper route on Cerro Torre: the Southeast Ridge.

On the summit they sat, soaking in the immaculate view and talking. Soon their discussion turned to the bolts. For a half-hour they had their first-ever real talk about removing them. Of course they'd considered it, even mentioned it here and there, as it's easy to do from afar, as so many others had done.

They'd been focused first and foremost on the climbing, and it wasn't overly difficult. They knew they'd gotten lucky with conditions, which is part of the game. They free climbed as much as possible, so their ascent went at around 5.11+ with some short sections of aid. But it would just as well go at 5.10+ A2, a grade that alpinists have been climbing in the mountains for more than half a century.

"When the bolts were there, that's all you saw," Kennedy later told me. "But the headwall is featured, beautifully featured."

HAYDEN KENNEDY looks like a gangly, awe-shucks, good-guy cartoon character. He was barely old enough to drink back home when he arrived in El Chaltén. He's about six foot one and 160 pounds soaking wet. He looks all tendon and bones, so you wonder where he hides the muscle that allows him to do what he does. He'd sport climbed 5.14c (a hair away from the top end of the scale at the time), freed El Capitan, and was increasingly drawn to the mountains. He's one of those guys everybody loves, and nobody says anything even remotely bad about. Well, not until Cerro Torre, anyway.

"We removed about 120 bolts with our ice tools to begin to restore Cerro Torre to a more natural state. We didn't ask our elders or anyone else for permission," Kennedy wrote.

On the way down they tried their untested bolt-removal technique: A few whacks of the hammer and some simple leverage using an ice tool's pick through the eye of the bolt, and *pling*. Sometimes, the few whacks so loosened the old bolts that they plucked them out with their fingers. Out they came, ten, twenty, fifty, one hundred... they cleaned the endless line of wholly unnecessary, but wholly utilized bolts from the headwall. The compressor itself still dangled, a behemoth too cumbersome to easily remove.

Another team, an Argentine and a Brazilian, had started down just before them. They'd been on the Compressor Route for three days, and they appeared haggard and worn. As Kennedy and Kruk paused every couple of feet on their way down, one of the climbers yelled up to ask what they were doing. "We're chopping the bolts!" Kruk replied. One of the weary pair shouted back: "Glad we climbed it today!"

Looking down the headwall after ignoring a line of Maestri's bolts during the first fair-means ascent of the southeast ridge. Photo: Hayden Kennedy

Kennedy and Kruk soon passed the duo, who, since they had climbed the original Compressor Route, didn't know the fair-means variation to the bolt traverse. "They were strung out for sure and we didn't want to hose them," Kennedy explained. They stopped removing the bolts when they passed them.

Kennedy and Kruk also left the anchors in place. Kruk wrote, "If the Southeast Ridge had been completed initially in a reasonable style there would be fixed gear for rappel *in situ* anyway."

Predictably, they were bashed for using Maestri's anchors. And many criticized their partial de-bolting as a "botched job." As if they would have been less reviled had they chopped them all and stranded the Argentine-Brazilian team. Regardless, the Compressor Route was no more.

"There continue to be just two independent lines to its summit," Kruk wrote, referring to the 1974 Ragni di Lecco first ascent route (El Arca de los Vientos, the 2005 route on the north face, finishes on the Ragni Route), and now, the fair-means Southeast Ridge. "Perhaps without Maestri's bolts the next generation of climbers will go in search of unclimbed terrain. On Cerro Torre, these futuristic routes lurk, waiting for the bold to disbelieve the impossible."

The pair returned to their tent at the Col of Patience, energized with excitement over their climb.

EARLIER THAT DAY, but hours before sunrise, Cian Brinker looked to the east and saw the lights of El Chaltén.

"I just wanted to ask someone else what I should do, like a second opinion," Brinker told me. "That was one of the worst parts, trying to go through and weigh options alone."

He had three choices. He could try to bring Norman down— a desperate proposition with an unresponsive and gravely injured person, especially given the broken terrain and loose blocks on the ledges. He could stay with her, but dying beside her would serve no purpose. Or, perhaps most excruciating, he could leave her and go for help.

Brinker had wrapped Norman's parka around her. "A few times I thought she was dead, and I was just sitting there, and I thought,

I guess maybe I should just go. And then I would hear her breathe or gurgle." In two hours, her level of consciousness hadn't changed. He remembers thinking that maybe if he removed her shoes it would help her circulation. Then he placed her inside their bivouac sack, propped some rocks underneath her shoulders and began descending, alone.

The lights down in Niponino were out; everybody in camp had gone to sleep. Across the valley, high on Cerro Torre, Brinker saw headlamps moving steadily up its southeastern flank. Sometimes he would pause and watch them for a moment, but they gave no comfort.

His ropes got stuck on his first rappel. He had to cut one, and continue down making shorter rappels. He rappelled through the night, and it was midmorning when he staggered down from the base of the route.

In the boulders below the spire's west face were four climbers who had just returned from their own exhausting climbs on Saint-Exupéry and Rafael Juárez. One of the climbers, Matt Hartman, remembers waking from the boulder on which he was napping to see Brinker, alone, looking utterly spent and distant. Hartman asked Brinker if he was OK. Brinker said yes, and asked the way to Polacos camp (a nearby bivouac area, with a small climber's trail to the glacier). Hartman, somewhat bewildered, pointed straight down the gully. He asked again if Brinker was OK. He nodded. "Talking didn't occur to me as something that I really wanted to do," Brinker later told me. "When I left her on the ledge I was just going to town, right now. I'm just going to town. That's my project right now."

Brinker continued to the glacier and trudged to town in a state of emotional shock, speaking to nobody else. He arrived in El Chaltén midafternoon on January 16, where he reported the accident to the park service. Carolina Codo, the town doctor and rescue coordinator, requested assistance from the Red Bull helicopter. It wasn't a rescue helicopter—there isn't one in El Chaltén—but it was there again to film David Lama and Peter Ortner. The pilot volunteered to fly over the accident site to record video of Norman's location. Brinker remembers describing the event a couple of times, and then someone gave him a sleeping pill to help him calm down, and he was out.

Meanwhile, many of the climbers camped at Niponino had an eerie sense that something was wrong. The buzz of the Red Bull helicopter filled the evening air, but Lama and Ortner weren't on Cerro Torre.

ON THE MORNING of January 17 in El Chaltén, the cameraman reviewed his footage and thought he saw Norman's arm move. That was enough.

A rescue team had to be assembled. For all of the changes in the massif, with the stable weather forecasts of New Patagonia, the mountains remain serious. El Chaltén is not Chamonix—there's no professional rescue team, no cell phone service, no rescue helicopter at the ready.

The El Chaltén rescue team is 100 percent volunteer and generally not trained or equipped for high-angle rescue. The volunteers are dedicated and valuable and have hauled many climbers from the bases of mountains. But climbers first have to get themselves down on their own, or hope for help from fellow climbers.

If anybody was going to try to save Norman, the rescuers had to be skilled, fast, and brave. High-angle mountain rescues are complicated. They take time. Time enough for the adrenaline to fade and rescuers to contemplate their own mortality, what they are risking, and what they are willing to lose in order to try to reach another person who might not even be alive.

Dr. Codo showed up at Rolando Garibotti's house. With all things climbing in the Chaltén Massif, including high-angle rescue systems, nobody has Garibotti's knowledge and expertise. Likewise, nobody comes close to Codo's medical knowledge and devotion. She asked Garibotti to assemble a team immediately.

In crucial situations you want to climb with people you trust. Garibotti asked Colin Haley—he was in. That season, Haley was climbing with Jorge Ackermann, Argentina's finest young alpinist. Also in. They asked Pep Masip, an accomplished Spanish big-wall climber who is also a nurse. In. The weather looked to be changing, and the helicopter was on standby—Red Bull had offered its help, including the helicopter. They had made a radio call to the crew at Niponino; everyone there was ready and willing. In town, Codo told Garibotti they had one hour to prepare. They were ready in forty minutes.

LATE MORNING on Cerro Torre, Kennedy and Kruk began a lei-
surely descent from the Col of Patience. They were thrilled, having just completed a phenomenal climb and feeling like they had done something that had been forty years overdue. At Niponino, friends broke the news about the accident. Their climb didn't matter, and their excitement gave way to tears.

"We gotta go. We gotta get a rescue going," Kennedy said. Kruk was more pragmatic, recognizing their fatigue and knowing a multi-tude of strong, better-rested climbers were ready to help. Hartman remembers Kennedy and Kruk's reactions: "They were ready to roll from minute one. They said nothing about their climb to anyone during this time. No one cared, especially them. We had to tell them to sleep and eat and that we might need them later."

Some of the climbers in camp were still exhausted from their own climbs, others had hoped to head up on ambitious routes, but all dropped everything to help. A sudden storm, brewing in the Pacific, added urgency.

American climber and videographer Lincoln Else, formerly a climbing ranger in Yosemite National Park, coordinated efforts by radio in camp. "At least from my vantage, it was a true collaborative effort—everyone dropping whatever climbing egos, baggage, or oth-erwise in the name of trying to save Carlyle."

A bunch of climbers, including Americans Matt Hartman, Joel Kauffman, and Chad Kellogg, Austrians Toni Ponholzer and Markus Pucher, and Norwegian Bjørn-Eivind Årtun, quickly rallied to carry extra ropes and supplies to the base of the route, where they would spend the night, waiting so that if the four primary rescuers could reach Norman, they could help bring her down.

The helicopter barely got the four climbers in before the storm, dropping them off, two at a time, on a large moraine on the east side of the Torre Glacier, near the old Polacos bivy camp ("old" because it had disappeared into the moraine a few years before), about an hour's hike from Niponino.

Ackermann, Garibotti, Haley, and Masip spent the next three hours hiking heavy packs through the rubble-strewn moraine, up boulder fields, a snow couloir, and scrambling to the col between Aguja Saint-Exupéry and Aguja de l'S. While the four geared up, the support crew from Niponino arrived.

Ackermann and Haley alternated leading, while Masip jumared with a pack full of bivouac and medical gear. Garibotti fixed ropes behind them, to facilitate bringing Norman down.

Soon, darkness fell. Ackermann and Haley continued by head-lamp, leading pitches of 5.10+ alpine rock as the wind rose and the rain fell. Spontaneous rockfall echoed and boomed in the darkness. They kept climbing. The rain turned to sleet, and then to snow. The wind worsened, plastering the rock with white. They led in their belay jackets, battling numb fingers, darkness, and the mounting storm. It was hard to know how much farther to go to reach Norman. It was her third night out, alone, exposed, with a fractured skull. Continuing upward grew increasingly dangerous; they had pushed far beyond where they would have retreated had they been simply climbing for themselves. They were at risk of breaking one of the cardinal rules of rescue: Never create more victims.

After eight or nine pitches, more than a thousand vertical feet above the col, the four stopped on a ledge for a short and frigid bivy. It was around 3:00 a.m. on January 18 and the weather continued to deteriorate. A few hours later, in the cloud-dimmed morning light, the rock was even more plastered. Over an inch of snow had already fallen. Even in their sleeping bags and bivy sacks, they had endured a frigid night.

At the col down below, the support crew waited in the cold and wet, dozing off as rain- and snow-loosened blocks teetered and tumbled down the walls, a chorus of rockfall that echoed throughout the valley.

"That's when we decided to retreat—in part because the rock was so snowed up, we weren't sure we could safely climb it, and in part because it would've been Carlyle's third night without bivy gear and food or water. Considering how miserable we were with bivy gear, it seemed like a slim chance that she would've still been alive," Haley recalls. It was more risk than any of them would assume in their own climbing, based on nothing more than a video showing a possible millisecond of arm movement, following a head injury.

Preparations for the rescue attempt had begun the previous morning in El Chaltén, when the helicopter crew reviewed the video from their flyover. The blurry, possible moment of arm movement on the screen was enough to initiate the rescue. Soon after, they showed the footage to Brinker. He was shocked by something much bigger: Norman had moved.

Brinker had left her, unconscious, encased in her warm belay parka and a bivy sack, on a big ledge. Now she was on a smaller ledge about forty feet down, on the very crest of the ridge. On the screen, Brinker could see a rope coming out of a pile of rocks on the upper ledge—the rope that he had cut after it got stuck on his first rappel.

"It was surprising, it made me think she's still alive then, right? Like maybe she's still fine," Brinker remembers thinking. "It was pretty rough because the first thing I thought was that I shouldn't have left her if she was good enough to move herself."

Amid the rapid rescue preparations, somehow nobody had told the rescue climbers that Norman had moved. But they had already pushed far beyond what any official rescue team would have done, putting themselves at severe risk. And the chances they could have saved her had they continued with the rescue were infinitesimal. Clues as to Norman's state were visible in the footage, which was taken over thirty hours before the rescue climbers retreated in the storm.

On the big ledge above, Norman had left her rock shoes and her approach shoes, the backpack, bivy sack, and her belay parka, which she must have removed herself.

The Patagonian wind comes from the west, and she was fully exposed. Although she'd regained consciousness, the fact that she left her bivy sack and shed her belay parka could suggest severe cognitive impairment, perhaps from her head injury, combined with almost certain hypothermia. Hypothermia victims are known, in their final states of confusion, to shed their warm clothes. She might have noticed the rope going down, and, thinking it a line to safety, instinctively descended it. But when she arrived at the smaller ledge, with no more ropes continuing below, and more than a thousand feet of vertical rock dropping away, maybe in her confused state she simply sat down.

A haunting screen shot from the helicopter's video shows the details. There's the rope, the scattered clothing, and then, only a couple of feet from the brink of the lower ledge, is Norman, lying alone, curled in the fetal position.

THE STORM BLEW THROUGH, leaving the tips of the spires

dusted in white that glowed orange in the morning sun. The forecast showed clear skies for the mountains. On January 19 Kennedy and Kruk packed up everything from their season of climbing. They'd originally planned to rest and then climb more, but they were reeling, especially Kruk, who had been friends with Norman. Late morning they began hiking toward El Chaltén, aswirl with conflicting emotions.

At one point along the way, they set down their backpacks, took a break and sat in the forest, sipping water. Coming up the trail were David Lama and Peter Ortner.

After all of the hype and controversy surrounding his previous attempts, young Lama had arrived without fanfare in El Chaltén only a week earlier, again intent on free climbing Cerro Torre's southeast ridge. After summitting via the Compressor Route in early 2011, he spent the rest of the year honing his alpine skills; it was the first year since he was a child that he didn't enter any climbing competitions. He'd planned to clip Maestri's bolts for protection if needed; the physical presence of the bolts didn't bother him.

"It's not the bolts that even bother me, so much as the idea behind them," he told me in 2013. "The line that you paint represents an idea, it's an expression of yourself. Maestri drew his line with his drilling machine."

Lama's focus, the line he wanted to draw for himself, was one of free climbing. The bolts, like them or not, were in place and he'd clip them if needed—after all, he'd already used them the previous season. But now, in the crucial psychological arena of hard climbing, the stakes had just skyrocketed. Keeping himself safe while free climbing was no longer a matter of clipping bolts whenever he wanted to; he had to find natural protection as he went. Gear used for aid climbing need only hold body weight. Gear placed for free climbing must be solid enough to hold the exponentially greater forces of a leader fall. Lama had the added pressure of a film crew and a major corporate sponsor who had poured hundreds of thousands of dollars into his story, and had again hired a helicopter to shoot footage of his climb.

Lama and Ortner had already heard about the chopping. "It was like, alright, that's fine with me, but I think I'm still gonna do this. Somehow I just knew I could protect up on the headwall, because I'd been there the year before and I knew there were flakes and features. It would work. It would have to work," Lama said.

When they met Kennedy and Kruk on the trail, the four exchanged only brief, awkward pleasantries, before Lama and Ortner continued to the Torre Glacier, and Kennedy and Kruk headed down to what awaited them.

WORD SPREADS QUICKLY in a small town. Everybody knew about the bolts, and everybody knew about Carlyle Norman.

In El Chaltén that morning, on a couple hours' notice, some local climbers had organized a meeting held, coincidentally enough, by the rescue equipment room in back of the hospital. But the meeting had nothing to do with the rescue—it was about the bolts removed from Cerro Torre. Maybe nothing could be done about Norman anyway.

Garibotti, Haley, and many others I spoke with didn't attend the meeting. "We were tired and had our heads in something else," Garibotti said. After their brief shiver-bivy during the attempt to rescue Norman, they retreated in a storm, but the helicopter couldn't fly due to weather so they had to trudge another eight hours from the base of the route to town. They'd been on the go with little sleep for nearly forty hours. And there was still talk of a second rescue attempt.

It was late in the day when Kennedy and Kruk finished their walk to town. Kruk dropped his pack and immediately headed to the phone center to call home to Canada about Norman. That's when the angry group of people cornered him and prevented him from calling. Kennedy, meanwhile, showered, ordered some pizzas from the joint around the corner, and waited for Kruk's return. He had no idea of Kruk's experience at the phone center.

The scene sounded far from pleasant from Kruk's description: "Man, it just seemed like a crazy mob mentality to me, everyone shouting and pointing, pretty much the worst experience ever. I was completely choked in that moment. Absolutely bewildered... so sad about Carlyle, just wanting my phone call." Kruk, of course, was emotional. Several people who were part of the group later insisted to me that, while upset, they were peaceful and respectful, and simply wanted to talk with Kruk. I saw one photo (taken by a member of the group) where, at least in that moment, Kruk was standing alone, surrounded by people who kept their distance.

For an overall feel of the scene, I talked with Miguel Burgos, owner of the call center and one of El Chaltén's first residents. He told me (through a translator) that a group of twenty or more people jammed into his shop, and while he confirmed that there was no violence, it was far from placid—he describes many of the people as being hostile, angry, and shouting.

Burgos said that what bothered him most, though, was that these people barged into his privately owned place of business. They invaded his space, they imposed. They were disrespectful and inappropriate. He doesn't care about the bolts. I suspect that few in the angry group recognized the irony of their behavior at Burgos's.

Back at their place, Kennedy was eating pizza and drinking a beer. At some point, he heard a commotion outside. A police car had pulled up, having come to the call center and escorted Kruk back to his and Kennedy's cabin. The mob, which had grown in size, followed close behind.

Kruk, three police officers, and a translator from the group entered the house.

Kennedy was shocked, "Uh, Jason, dude, what's up?"

The translator was indignant: "We feel like you have stolen the bolts from us. This route is part of our cultural heritage and you have taken them, and you have no right. We want the bolts."

One of the cops asked, "Where are the bolts?" Kennedy and Kruk, stunned, emptied a backpack and handed them over. They talked briefly with the police, who said, "You're coming with us."

The police never explained the reason for detaining them or for confiscating the bolts.

As the police escorted Kennedy and Kruk to the police car, the mob started clapping. That's when one person, who was a de facto ringleader of what were loosely self-titled the "Climbers of El Chaltén," approached the police car.

"I will fuck you in the ass like you fucked me in the ass! Remember the name Jimmy!" he shouted through the police car window.

The cops took the two climbers to jail, while the mob stayed and taped homemade signs on the cabin door and windows that read, "Jason y Hayden go home," "Irrespetuosos Fuera de Chaltén" [Disrespectful, Out of Chaltén], and, somewhat curiously, "¡Miserables Violentos!"

UPON HEARING of the accident with Carlyle Norman only a couple of days earlier, Joshua Lavigne immediately flew down from Canada; he and Norman had been a longtime couple and, though no longer together, they'd maintained a strong connection over the years.

He and Garibotti had never met, but he found Garibotti's cabin straight away. Several climbers were discussing options. Those involved in the harrowing rescue attempt the previous day were still recovering, but the weather had cleared and they'd left fixed ropes in case of another rescue attempt.

Lavigne, an accomplished alpinist and mountain guide, knew the reality of the situation. But maybe there was a slim chance she was still alive. Someone competent, and ideally familiar with the route, needed to climb with Lavigne. "I didn't really have a plan," he said. "My intention," his voice beginning to tremble, "was just to climb up and see her, and to be up on the ledge with her."

The Red Bull helicopter (they generously absorbed the expenses of the rescue-related flights) had offered to fly up again, saving the climbers valuable time and energy. But many of the most competent climbers were still in the mountains, and Garibotti and Haley were worked from the rescue attempt. Garibotti was limping badly from a degenerating hip. Haley thought of Kennedy and Kruk. Despite their long hike out of the Torre Valley earlier in the day, they were better rested than he or Garibotti. He bicycled to their place, planning to ask.

Haley recalled the scene when he got to Hayden and Jason's cabin. "There was a group of about twenty people outside their door, in the street, yelling and putting signs up on their place like 'gringo go home.' Lots of familiar faces to me."

He didn't know where the two were at the time, and he noticed that the lights were off inside. "I kind of looked at the mob in amazement, and I think I shook my head, but they didn't bug me."

Kennedy and Kruk were in jail, Garibotti was hobbled, and the self-proclaimed "Climbers of El Chaltén" seemed somewhat preoccupied. Haley, though fatigued, was the last man standing. In the morning, the Red Bull helicopter would fly him and Lavigne to the edge of the glacier below Aguja Saint-Exupéry.

Back at Garibotti's house, while the small crew was still discussing plans for the next day's mission—whether rescue or body recovery—there was a knock on the door. Jimmy the angry dude and a group of twenty people were standing in front of Garibotti's yard; they'd decided that he had been behind the removal of the bolts. Though Garibotti had nothing to do with it, for years he'd been outspoken about the route. A local climber and guide, who was inside helping with the rescue plans (who also happened to be against the de-bolting, but, as with many, put it aside for the time being), answered the door and explained the situation. The mob moved on.

Later that evening, after Lavigne and Haley made a plan for the morning and went home, Garibotti got a message that Kennedy and Kruk were in jail. Garibotti went to find his friend Sebastián, who works fall through spring as a lawyer in Buenos Aires and in summers runs the Aylen Aike hostel. Garibotti grilled him for details, and indeed the police had no authority for the detainment, as no crime had been committed.

Garibotti, fuming, went to the police station and confronted the chief officer with this information. "He told me that if I wanted to play hardball, he would keep them for a criminal background check, which under some shit Argentine law he had the right to do for up to twenty-four hours," Garibotti said. He went back to Sebastián, who confirmed the existence of the rarely enacted and archaic law. Garibotti returned, played nice, and waited for a couple of hours until Kennedy and Kruk were released.

"I thought it was mind-blowing that [the police] could act in such an illegal manner," Garibotti told me a year later, still incensed. "They claimed to have arrested them for their own safety, but what they should have done was disband the mob and leave a policeman at their front door. It was one of those civil rights issues that I feel one cannot let pass by if one wants society to advance."

Garibotti walked out of the police station with Kennedy and Kruk and offered to drive them home, but they were shellshocked and preferred to walk.

"OUR PLAN was to try to recover her body, but I remember Josh saying he thought there was some, some tiny chance she could still be alive," Haley recounts.

On January 20 Haley and Lavigne were onboard as the Red Bull helicopter circled the ledge where Norman had been seen four days before. She was gone. Lavigne said, "It was kind of freaky, I didn't really know... I knew, obviously, but I was also like, where did she go?... maybe she had crawled into some sort of crack or something to find shelter, and my thoughts were, maybe we'll still go up there." As the helicopter scoured the area, they could see her backpack and articles of clothing on the upper ledge, and some items on a ledge below. Much farther down her jacket was hung up on the east face. Norman's ledge was on the very apex of the south ridge—she could have fallen to either side.

"We need to look on the glacier below the east face," Haley said, remembering the sound he heard two nights earlier.

During the night of the rescue attempt, as Ackermann, Garibotti, Haley, and Masip shivered for a few hours three pitches below and just west of Norman's ledge, Haley heard a sound. The other three didn't hear it, and sometimes, when Haley thinks back, he wonders if it was real.

Chad Kellogg and Joel Kauffman, bivied a thousand feet below with the other support climbers, described hearing something similar. It woke them from their semi-sleep. It was the sound of a large object falling from above, but it was different than the normal terrifying, loud collisions of rockfall. Haley, high up and closer to Norman's ledge, heard it too. But he also remembers the sound of fabric flapping in the wind.

IN THE PREDAWN HOURS of January 20, David Lama and

Peter Ortner left Niponino. By 7:30 a.m. they had gained the Col of Patience, where they brewed up and rested before launching onto the true climbing of the Southeast Ridge. They swiftly cruised the opening ten or eleven pitches until encountering the ninety-meter bolt traverse angling off right. Above rose the thin seam first climbed by the Anglo-Argentine 1968 team and last climbed by Kennedy and Kruk four days earlier. In between, you could count on one hand the number of teams who eschewed the bolt traverse for the natural line. Lama himself had used the bolt ladders the year before, but now he was exploring a new possibility.

Even the tiniest fingertips couldn't latch the 1968 crack well enough for free climbing. Someday, someone will look at it differently, but, for now, it remains an aid pitch. Just around the arête to the left, where Smith and Wharton climbed in 2007, is well-featured rock. Lama started up, and as he climbed higher, a thin crack appeared and then ended. At its top was a fixed knifeblade piton—Wharton had left it in 2007 as a pendulum point to swing back right, to the 1968 crack. Lama placed several small cams and nuts just below, backing up the knifeblade. Straight above, blending onto the prow, tiny edges and minuscule footholds speckled the granite. Lama climbed carefully, spiderlike and smooth, working meticulously upward as the angle steepened and the holds nearly vanished.

Lama contorted his body, grasping microscopic edges and smearing his feet ever-so-precisely to maintain body tension while, somehow, relaxing just enough to conserve energy. The Red Bull

left The southeast ridge of Cerro Torre. Dots represent hidden portions;
diamonds represent de-bolted portions.
1   Compressor Route, which ascended headwall (debolted in 2012) near line 5 and diamonds
     above (Alimonta-Claus-Maestri to near summit, 1970; Brewer-Bridwell to summit, 1979).
2   1968 Anglo-Argentine highpoint (Boysen-Burke-Crew-Fonrouge-Haston).
3   Mabboni-Salvaterra 1999 variation.
4   Smith-Wharton 2007 variation, reached via 3 below.
5   Geisler-Kruk 2011 fair-means headwall variation, via 3 and 4 below, retreat near top.
6   Kennedy-Kruk fair-means variation, via 3, 4, and 5.
7   Lama-Ortner free fair-means variation, via 3, 4, and 5.

right Headwall variations.

Photos: Rolando Garibotti

helicopter buzzed above, filming him as a speck on the granite mono-
lith with the ice cap disappearing in the distance.

Suddenly Lama fell, soaring twenty feet through space, the rope
stretching and slowing him to a halt. He tried again. Fell again. And
again. Each time he got slightly farther, sometimes progressing by
only a few centimeters. Soon, he had unlocked a series of cryptic
sequences, in the process going farther and farther above that old
fixed knifeblade and his nest of thin gear. Then he fell again. His
falls grew to nearly thirty-five feet. He started to doubt if his dream
of freeing the Southeast Ridge was possible.

"I tried again. A minimal adjustment to my hip-position, a few more
millimeters of reach. My right hand wandered over the polished surface of the wall, and fingers became my eyes," Lama wrote. He
delicately worked upward, linking the moves until reaching the anchor.
Then he lowered back down.

Before starting up again he clipped himself into the anchor,
untied from the rope, pulled it down, and then tied back in. He would
retry the pitch from the start, because it isn't a proper free ascent
until you do it without aid or falls. It was as if he was red-pointing a
sport pitch. Only, the twenty-one-year-old was nearly a mile above
the Torre Glacier. It's unfathomable to most alpine climbers, and virtually all older alpine climbers, who willingly yarded on gear whenever
needed. Not only that, but the crux sequence came between fifteen
and twenty feet above his protection. Not much higher and a fall
would have been catastrophic, onto a ledge below—but he wouldn't
fall up there, as the climbing had eased to 5.10.

"With the choreography in my head, I climbed the pitch without
falling. The way to the ice towers was free."

It probably checks in at 5.13b—by far the hardest free climbing
on Cerro Torre—and with a heady runout. Lama was initially reluctant to attach a grade, writing, "A free ascent of Cerro Torre's
southeast ridge goes far beyond grades. Everybody who has been
there knows what I mean, and I think that's all that needs to be said."

But they weren't done yet. Free climbing the headwall still
remained—now without the option of clipping Maestri's bolts
for protection.

A handful of easier pitches brought them to the ice towers, where they chopped ledges and sat out the night, nestled in sleeping bags, watching the alpenglow settle over southern Patagonia.

Lama and Ortner started at 6:00 a.m. on January 21, swinging leads through the remainder of the ice towers, finishing with the Smith-Wharton ice chimney variation. By 9:00 a.m., they were at the base of the headwall. A film crew comprising stellar climbers and guides hired by Red Bull had climbed the Ragni Route the day before and bivied on the summit, planning to rappel in and shoot photos and video. The Red Bull helicopter hovered above with a Cineflex camera mounted and ready. Baffling as it seems to those born of Old Patagonia, the media team was poised to capture history on Cerro Torre's headwall.

Lama and Ortner had not only avoided all of Maestri's progression bolts (the two hundred or so that remained), but they hadn't even used his anchors. At the base of the headwall, Lama rigged a less-than-perfect anchor, stringing together pieces, equalizing cams behind flakes, while within arm's reach was one of the Compressor Route's bolted anchors. "This is stupid," Lama remembers thinking, "so contrived." After that, they used the remaining fixed anchors.

They were the first party since Cesare Maestri to gaze up at the headwall of Cerro Torre and see it without bolt ladders—though the rusting engine block still hung in isolation above.

Lama started upward, climbing hollow flakes and incut edges, tiptoeing past stacked blocks, placing natural protection when he could find it and running it out when he couldn't, stringing together the natural features of the route.

Just below the compressor, where Kennedy and Kruk went left, Lama angled right, into a system of corners and discontinuous cracks that looked like it might allow free climbing. But, soon, reliable holds and reliable protection vanished.

Only a hundred feet from the easy ice slopes leading to the summit, Lama faced the most difficult climbing of the headwall. He climbed fifteen feet before getting good protection, then unlocked a sequence that included a traverse and tenuous climbing for another thirty feet without protection. Then he found a good cam placement and ran it out again, occasionally fiddling in borderline-trustworthy gear on 5.12 terrain. Thirty feet below the summit icefield, he tied together a nest of questionable protection—a piton, two nuts, and a cam—and climbed over huge teetering blocks, somehow perched in balance on the vertical wall. A series of crimps finished the headwall, and twenty-four hours after leaving the Col—including their bivy in the ice towers—they climbed the final ice to Cerro Torre's summit.

The summit mushroom was in easy condition that year, the same mushroom that in some years had shut parties down, the same mushroom Maestri said would someday blow away. The helicopter flew off, the on-mountain film crew congratulated Lama and Ortner (Ortner had freed most of the route, while seconding the harder portions), and everyone threaded their rappel devices and began their descent.

In the course of five days on Cerro Torre, the Southeast Ridge evolved forty years and beyond. It had been climbed by fair means (not using Maestri's progression bolts); it had been climbed free (without aid); and in the sometimes controversial realm of story-telling, those documenting this serious alpine climb captured phenomenal imagery.

If there was doubt about David Lama's qualifications as a legitimate alpinist when he came to Cerro Torre in 2010, there can be no doubt that by 2012, he'd evolved as a climber and more.

"It's a matter of your style, the way you look at climbing, the way you respect these mountains. It's a mirror of yourself, I guess," Lama later told me. He paused and stared ahead for a moment, before adding, "Such a crazy mountain."

LAMA'S FREE ASCENT has brought about ideas of personal evolution, next-generation abilities, and questions of a new kind of impact: that of media productions on the resource, on other climbers, and on the ascensionists themselves.

David Lama on his variation to the headwall during the first free ascent (also by fair means) of the southeast ridge. Photo: Lincoln Else–Red Bull Content Pool

Climbing is no longer the fringe pursuit of the past, and nowhere in the alpine climbing world has change come as rapidly and as profoundly as it has in the Chaltén Massif.

As with Lama, Red Bull transformed their approach and, in the end, captured their footage without leaving a trace on the mountain. Their film is sure to inspire scores of people, climbers and non-climbers alike.

At the same time, the continual buzz of a helicopter, filming overhead, indisputably impacts the experiences people seek in wild mountains. What about when that same helicopter proves instrumental in the attempts to save a life? And how does our relationship with risk, that integral component of alpine climbing, shift when we are on camera and when the possibility of rapid rescue exists?

It's impossible to quantify. Of course, we find risk and commitment easy things to discuss in theory. Does that nuanced term "fair means" include the shift that occurs when a sort of on-route safety net is hovering overhead? Should that be considered when we compare and contrast ascents? Climbing a route while others are on the same route or with more climbers in your own party also provides an added sense of security. A team of mountain guides nearby, specifically focused on you (to rig and film), along with a helicopter, surely affords a different level of security and therefore a very different state of mind—even if it's subconscious—while climbing.

And still, Lama did all the moves, and he alone was running it out over 5.12 terrain on the headwall. Yet if he took a hundred-foot leader fall and injured himself, he faced an entirely different scenario than when Brinker and Norman got into trouble. I've seen Lama climb, and followed his career; I doubt if it would have mattered. Safety net or not, I think he still would have freed the Southeast Ridge.

WHEN HALEY AND LAVIGNE flew over in the helicopter, they didn't see anything on the Río Blanco Glacier, below Saint-Exupéry's east face. The helicopter's camera was filming, though, and when they returned and studied the footage, they saw distinct colors in the snow.

That same afternoon, Lavigne and a local friend hiked to the Río Blanco Glacier. It was a warm day; rockfall boomed throughout and ice shed from the walls. "It was like being in the mouth of a shark and waiting for it to slam shut," Lavigne recalled. They found Norman's remains, but little was left, and the area was extremely dangerous. He retrieved what he could, and buried her under a cairn at the edge of the glacier. Lavigne later said, "I think about those twenty-four-plus hours that she was up there before she passed away, and one of my only kinds of solace in knowing that she was alone when she died was that in some way she wanted it as her last challenge, to experience her death."

Jason Kruk (left) and Hayden Kennedy outside their
rented cabin in El Chaltén. Photo: Mikey Schaefer

chapter 28

AFTERMATH
2012

After the de-bolting, some of the anger in El Chaltén boiled into rage. Yet many of the people who were most furious couldn't even point to the Compressor Route on a photo of Cerro Torre.

"Town was ugly afterward. Locals were pissed," one visiting climber told me. "It reminded me of when locals in a mountain town get pissed at tourists. It wasn't about the route. It was about the fact that they were [North Americans]. The younger South Americans were pretty quiet though. I think they really looked up to Hayden and Jason."

One day in town, while Colin Haley was in a small grocery, two guys he'd never seen before began yelling at him about the chopping—they were getting disruptive, and people stopped to watch. Haley, who isn't aggressive, suggested they calm down, and talk outside. One of the workers at the grocery was so disgusted that he wanted to punch the guys.

Haley had nothing to do with the chopping. He was in favor though, and he's a gringo. Apparently, that was enough. He'd likely spent more time in El Chaltén than the guys yelling at him, and Haley knew more about the history of Cerro Torre and the climbing in the massif than practically anybody except Rolando Garibotti. But none of this was about rational thinking.

There seemed to be a powerful influence of a small, vocal minority in the normally relaxed town—in cases like these it often takes only a few enraged people to roust latent anger and impact attitudes. The morning after the desperate attempt to save Carlyle Norman, two local climbers were seen riding bicycles around town rallying support against the de-bolting.

On January 26, the local alpine club, Centro Andino, organized an open meeting to discuss the bolt removal. About a hundred and fifty people showed up, and, afterward, rumors spread that the town had declared Kennedy and Kruk "personae non gratae." I checked with several people on the issue, including Adriana Estol, editor of the local newspaper, *La Cachaña*, who was very clear. "The Centro Andino declared Jason and Hayden 'non grata' and they decided before the meeting, but they put the decision under consideration in the meeting. There wasn't any vote. The people in the meeting were divided about that. Only the Centro Andino declared them 'personae non gratae,' not the town!"

Estol reminded me of how influence can spread: "In El Chaltén live the sons of Cesarino Fava, and they are part of the climbing community. El Chaltén reacted like Italy."

Kennedy said that among the more experienced local climbers who disapproved of their actions, most recognized the nuances involved and were willing to have discussions—to disagree with civility. But they were a minority. "I would say that 90 percent of people [who disagreed] just wanted to rant and yell."

"We'd just be walking down the street and people would flip us off," Kennedy recalled. "I couldn't believe how people turned on us. People I thought were friends, who we'd hung with, gone bouldering with, had dinner at their houses, were just like, 'Fuck you!' It seemed really weird to me."

Another climber who visited Kennedy and Kruk in their rental cabin said, "Cars would stop and creep by the house and then speed up again, all the time. They were worried about sitting by the window. People that you kind of knew—like the girl from the climbing store by the bakery was *super* pissed at Hayden. I walked by to say hey because I saw Hayden in there, and she's *screaming* at him in the shop. He's just sitting there."

"It was an emotional thing," Kennedy said. "I don't think our deal on Cerro Torre was a real reason for them to get so mad. A lot of things have caused frustration in El Chaltén over the last five years—a crazy amount of tourists, they can't sustain it, there are generators running, they're dumping into the river, all these things, and Jason and I were just the excuse to get people fired up."

Kennedy and Kruk stayed the length of their planned trip. They left the signs up on their house. "I think we had to be a little bit strong headed," Kennedy told me. "We were getting so much pressure, we had to stand our ground at some level. We weren't dicks to anyone but we weren't submissive. We'd go bouldering and hang out and if people came up to us and started ranting we'd start going with it, counter-arguing their points, and be like, 'You don't know what you're talking about.'"

"That's where it comes off as arrogant," Kennedy said of some of the common sentiment, "and they're right—'You two gringos are saying that if you're not good enough, you can't climb Cerro Torre, and you're elitist.' It is true at some level. We did limit people's ability to get up Cerro Torre. Ultimately, we're not entitled to climb every mountain. If that's the argument, why isn't there a continuous bolt ladder up the east pillar of Torre Egger, or the east pillar of Fitz Roy, or Uli Biaho [a peak in Pakistan]?

"It's true that Jason and I don't have any more right than anyone else, but we just had the balls to make the decision that a lot of people talked about but that nobody else would do. The mountains belong to everyone. Maestri had the right to put it up just as much as we had the right to take it down."

The object of anger? Photo: Mikey Schaefer

chapter 29

EVERYBODY HAS AN OPINION

Italy went nuts. An article published on Italy's most prominent climbing website called Kennedy and Kruk "Taliban on Cerro Torre." The article was signed by a laundry list of influential Italian climbers, guides, and climbing media.

Reaction in the U.S. and Canada was mixed. Same in Argentina. Older climbers in particular seemed opposed to the chopping.

Newspaper articles appeared not only in Argentina and Italy, but in the *Guardian* (in the U.K.), American and Canadian newspapers, mainstream outdoor magazines, and, of course, practically every climbing magazine, journal, and website in the world. Web forums exploded with thousands of comments, many of the predictable inflammatory sort. Respected author and climbing historian David Roberts called it "the most explosive mountaineering controversy of the last decade."

Not surprisingly, a thorough ignorance of alpine climbing's "rules" (or absence thereof) and of Cerro Torre stopped nobody from spouting an opinion. The no-barrier-to-entry character of the

Internet, and associated absence of critical thinking, was on display in all its glory. For every well-informed and well-reasoned post, dozens of simplistic rants appeared. Soon those interested in a conversation about the complex topic lost interest amid the online shitshow: bad spelling, problems with caps lock, too many exclamation points. Often it seems that the surest way to halve your IQ is to get emotional and get behind the keyboard.

Many seemed to have trouble accepting the idea that Kennedy and Kruk had acted on their own, regardless of their extensive climbing experience and accomplishments. Many insisted they were pawns manipulated into action by Rolando Garibotti. Irrationality abounded. Someone on an Italian web forum posted Garibotti's Italian address (he lives in Italy part of the year) and a description of his vehicle, with suggestions that his tires be slashed. Threats of bodily harm were leveled against him, Kennedy, and Kruk. It was climbing's version of soccer hooliganism. Often it seemed like anger for the sake of anger; anger at something, anything, amid the challenges of a changing world.

A prominent German climbing magazine ran an opinion piece on the issue that included a cartoon of the statue of liberty holding a cutting device in one hand and a handful of bolts in the other. The implication was obvious, and one voiced far and wide, drawing connections to American imperialism. Never mind that Kruk is Canadian.

Given the furor afterward, much of it on American web forums, Kennedy was somewhat concerned that he'd face harassment while out climbing when he got home; but nobody so much as approached him about it. "One thing I respect about the Argentines—they call it like it is. People come up and say, 'What the fuck?' They'll talk to you about it. Americans won't come up and say it, they'll just talk shit on Internet forums."

Perhaps the puzzling thing about the outrage over the de-bolting is that it affected so few people and in such utterly inconsequential ways. The same could be said of the initial bolting and the presence of the bolts, but nobody then reacted with the irrational hostility as people did when the bolts came out (granted, the Internet hadn't been invented in 1970). The bolts can't even be seen from the base of the mountain, and the route had been fading into oblivion. I always thought it would have been a brilliant prank if Kennedy and

Kruk were only joking about removing them; how long until the enraged would even know?

For those who climbed the route while it existed, their memories remain. For those who still wanted to climb it, their disappointment is understandable. Now they'll have to climb something else or up their game for the Southeast Ridge.

As I wrote soon afterward: Why should the default setting be to leave a contentious installation rather than remove it, when the latter is far closer to the original, non-controversial state?

Through the chaos, questions and counter-questions continually emerged. Did the route deserve to stay? Is forty-two years long enough that the bolts are historical artifacts worth keeping? If so, shouldn't they be in a museum, for public appreciation? Or should Kennedy and Kruk have just left the bolts? Climbers who objected to them could have ignored them. Or would that be like asking someone to ignore litter in a field of flowers?

In El Chaltén, the Compressor Route had zero impact on how residents made their living. Not only because the thousand or so climbers coming to Chaltén each season represent a small fraction of the 100,000-plus annual visitors, but because, at the time of the bolt removal, Cerro Torre had never been guided. Even the Compressor Route was too hard for guiding—the "easy" lower parts of the route, the natural climbing sections that offer moderate climbing to serious alpinists, were beyond the ability of most clients.

During my travels and research I had countless discussions with people on the issue, from Maestri's friends in Italy to residents of El Chaltén and climbers everywhere between. Throughout, it seemed as though the more informed the person, the less the outrage (even if they didn't like the chopping) and the more likely the support.

Seba de la Cruz, one of Argentina's greatest climbers—he climbed Fitz Roy in 1985 when he was fifteen, and at age sixteen made the first winter ascent of the peak—was outspoken. In an email, he told me, "History is still rolling on and we are all just witnesses and/or actors. Cerro Torre is getting back its magic just by the laws of entropy and the passage of time."

Carlos Comesaña, another of Argentina's greats, who made the first ascent of Fitz Roy's Supercanaleta with José Luis Fonrouge in

1965, wrote an impassioned post on the Supertopo.com forum. He talked about his time in the area, and how in early 1970 Maestri had come to him and Fonrouge in Buenos Aires to ask for information (since Fonrouge had attempted the southeast ridge in 1968), but never let on about his plans to use the compressor. Comesaña expressed his disapproval of the route and his support for the bolt removal.

Garibotti, in response to the mounting outrage, rallied a petition in support of the de-bolting—a list of nearly a hundred climbers who had established many of the most significant climbs in the area. Those opposed to the chopping dismissed Garibotti's petition as "elitist"—as if to say that knowledge and devotion to the craft were attributes deserving of contempt.

Part of the issue surely related to some sort of blinder effect. Josh Wharton notes an issue in hyping the fair-means ascent as groundbreaking or of cutting-edge difficulty: "This misses an important point. The southeast ridge could have been climbed in a very similar style, although probably a bit slower, in the '70s with the gear and skills possessed by the climbers of the day. Categorizing Jason and Hayden's climb as groundbreaking lets people easily argue that chopping the route is elitist and disrespectful to the climbers of the past. It's simply not true, and many of Maestri's contemporaries viewed the climb as an abomination. Taking nothing away from Jason and Hayden, they are clearly great climbers. Having nearly completed the climb they finally finished, I can tell you from experience that it is not especially hard."

Wharton's last sentence reflects relative terms, of course, but his comment raises an important point. Does anyone think that Cerro Torre should *not* be exclusive? Only a quick glance with the naked eye reveals that Cerro Torre's natural challenges are those of elite-level climbing.

A photographer named Peter von Gaza was hiking and shooting in Patagonia at the time of the chopping. At first he was against it, but, as he reconsidered, he offered another perspective:

*When everyone calms down I can't but think that the consensus
(what an evil word these days!) will be that it is a good thing that
most of the bolts are gone and that it is a good thing that the
mountain reverts back to being the playground of highly talented
climbers. But I am upset because while the bolts were in place
I could dream that I could make it to the ice mushroom, even
though it has been ten years since I climbed anything hard. Now
that phantom dream is dead—forever. That is what is interesting,
that while the bolts were in place, hundreds, if not thousands of
climbers all around the world whispered to themselves (mostly at
night, after a bottle of wine) that they were good enough to climb
Cerro Torre.*

Many accused Kennedy and Kruk of simply seeking publicity,
while others went the opposite direction. At a climbing gym in
Boulder, Colorado, Kennedy ran into a well-known sponsored climber
and videographer who said, "Man, I can't believe you guys did that.
That's gonna look really bad for your image." When Kennedy
recounted the moment to me, the look on his face said as much as
his words. "I was like, really? That's what you think about?"

At the 5Point Film Festival in late April 2012, in Hayden
Kennedy's hometown of Carbondale, Colorado, I introduced him
before his brief talk. He presented images of his adventures and
talked about what climbing and adventure have meant to him. How
his parents brought him up with a love of the outdoors and a
respect for the mountains.

Toward the end, after multiple interruptions for applause,
Kennedy talked about his and Kruk's time spent hanging out on the
summit of Cerro Torre. "Climbing is not a democracy. It never has
been. That's one of the things we love about it. Climbing is about
freedom, and just as Maestri scarred Cerro Torre when he put in all
those bolt ladders, Jason and I removed about 120 of his bolts on
our descent." The house erupted.

Kennedy ended his presentation with a dedication to Carlyle
Norman and Bjørn-Eivind Årtun (Årtun was a world-class alpinist
who had helped try to rescue Norman; at home in Norway three

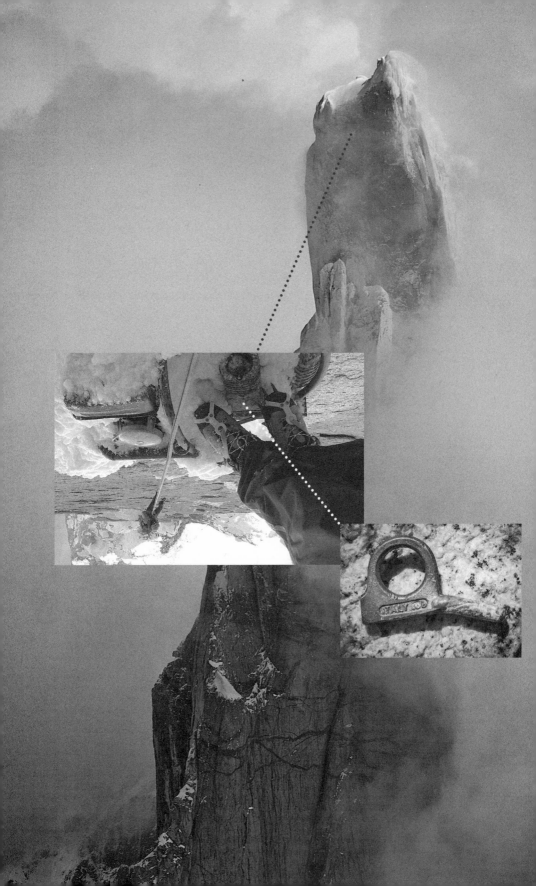

weeks later, he was killed while climbing), and finished with a gorgeous photo of Cerro Torre, projected on screen. Just before setting down the mic and walking off stage, he said, "Let's have a round of applause for Cerro Torre." The standing ovation lasted for several minutes.

IN NORTHERN ITALY, also in spring 2012, a few months after the de-bolting, the University of Verona awarded Maestri an honorary doctorate degree. In an article in the university's magazine, an official praised Maestri for climbing Cerro Torre, calling him an "innovator" for his tactics on the Compressor Route, and celebrating his pointed refrain, "There are no impossible mountains, only men who are not able to climb them." Photos showed the eighty-two-year-old smiling on stage. Maestri grew tearful with gratitude. An old film showed him climbing during his younger years and plucking a flower from the rock. On stage Maestri told his audience, "Do not ever do it again, the flowers must be left where they are."

The following spring, at the Piolets d'Or in Courmayeur, Italy, celebrating the world's best alpine climbs from the previous year, the jury assigned "Special Mention" to Kennedy and Kruk, and Lama and Ortner, for their accomplishments on Cerro Torre—including Kennedy and Kruk's de-bolting. The jury comprised an international panel (none Italian) of esteemed alpinists. They released a statement that included these two paragraphs:

> In 1970 Cesare Maestri placed over 300 bolts on the southeast ridge, a manufactured path that unequivocally altered the character of this spectacularly untamed peak. In January 2012 Hayden Kennedy and Jason Kruk climbed the southeast ridge by fair means and removed many of Maestri's bolts during their descent, taking the first step to recover the mountain's natural challenge, an act that also implied restoring it to an uncontroversial state. A few days later David Lama and Peter Ortner managed to complete a free ascent of the "fair-means" southeast ridge, overcoming an even greater natural challenge.

Cerro Torre, showing the location of the compressor and one of Maestri's bolts. Compressor: Kelly Cordes. Others: Mikey Schaefer

In his book Duemila Metri della Nostra Vita *Maestri agreed with Kennedy and Kruk's actions, recounting that before making the first rappel he decided to, "take out all the bolts and leave the climb as clean as we found it." Unfortunately, after chopping twenty bolts and confronted by the magnitude of the enterprise, Maestri gave up. The bolts blinded possibilities: by returning Cerro Torre to a more natural state those blinders have been removed, as witnessed by the countless teams that climbed the west face this year. It turns out that the physical presence of the bolts was not nearly as important as their psychological impact, and their tendency to focus attention on the manufactured path, rather than on the mountain's natural features that allow pas-sage. Maestri's odyssey and the Compressor Route will live on in history books as a testament to man's potential for hubris and incredible drive, while Cerro Torre has recovered its standing as an icon of wilderness adventure.*

At the event's press conference, many of the usual questions were asked of the climbers. Yet, being in Italy, the question-and-answer session quickly turned to the Compressor Route de-bolting. The Italians grilled Kennedy over Cerro Torre.

The issue soon became a debate of "the dignity of the mountain" vs. "the dignity of man," Italian climbing historian Luca Signorelli told me.

Perhaps this touches upon a core issue. Some people seem to more heavily weight the importance of humans, while others more heavily weight the value of nature. Taken in extremes or as abso-lutes, neither work. Dignity of humans must relate to their behavior; likewise, dignity of mountains or nature requires compromise if we are to experience its grandeur. Maybe this oversimplifies the differ-ing perspectives and the de-bolting hysteria, though. Often, none of it seemed to make much sense.

Signorelli told me, "The 'Special Mention' of the jury was badly presented and explained, and almost everybody on this side of Mont Blanc perceived it as an arrogant, ill-conceived claim that vandalism in the mountains is OK, particularly if this happens without the approval of locals."

It's strange that some used the term vandalism, when Kennedy and Kruk left the mountain closer to the natural state that Maestri initially vandalized. Can you desecrate a desecration?

Another frequent accusation was that Kennedy and Kruk "destroyed" or "erased" history. But removing 120 bolts didn't negate Maestri's installation of them. Maestri's bolt project is part of history. So is Kennedy and Kruk's removal of them.

"When Maestri put the bolts in, the world gave him a lot of shit. When we took them out, the world gave us a lot of shit. You can't win," Kennedy said, shaking his head.

At the Piolets d'Or, eventually questions shifted to other climbers, including American Kyle Dempster. Dempster and Kennedy were nominated for their phenomenal new route on the Ogre, in Pakistan, in the summer of 2012, which came just a few weeks after they climbed a new route on K7 with Slovenian Urban Novak. Both routes were huge, difficult, and climbed in perfect alpine style—Kennedy had a good year.

A woman from the press asked Dempster how frightened he was on their somewhat epic descent from the Ogre. He paused, contemplated the question as the audience waited quietly, then answered, "The scariest part for me was keeping an eye on Hayden to make sure he didn't remove the anchors."

Only a few people laughed. "The Italians didn't think it was very funny," Dempster later told me.

Cesare Maestri in 1972. Photo: Leo Dickinson

chapter 30

CESARE'S LETTER

Everybody had warned me that Cesare Maestri would not meet with me. He refuses to talk with anyone about Cerro Torre. His friends say they don't even mention it, because it causes him too much pain.

I'm not convinced that we can ever truly know anybody else, or even ourselves, but I had hoped to get a glimpse of Maestri. More than Cerro Torre specifics, I was interested in hearing some of his thoughts, philosophies, and reflections on life—I had been studying this man through the lenses of his friends, his critics, and publications, but had never met him in person.

Mirella offered to tell Maestri about my desire to speak with him and offered to serve as translator. She said, "He trusts me and it is not completely impossible that he accepts. He is really a legend, Cerro Torre aside, for his more than one thousand solo ascents and solo descents and other incredible deeds."

Mirella had called him for me, but he was having personal difficulties and his spirits were low. "I felt it inappropriate to inflict on him the torture of hearing Cerro Torre mentioned," she said. "I am not exaggerating, Kelly. I hope you meet him so that you can understand how much the Torre controversy has devastated his life."

Maestri doesn't email, so I wrote him a letter. I told him I was writing a book and invited him for a cappuccino and conversation. I invited him to talk about anything at all, about life—it didn't have to be Cerro Torre. Mirella translated my brief letter and sent it to Elio Orlandi, who then hand delivered it to Maestri. Maestri called her to say he appreciated my interest, and though he would not meet with me in person, he had something he wanted me to read.

Maestri's letter arrived while I was still at Mirella's house, and she translated for me. It was a new chapter to be added to his 1997 book, *E se la Vita Continua* (And if Life Continues), which was to be re-released in Italy under a new title, "Una Vita di Emozioni" (A Life of Emotions). Publication was subsequently delayed when the publisher closed. The chapter is brief, maybe a thousand words.

He opens by saying that although he has never defended himself against the "defamatory accusations" made against him by "the South Tyrolean mountaineer"—meaning Reinhold Messner—he wants to clarify some things.

He repeats what he's said for more than fifty years, but with a few new twists. Or, more accurately, new targets.

He says he's always felt revulsion toward those who think themselves perfect, and who "think they have the key to the truth." That Messner should deal with his own problems instead of attacking others, and that he's never responded to Messner's accusations because it would only help Messner gain publicity at his expense. (Much of Messner's 2009 Cerro Torre book focuses on the 1959 affair.)

More importantly, he says, "since the first time I went to the mountains I have always maintained that the moment somebody doubts the word of any mountaineer, we should automatically doubt the entirety of mountaineering, since from its birth it has been based on trust." He notes that several Himalayan ascents have been accepted without definitive proof.

Then he urges Messner to re-read the article he (Maestri) published in the Italian Alpine Club journal in 1991. The next page and a half—the majority of this new chapter—is that 1991 article, "Dogmatism and Mountaineering." He starts by blasting Messner for his involvement in Werner Herzog's film, *Scream of Stone*, which Maestri didn't like (neither did anyone, really; Herzog even tried to distance himself from it afterward). The idea for the film loosely

left Cesarino Fava near Laguna Torre, 1972.

right Cesare Maestri in 1972. Photos: Leo Dickinson

originated from the 1959 story, though it bears no resemblance to the actual events or the tragedy. Maestri writes that the film caused him great pain by way of the "cynical reference to the tragedy that has devastated my life."

And then, he says, for the last time, he wants to be clear:

In January of 1959 Toni Egger and I reached the summit of Cerro Torre, climbing in part the difficult east wall and, from the col, the easier but very dangerous upper north wall which, due to the heavy snowfall of the previous days, was covered by snow that had transformed into a steep wall of ice.

Maestri adds that nobody had repeated their 1970 efforts on the southeast ridge (Compressor Route) for years, although others had tried but were unable. Along the way, he says, he and his teammates were "asking ourselves every moment why those very strong climbers had retreated." As with his other writings and interviews, he elaborates on the compressor and their 1970 efforts far more than the alleged 1959 ascent.

He emphasizes 1970, "not only to honor the devotion of my partners of the expedition, but to say once more that with that victory I did not want to demonstrate that in 1959 Toni and I had reached the summit, but only and exclusively to reiterate my belief that impossible mountains do not exist, but only mountaineers who are not able to climb them."

I asked Mirella to confirm, in case I heard it wrong. *Not* to demonstrate that in 1959 he and Toni Egger had reached the top? Correct. He only went to the southeast ridge, using four hundred pounds of internal combustion engine and associated equipment, throughout a two-trip, multi-month siege, to show that impossible mountains— such as Cerro Torre via the harder line of his and Egger's rapid ascent a decade earlier—do not exist. Only mountaineers who cannot climb them.

Then he returns to the present, and the recent climb fueled by a "witch hunt" against him. He mentions newspaper reports about the "stupid stunt made by two young American [*sic*] climbers who have completely unbolted our route of 1970 along the southeast ridge, also known as the Compressor Route."

Eventually, he concludes: "An ignoble and stupid theft that once again has deeply humiliated and offended the history of mountaineering, confirming that all of those maximalist fanatics continue to be dangerous for humanity, those who believe they hold the 'absolute truth,' giving rise to the most horrible tragedies in the bloody history of humanity."

Mirella shook her head and said, "It's pure rhetoric, but that's the translation."

On the way to El Chaltén. Photo: Kelly Cordes

chapter 31

GROWING PAINS

Long ago, there were spectacular mountains, then nomadic Tehuelches, and, later, a few scattered estancias. And now?

"Patagonia is becoming a victim to its own attractiveness. The solitude remarked upon by earlier visitors is largely gone. But go in winter or travel away from the more popular trails, and you will still find the true Patagonia," Chris Jones writes in the introduction to Alan Kearney's book, *Mountaineering in Patagonia*. Funny thing is, he wrote that in 1992.

Tourism, not sheep ranching, now funds the area. Visitors arrive in droves to marvel at the landscape, and climbers come to scale the spires. El Chaltén epitomizes the relaxed South American "mañana" attitude, the chill vibe that's nearly impossible to find anymore in North America or Europe.

Lurking just beneath the surface, however, is a relatively new tension, one long known in tourist towns. Several climbers I've spoken with, who have visited El Chaltén regularly over the years, note the different feel, which was palpable when I returned in January 2013, six years after my first visit.

It's a tension that's quite familiar to me. I live in Estes Park, Colorado, the gateway town to Rocky Mountain National Park. It's tourist-mecca mayhem every summer: complete madness. Tourists waddle the sidewalks wolfing down ice cream cones and buying T-shirts. They block your driveway. They stop in the middle of the road to video the elk eating grass. Their obliviousness is tolerated—sometimes barely—for one reason: It's how the town survives. Then, come fall, we get our town back. It stays quiet through spring, then tourist hell resumes. It's been that way for ages, for far longer than the fifteen years I've called Estes home.

Change came fast to El Chaltén, and they're still in it. "Think about how beautiful it is and how amazing the peaks are, it's inevitable. The world got smaller," John Bragg said. On his first trip, in 1974, he took months to get there. The last time he went, a handful of years ago, he flew out of New York City and was in El Chaltén within twenty-four hours.

Visitation has skyrocketed in the last decade. In midsummer (January and early February) the tiny town, with a year-round population of about six hundred, is at full capacity and the trails are crowded. Over 100,000 tourists come each summer. Although they paved the road from El Calafate in the mid-2000s, then paved town a few years ago, you can't sit on your ass for a drive-through experience of the surroundings. There are still no roads into the park and no stoplights in town. But today's El Chaltén has an ATM (it's usually out of money), satellite and radio-wave snail-speed Internet, and cell phone service is supposed to come next year (a rumor that recycles every year).

Half-built structures, in various states of repair or disrepair, offer reminders of a building boom-and-stall in town. The cost of goods keeps rising—inflation in Argentina is upward of 25 percent in recent years—yet wages remain low. Groceries cost almost as much now as they do back home, yet the labor for my bicycle repair was only a few bucks.

Prices had more than tripled since my 2006–07 trip when I spent barely three hundred dollars in a month while living large. We camped by Laguna Torre most of the time, but some nights we camped in town and ate steaks.

Nobody stays in the mountains anymore, though—too much usage, too many people wandering through, too much impact. The free, dirtbag-climber campground in town no longer exists. These days, everybody rents apartments, goes bouldering on the excellent rocks near town, and makes quick blasts to the mountains in good weather. Which is great, but expensive—a part of Old Patagonia's appeal was that even with airfare it was damned near cheaper to winter there than to stay home. Today, visitors increasingly hit El Chaltén for only a day or two, zipping in and out on the huge tour busses from El Calafate.

Ivo Domenech, owner of La Senyera restaurant and the adjacent grocery, first came to the area with his parents in 1963, and has been living there year-round since January 1986—soon after the Argentine government created the town. When we talked, he looked tired. While business is good, he talked openly about the stress and the pace. Back in the old days, it was all climbers and ranchers. They had this interesting connection, he said. Neither had any relation to what the other did—completely different worlds, it would seem—but both were based on an intimate connection with the land. It's different now in El Chaltén, and the tourist influx is how the town survives. "It's like in Ushuaia," he said, referring to the outpost down south in Tierra del Fuego. "Go there, get the sticker, turn around and leave."

Most locals and seasonal workers alike came to El Chaltén to escape the same rat race that now provides their income. It makes for an interesting mix of relaxed vibe and underlying tension.

Of the multiple restaurants I visited, for example, while a few were prompt, there's no way that most of them would last two weeks in a popular tourist town in the U.S. or Europe. In one restaurant, on a night that wasn't even remotely busy, we waited two and a half hours for our food (they kept bringing wine, at least).

I walked to the post office in the late morning one day. I needed stamps for a postcard. Closed, with nothing indicating their hours. There was, however, one sign on their door. It was sloppily pasted with a ton of postal service tape, and in all-caps it read: "NO STAMPS!!!" As if they got sick of people bugging them for something so absurd as, well, stamps.

Don't even think of getting anything done that relies on an open business before nine or ten in the morning. And then, good luck buying groceries—or most anything—in the early afternoon, when most shops close for a three-hour siesta. Anybody who's spent time in El Chaltén will nod their head in acknowledgement, and probably smile. It's not the U.S., Paris, or Buenos Aires—and that's a big part of its charm.

At first it's frustrating, but you adapt. You appreciate the relaxed pace that's absent back home. Besides, on the flip side they stay up late, blending work and play—*comida, buen vino, música*—since shops often don't close until nine, ten, midnight, or whenever they get around to it.

And still, each year more and more high-strung tourists arrive— along with their money.

The conflict between the two worlds doesn't make for a relaxing summer for some of the locals, who struggle with the massive influx and rising costs in a shaky economy, while yearning for the slower pace they came there for in the first place.

WHEN I ARRIVED IN EL CHALTÉN in January 2013, I had a hard time seeing the outrage over the debolting I had heard and read about. Climbers and trekkers were everywhere, locals were busy dealing with the tourists, and unprecedented spells of good weather had settled over the massif.

Nearly everyone I met was kind and welcoming, despite many being stressed and overworked. One day, I spoke with a year-round resident named Poli. Her observations matched those of most non-climbing locals. She said she doesn't know anything about climbing— these "nails" [Maestri's old bolts] everyone was talking about last year were things she couldn't even identify. Of course she knew about the controversy, everyone did, but to her it didn't matter. She would never go to Cerro Torre, she said.

"In El Chaltén, we have much bigger problems to worry about," a local schoolteacher told me. "The mountains do not belong to the town," she said. "I am not a climber, I don't know about what happens with climbing in the mountains. But it is great what climbers do; they go and climb amazing things and tell us stories that apply to life. Sometimes it can be like an inspiration."

IN THE TORRE VALLEY, many climbers leave gear caches, often shared among friends and climbing partners, hidden in duffels and barrels under the rocks to save lugging gear back and forth to town between attempts. Sometimes they leave their caches between seasons. Early in the 2012–13 season, somebody looted the gear bin that Kennedy and Kruk had been using the prior season. The cache actually belonged to Josh Wharton, and contained mostly his gear. The thieves smashed the lock and stole everything, several thousand dollars worth of climbing equipment.

They left a hand-scrawled note:

> *You guys have showed us you don't have respect for this place and its people, therefore neither we will have respect for you! The same way you rule your world crazy here; your funny way of putting your hands into everybody's business, the way you want to replace our own history for your deep ecology of 'fear (sic) means,' this same way we will do our best to erase the track along your way, until, we hope, some day you will long to go back to what remains of 'your' own world.*

> —El Chaltén climbers community feelings and many other people who is concerned about this matter.

IN DECEMBER 2013, just shy of two years after the de-bolting, Jason Kruk returned to El Chaltén for a climbing trip. Soon after, the Centro Andino released an official-looking "Persona Non Grata" poster with a photo of Kruk's face, the club's logo on all four corners, and text in both Spanish and English, giving notification that Kruk was in town and that he had committed "an act of violence and invasion over our community and heritage."

The poster had little effect, as most people either didn't care or didn't remember what the trouble was about. "A customer is a customer," the editor of the local newspaper told me (she refused to publish the poster), noting that the locals were too busy making money to discriminate against a visitor who did whatever that guy did a couple of years ago.

The poster had a short timeline of Compressor Route–related events, including reference to the 2007 meeting that was the impromptu discussion after a slide show. "It was decided in a meeting integrated by climbers from the whole world that the bolts must be leaved untouched," the poster read. The timeline also listed the initial attempt to remove the bolts, in 2007 by "Josh Wharton and Zach Martin." (An American climber named Aaron Martin made an extremely rapid solo ascent of the Compressor Route in 2005. Josh Wharton and Zack Smith were the two who considered cleaning the route in 2007.)

Given all of the talk about respect for history, the irony stacks atop itself.

SOME OF THE ARGUMENTS sound perfectly logical at first,

like "they didn't have a consensus" or "they needed the approval of locals." But they're essentially variations of the straw-man argument, where an inherently false notion is held up as truth, as something legitimate, that was subsequently violated. Here, the false notion is that climbing is some kind of democracy.

To the outside observer, or even the climber who hasn't thought it through, it sounds like a good idea. Democracy always does. But step back for a moment and you realize that democracy doesn't exist in most areas of our lives. The farmer doesn't require an Internet vote before he plows the field. The surgeon doesn't consult with the hospital cafeteria on operating techniques. The football coach doesn't survey the local fans and community before calling plays. None of these are exercises in populism, and neither is alpine climbing.

That's the hardest thing to take: that your opinion doesn't matter. My opinion doesn't matter. Nor the baker's, the schoolteacher's, or even the rescue volunteer's.

We can complain, talk, discuss all we want, reinvent history and pretend that climbers need to check with us, or with somebody, anybody, before conducting unilateral action. But they don't. To paraphrase a statement from the illustrious Yosemite climber John Long: The vanguard doesn't give a damn what you think.

What brought us Maestri brought us Kennedy and Kruk and every single climber between, before, and after. Sometimes we don't like what they do, but it's the price we pay for our self-regulating system.

"For me, climbing is freedom—the maximum freedom available to anyone. And this freedom should not impose on the freedom of others," nonlocal Cesare Maestri said in a 1972 interview.

"Climbing is not a democracy. It never has been. That's one of the things we love about it. Climbing is about freedom, and just as Maestri scarred Cerro Torre when he put in all those bolt ladders, Jason and I removed about 120 of his bolts on our descent," nonlocal Hayden Kennedy said in 2012.

Ermanno Salvaterra outside a snow cave on the upper Torre Glacier.
Photo: Rolando Garibotti

chapter 32

ALONE WITH THE TRUTH

Ermanno Salvaterra sat down and wrote a letter to Cesare Maestri. It was early 2006, a few months after he, Alessandro Beltrami, and Rolando Garibotti became the first to climb Cerro Torre from the north. Forty-seven years after Maestri's claim.

Salvaterra was born and raised just down valley from Maestri, lived and climbed in his shadow. He now knew the face Maestri claimed to have climbed better than anybody on earth. Forever he had believed Maestri, was one of his strongest defenders.

But no more. When he reported what he found—and didn't find—on Cerro Torre, Maestri hired a lawyer and threatened to sue him for defamation. Salvaterra was called a liar in newspaper articles. Fava and Maestri called him insulting, vile names.

In his letter to Maestri, Salvaterra spelled out everything he now knew. It was time for Maestri to tell the truth. "We can lie to others but not to ourselves," Salvaterra wrote.

Members of the Compressor Route team, from left: Cesarino Fava, Cesare Maestri, and Carlo Claus. Photo: Leo Dickinson

BACK IN 1999, in the charming mountain village of Malè, in Italy's Trentino province, a gathering commemorated the fortieth anniversary of Cerro Torre's supposed first ascent. It was also a celebration of the mountain, and many of its greatest climbers were invited. Ben Campbell-Kelly recalled a private chat that he, John Bragg, and Brian Wyvill had with Cesare Maestri. All three had climbed past terrain that Maestri supposedly climbed in 1959, and contributed to the knowledge base that eventually debunked Maestri's claim.

"It was very amiable as we're all nice guys, and we were on his turf. We weren't going to attack him," Campbell-Kelly said. "It probably softened him up because Maestri made the following comment, or something like this, 'You guys are amazing climbers.' It was said in such an honest and melancholic way that you knew he meant it."

"After thinking about it for a few months," Campbell-Kelly said, "I decided that this was his way of saying 'You guys are younger and

Cesare Maestri talks about Cerro Torre in Malè, Italy, on the fortieth anniversary of his claimed first ascent. Photo: Leo Dickinson

better than me and climbed the things I wanted to do and in better style.' It's the nearest thing to a confession we are likely to get."

The Malè event had not gone well for Maestri. On an impeccable seven-foot-high model of Cerro Torre that his friend Elio Orlandi sculpted, Maestri was unable to identify the route that they were there to celebrate. Orlandi and another friend, Maurizio Giarolli, came on stage to help show Maestri his supposed line.

Bragg, in private emails soon after, wrote of the hospitality shown by his Italian hosts, though noted, "What was very interesting was how little the 1959 climb was talked about directly. When Maestri was asked questions, they were all softball questions from the moderator... and he either talked about the Compressor Route, told jokes, or deferred to Fava. Fava is of course a local hero, and no one seemed interested in challenging him at all... everyone else seemed content to have a good time.

"Maestri's behavior and body language were interesting—not at all what I expected. He did not seem the conquering hero, the man who did what might very well be the greatest climb of the century. He seemed very insecure, emotional. He seemed to need the approval of the other climbers. Where was the pride, the strength, the arrogance, that I expected?"

English climber Phil Burke was also invited to the Malè meeting. In 1981, he and Tom Proctor climbed to within a hundred feet of the snow mushrooms atop the north face, climbing very close to one of Maestri's claimed lines, and found no evidence of his passage. Burke told me that later that evening in a bar, Maestri approached him and asked if they could talk.

"I think he just wanted to share a few memories with someone who was familiar with the mountain. He didn't ask me what we'd found or comment on the route, just that everyone was against him, especially from the U.K. and America. I said that as I was no longer an angry young man and had no ax to grind, that if he was telling me he climbed Cerro Torre, then I believed him. He was completely overcome and emotional, throwing his arms around me and crying (he is Italian after all!). I felt very sorry for an obviously old and distressed man, but perhaps the truth should and has been outed, allowing others full recognition of their own achievements."

HERE'S THE BIGGEST IRONY to the tragedy of Cesare Maestri: All of his defenders, every person who feeds the delusion—there is a T-shirt, still for sale in a gear shop in Cortina, that has his name on it and says "Twice on the top of the most difficult mountain in the world, Patagonia, Cerro Torre"—all of those clamoring about respect and dignity of man, share the blame for his misery.

The worst his "attackers" have done is call for the truth. Nobody is calling for his head. Nobody is protesting outside his house. Nobody is violating his human rights.

Every time he heard the praise, saw the articles, attended the celebrations of 1959 in each successive decade, and accepted his honorary doctorate, it reinforced the myth.

As Salvaterra wrote to him, we can't lie to ourselves. Perhaps his defenders are protecting a time, a place, a desire. Something of their own.

In a 1972 interview, soon after he'd installed the Compressor Route, Maestri made a statement that he repeated forty years later, after his bolts were removed: "If I could have a magic wand, I would erase Cerro Torre from my life."

IN EARLY 2006, not long after mailing his letter, Salvaterra received it back, marked "return to sender." On it was a hand scrawled note from Maestri, saying "I do not open this letter because I am sick of it all" and ranting of the "evil you are doing to my family." But the envelope had clearly been opened, and then sealed again.

Cerro Torre. Photo: Kelly Cordes

chapter 33

THE MAN AND THE MOUNTAINS

"You have to respect the story, and what they *did* in the time," César Fava (son of Cesarino) told me in February 2013, toward the end of our talks. "What's done is done, the history is history, so let us know it, respect it, and try to build."

In a short time I'd come to like him and admire his sincerity and reverence for times before his own.

Between César's words, I again noticed the black and white images lining the walls of Patagonicus restaurant, old photos of Cesarino Fava and Cesare Maestri's expeditions. I had seen them before, about a month earlier, and while staring at the photos and trying to imagine what it must have been like, I'd noticed that the credits on a couple of the climbing images had been blackened out. Strange. They were old shots of a climber on snow mushrooms, which I recognized as being just below the summit on the upper west ridge. They looked similar to the other images in rustic graininess and old-school gear, though they were far enough away that you couldn't identify the subject.

Later I heard this story from Ermanno Salvaterra. One day in 2009, he was studying the photos, as everybody does. The now blackened out photo credit read: Cesare Maestri. But how could they have photos from the 1959 climb if their only camera disappeared with Egger? Summit mushroom photos would have practically proven their ascent.

Salvaterra pulled out his camera and snapped photos of the photos (which he sent to me), showing the phony attribution to Maestri. Just then, an employee scolded him, "No photos." Salvaterra gave her a look—it's easy to imagine him casting a sly, half-grin, raising an eyebrow—and then looked back at the picture. Two days later, the forged photo credits were blackened out with a marker. Same as they are now.

In reality, they're summit mushroom photos from the 1974 Ragni expedition, originally published in Ferrari's book, poached and placed among the 1959 photos with Cesare Maestri's name on them.

"IT'S GREAT WHAT THEY DO NOW, it's great, very strong young people," César Fava continued, "but I think as Pink Floyd said, we just put another brick in the wall. And the wall is made of many other bricks from others, and we put our bricks and someone next put another. We all just pass through in this life. Sometime our breath will take out, we have no breath anymore, and the life and the story keep going, so we have to build, to build positively."

I suggested that the chopping controversy was just another brick, huh?

"No, that is not another brick," he said, with a serious tone. "I'm sorry, what is your name again?"

"Kelly."

"Kelly, Kelly, I'm sorry. No, that's not built. That's unbuilt."

"I agree," I said, without thinking it through. I liked César, I wanted to agree.

I know what he means on the surface. But dig slightly deeper and there's another way to look at it.

Destruction and creation can be the same thing. Cerro Torre was unscarred by Maestri's compressor for sixty-five million years. He destroyed one thing to create another, but history does not begin and end with Cesare Maestri. His story—history—remains, and the story of Cerro Torre, as with the world, is forever changing.

Call it another brick, or another chapter.

Page 6 of the March 3, 1953, issue of the Buenos Aires *Standard*, with a significantly different version of Aconcagua events than those from Cesarino Fava's famous story. Photo courtesy of Special Collections and Archives, Universidad de San Andrés

chapter 34

FACT-CHECKING INTERLUDE

While editing the *American Alpine Journal*, I didn't scrutinize the veracity of every new route claim. For the most part, we'd trust climbers who submitted reports. I believe that most climbers, and most people, are honest—but we probably get duped more often than we realize.

Usually, you scrutinize only when red flags arise. Other times, though, you stumble upon stories that don't add up, and that lead you to question somebody's credibility.

As with many climbers familiar with the name Cesarino Fava, I knew the story about Fava's selfless attempt to rescue a stranded American climber high on the 22,841-foot (6,962-meter) Aconcagua in 1953. The well-known story went that he and his fellow Italian expat climbing partner, Leonardo Rapicavoli, came upon American Richard Burdsall, alone high on the mountain, after his guide had abandoned him. In Fava's 1999 autobiography, he called the guide "Un grande canaglia. Un assasino potenziale"—a great rogue, a potential murderer. They tried desperately, but in vain, to rescue Burdsall. The heroic attempt cost Fava his feet—all of his toes were amputated from frostbite.

Fava, who died in 2008, had explained in one interview: "Burdsall was ill and I tried to get him down to a ditch where we had two sleeping bags. I lifted him onto my shoulders but I was exhausted and my legs gave way."

One day, while reading the 1954 book *K2: The Savage Mountain*, by pure coincidence, I noticed a footnote. Richard Burdsall, it turns out, was a member of the first American expedition to K2 in 1938. The footnote read: "Burdsall died on Mount Aconcagua in Argentina on February 20, 1953, after climbing the mountain and making a futile effort to descend to help rescue two Italians exhausted near the summit."

I looked up the book's authors, but both are dead. Dead end for me, too, I figured. Anyway, I wasn't researching Aconcagua, a different mountain in a different range. Plenty of mistakes make it into print. Then again, Fava's credibility has long been a key element to the 1959 Cerro Torre affair. Cesarino Fava, so believable, so sincere, and so beloved.

The 1953 *AAJ* ran an obituary for Burdsall. Included was text from the March 3, 1953, issue of the Buenos Aires *Standard*, which I checked for verification. The article relied on reporting from the guide, Jorge Washington Flores, who said that Burdsall had been struggling with altitude illness. "They [Burdsall and Flores] reached an altitude of 6,600 meters and late in the afternoon reached the Juan José refuge where they found Cesar[ino] Fava and Leonardo Rapicarell*i [Rapicavoli]* of the Club Alpino Italiano. These two were in a rather bad state of health."

The article states that they all continued to the summit together, and, on the descent, all but Flores, the guide, were forced to stop from total exhaustion. Flores descended to retrieve food and drinks for the fatigued climbers, and when he returned he found Fava and Rapicavoli "descending with great difficulty, being almost blinded by the snow which had been whipped by the wind against their eyes." Burdsall was not with them. After helping Fava and Rapicavoli to safety, the guide returned, found Burdsall and tried to help him down, but Burdsall died along the way.

Who to believe? Flores, the guide, or Fava? If, as Fava claimed, the guide abandoned Burdsall, or if something simply went wrong under his care, maybe the guide was saving face, covering up his actions. If, as the guide claimed, Fava and Rapicavoli were the ones in need of help, maybe Fava was covering a bruised ego.

I struck out in all attempts at information on Flores, eventually learning only that he died in 2010. There was nobody still alive to shed light on the story, so I let it go.

EIGHTY-EIGHT-YEAR-OLD Orlando Modia, of Ivrea, Italy, formerly of Argentina and various places in South America and Europe, hasn't been connected to the climbing world since 1953.

Flash forward almost sixty years to 2012, when, out of nowhere, Ermanno Salvaterra received an email from a man named Alessandro Modia Rore, Orlando Modia's son. They'd never met, but Modia Rore had a sense of Salvaterra's credibility from articles he'd read. Modia Rore wanted someone to know about his father. Ever since he was a child he had heard stories about the crazy rescue on Aconcagua in 1953.

"The only thing that I want is for somebody to recognize what he did, before he dies," Modia Rore told me. "It is just disturbing for him to discover that in all these years there were so many lies about that experience that involved his life. Especially to discover that a 'little and insignificant' man presented himself as a hero."

When Salvaterra heard Modia Rore's story, he drove to Ivrea and filmed and recorded an interview with the elder Modia and his son. Salvaterra shared the interview with me, and I followed up extensively with Modia Rore.

Here is Orlando Modia's story.

Orlando Modia was born and raised in Buenos Aires, and was never a serious climber. But in February 1953 he happened to be on Aconcagua at the same time as Cesarino Fava and Leonardo Rapicavoli. They had never met.

Modia was with his good friend and mentor Gino Corinaldesi, a more experienced climber twenty-five years his senior. Both were adventurers, and Corinaldesi convinced Modia to train with him and to attempt Aconcagua together—which they did twice, neither time reaching the top.

They were on their second attempt when, at a camp high on the mountain, through binoculars Corinaldesi saw two people clearly in trouble. They were in an area known as the Gran Acarreo, at about 6,500 meters (21,320 feet). "One was trying to walk, but actually falling every two steps. The other was standing, but like a zombie," Modia Rore recalled his father describing.

Corinaldesi and Modia ascended as quickly as possible to try to help. The two distressed climbers were Cesarino Fava and Leonardo Rapicavoli, both completely snow blind and exhausted. In Salvaterra's video, Modia says the two were "walking in circles around a rock." Corinaldesi and Modia asked them how many were in their party. "Three," they replied. A third? "A yankee we met. He was with us, but now we don't know."

Burdsall was stranded above. Corinaldesi instructed Modia to lead Fava and Rapicavoli down to safety—the terrain is nontechnical. Corinaldesi headed up by himself, searching for Burdsall.

Modia managed to get Fava and Rapicavoli down to a place called Plaza de Mulas, where a mule team owned by a man named Mr. Carmodi was waiting, prearranged, for Burdsall. Modia explained the situation, and Carmodi told Modia to take Fava and Rapicavoli, on his mules, all the way down to Puente del Inca (about twenty-five miles away), while he would wait to help Burdsall and Corinaldesi. At Puente del Inca, soldiers and others in the area helped the three.

Higher on the mountain, Burdsall was not so lucky. When Corinaldesi found him, he was barely alive. He died soon after.

Weeks later, Modia talked with Flores (Burdsall's guide), who told him that since they were on the mountain at the same time as Fava and Rapicavoli, they had joined forces. But at high camp the weather was turning bad, and Flores insisted they retreat. Burdsall was hungry for the summit, and Fava and Rapicavoli berated Flores for wanting to descend, questioning his courage. "They were very arrogant," Flores told Modia. "I was the poor guy from Mendoza, they were the expert climbers." Burdsall chose to remain with Fava and Rapicavoli for a summit bid, while Flores descended.

"Let's make something very clear," Modia says on the video. "The two Italians [Fava and Rapicavoli] abandoned the American. To save their own lives they abandoned the American."

It's impossible to know who is telling the truth: Fava, Flores, or Modia?

MODIA and his son report that there is more to the story with Fava.

In Buenos Aires afterward, Modia was given an apartment by the popular president Juan Domingo Perón, whom he knew. He says a newspaper article was published about his and Corinaldesi's involvement in the rescue, and, at that time, the government was looking for heroes. Modia says that Rapicavoli returned to Italy, where he later died of lung problems resulting from his trials on Aconcagua, but Fava wanted to stay in Argentina. Modia felt sorry for Fava, who now had stubs for feet. He asked Perón if they could help Fava. As a result Fava was given a small kiosk in the Primera Junta subway station in Buenos Aires. (It was well known that Fava worked as a street vendor in Buenos Aires.)

In 1955 a military coup d'etat overthrew the Perón government. It was of unprecedented brutality, with persecution and murders of Perón party members and sympathizers. As the new regime grew more dictatorial, on June 9, 1956, army moderate General Juan José Valle led a group of Perónists—including Modia—in a counter-coup attempt. It failed, and over the next three days, around thirty people suspected of involvement were executed.

Modia had fled, fearing for his life. He hadn't eaten in five days and had barely slept. He considered whom he could turn to for help. Cesarino Fava owed him not only his life, but also his new life. Modia says he knocked on Fava's door. But Fava refused to let him in. Modia, afraid that people might hear Fava shouting at him, ran away.

Modia managed to escape Argentina and for the next six years was a refugee in Uruguay, Brazil, Paraguay, Bolivia, Chile, and Spain. In 1975 Modia moved his family to Italy, settling in the town of Ivrea.

Around 2006 or 2007 at the La Serra Conference Center in Ivrea, a climber was giving a slide show about his attempt on Cerro Torre.

The flyer caught Modia's eye, particularly where it said that a special, honored guest would be present: Cesarino Fava.

Neither Modia nor his family had read Fava's autobiography, and only later did they learn of Fava's version of events on Aconcagua. As they aren't involved in the climbing world—Modia never climbed after Aconcagua, and eventually became a successful businessman—they were unaware of Fava's relative fame. But Modia remembered the door slamming shut in his face in 1956.

Modia's son, Alessandro Modia Rore, remembers the evening in Ivrea: "All my family went that night and during a pause, I went close to Fava and I introduced myself. At first he didn't understand, then I told him who was my father. Even if he was with some wine in his body, he became white like a piece of paper.

"In the meantime, my father came forward, in front of that small, insignificant kind of man. I said to him: 'This is my father, do you remember him?'

"He hugged my father, crying. My father was like a stone! Then they start to talk, and he was making excuses, that it was his sister who pushed him to not help my father, blah, blah, blah. My father listened, with a smile, all the time.

"He promised that he would invite my father to his 'Circolo Alpino' to talk about him, about what my father did for him, that he would write about him, etc., etc. Nothing happened."

WHEN CESARINO FAVA WENT to Aconcagua in 1953, he was a poor immigrant. And afterward, he was a poor, disabled immigrant. After some initial newspaper articles, in Argentina the Aconcagua story faded; it wasn't until later that Fava's version became widely known and grew into legend. During his long recovery from his amputations, Fava saw the article with Maestri soloing back home in the Brenta Dolomites. That's when he wrote his famous letter, inviting Maestri to come to Cerro Torre. Soon Fava became a hero via his connection to the greatest ascent in history.

The Chaltén Massif, jutting skyward from the pampas.
Photo: Kelly Cordes

chapter 35

MY
TRUTH

In Buenos Aires in 2013, after leaving El Chaltén but long before learning Modia's Aconcagua story, I visited the Biblioteca Dante Alighieri. The librarian who helped me, Liliana, knew of the story I was researching— a series of 1959 Cerro Torre articles from an Italian language Buenos Aires newspaper. Her mother was from Malè, Italy, and was friends with Cesarino Fava and his family. Amazed, I told her that I had just spoken with his son César in El Chaltén, and how I enjoyed his company. She told me that she had held young César in her arms when he was a baby, and fondly recalled his family. Liliana asked if I could put her and César in touch.

~ Once I returned home I emailed César to thank him for his time, and to tell him that I had met Liliana as well as Juan Pedro Spikermann, one of the young students who helped carry gear for his father and Cesare Maestri on the 1959 Cerro Torre expedition (and on the first 1970 compressor trip). They had enjoyed memorable times together in base camp, and Spikermann remembered Cesarino as being very funny, and with a great personality.

César wrote of those I mentioned and of their relationships— though time had passed, the bonds remained. It had been awhile since he talked with Liliana, but he was enthusiastic, and he wrote of Spikermann's son, a national park ranger in nearby El Calafate, and their friendship borne of the friendships of their fathers. He expounded upon the heritage of relationships among other local climbers he knew whose fathers knew his father. He thanked me and told me that I was the "bridge" for connecting him and Juan Pedro and Liliana. He even wrote, "That is what I feel you'll be in all this story Kelly... a bridge that will overcome its crevasses."

Damn, I thought to myself. I like César, just as I like many supporters of his father and of Cesare Maestri. But I won't—I can't—ignore the evidence from 1959.

All the talk, all the great stories told and shifted and re-created later do not change your actions. To me, the truth matters. And while it's true that I don't know "the *man*" in either case, maybe these people don't truly know them, either. I'll base my judgments on behavior, not on words—no matter how romantically spoken.

I would love to be a bridge. But as I read César's words, I felt a twinge of sadness, knowing that what I would write might be perceived as a betrayal.

I would write the hard facts I'd discovered in the mountain of evidence surrounding Cerro Torre. Facts that many people chose, and still choose, to ignore. The lies that never gave Toni Egger's family an honest answer about his death. Lies that perpetuate a mindset where people distort history and reality to protect their beliefs at any cost. Lies that undermine those who conduct themselves honestly.

I would write my belief that all that followed the lie of '59—the beauty and the ugliness—could be traced back to that story, almost like original sin. Though I admire the courage and vision required to even venture to Cerro Torre in 1959, the story remains fatally flawed, and not because they didn't climb the mountain. It remains flawed because it lacks truth.

That is where Cesarino Fava and Cesare Maestri failed. They failed themselves, they failed those who believed in them, and they betrayed the code of trust that is essential to climbing mountains.

I believe the ways we treat the things and people we profess to love are expressions of who we are.

The mountains are sacred, transcendent places, places of inspiration and consequence, where trust and actions and honesty matter. Places where, in fleeting moments, I've known the beauty of belief to merge with the power of truth. Moments as fragile and precious as tiny crystals of rime, carried off by a furious wind.

The Torres, as seen from just below the summit of Fitz Roy.
Photo: Kelly Cordes

EPILOGUE

When I came to El Chaltén in January 2013, I came with no expectations. No real climbing plans, aside from something easy if it worked out. I had two months, and, first and foremost, I needed to try to understand the frustration and anger over the de-bolting of the Compressor Route. If I could frame it right, this was an opportunity for me, a chance to shift gears. I'd known for a couple of years that I needed to transition to different types of climbing—maybe to different adventures altogether. Ones that don't exact such a toll on my aging, injured body.

When my friend Craig and I booked our tickets, I warned him not to count on me for any big routes, and that he might need to climb with some of our other friends. For me, this was primarily a work trip.

My body's just too wrecked, ever since destroying my lower leg in early 2010. That day in the mountains of Montana, while lowering off an ice climb—it was our first route of the day, our warm-up— I dropped my guard. Just for a second. I'd been climbing well, had big plans for the coming spring and summer. I was on the road, climbing with friends in various locales, in love with the flow, the challenge, the natural beauty of wintertime in the mountains.

I'd just finished leading the pitch and was out of sight of my belayer. He'd paid out slack, as he should, while I anchored the ropes to a tree. I returned to the edge of the cliff and paused, smiling, marveling at the spectacular landscape. I thought the rope was tight and I was ready to lower. But I didn't make sure of it, I just leaned back. One moment and everything changed. I accelerated through space until, maybe ten feet down, the rope pulled me back into the wall. As it did, my crampon points locked my outstretched right leg onto an icy ledge as my body continued. In an instant, my leg was flopping off to the side.

I still remember sitting in the snow afterward, wincing in pain, knowing my climbing life had just taken an irrevocable shift. But I also remember looking off to the snow-blanketed slopes and trees and the glimmering ice pouring over the cliffbands. At a beginner area across the canyon—one of the places I first learned to climb—I could see a couple of parties top-roping the ice, and I remember hoping that they were having the time of their lives.

My tibia had shattered to dust at its distal end—the upper half of the ankle joint. I had four surgeries on my leg, plus a knee surgery and a massive shoulder reconstruction, making for six surgeries in thirteen months and an overwhelmingly horrible year. I received great medical care, but still, some days my leg hurts so bad I can barely make it from my bed to the coffee grinder. No matter how hard I beat my head against the walls of the past, it will never change.

While the rest of the world is version 2.0, Patagonia approaches are too much for Kelly 0.75. The actual climbing usually feels good, but the pain on approaches and descents steals too much of the joy. Sometimes, though, I get these moments, these glimpses of my old self—sometimes just a flash but sometimes days at a time—times when I don't hurt and when everything flows and moves and transports me to a different place.

God, how I miss the wildness, the unpredictability, the way my energy moves unencumbered with the mountains and the way their ever-changing moods gives gorgeous contrast to our static, pre-packaged world, where adventure comes when the TV station changes the lineup without warning you.

In the weeks leading up to my Patagonia trip the good days started to outnumber the bad, so I packed my full alpine climbing kit just in case.

When you fall in love, it's hard to let go.

IN MID-JANUARY, Craig and I stood on the summit of Fitz Roy. *I should appreciate this moment*, I should have been thinking. But the weather was shifting, daylight was dwindling, and we had to get down.

In a way it all started here, on Fitz Roy's summit. The same place from where, sixty-one years earlier, in 1952, Frenchmen Guido Magnone and Lionel Terray peered over at the impossible-looking Cerro Torre.

Time paused as I stared west, across the valley to the Torres, aligned like chess pieces, incomprehensible works of art born of nature's chaos, jutting skyward against the backdrop of the ice cap.

Had I been thinking, I'd have remembered Terray's words from his acclaimed 1961 memoir, *Les Conquérants de l'inutile—Conquistadors of the Useless*: "The ascent of Cerro Torre, a more difficult neighbor of Fitz Roy, by Toni Egger and Cesare Maestri, seems to me the greatest mountaineering feat of all time." Terray never saw how the rest unfolded—he died on a rock climb just four years after his book was published.

The wind kicked up and the sun dropped. Craig and I snapped a couple of summit photos and began down the cold south face, taking a variation to Magnone and Terray's first ascent route.

FUCK. FUCK, FUCK, FUCK. I couldn't tell if my ropes touched or if they were just dangling in space.

We should have bivied on the summit. Should have just stopped, waited for daylight. Over the previous two and a half days we'd climbed Fitz Roy's northwest ridge, the Afanassieff Route—not a hard route but one of the longest routes in the massif, rising five thousand vertical feet from base to summit, forty-some pitches of climbing. Neither of us had ever been on Fitz Roy, so we didn't know the descent. But the weather threatened, the wind rose, and we started down at dusk.

They have to touch, I thought. The ropes had to connect with the rock wall below so I could build an anchor. But it was pitch dark and I couldn't see. My headlamp didn't shine that far and my eyes were too blurred by fatigue. We had three thousand vertical feet of descent to go. From the blackness below I pulled up coils of rope and dropped them. Wait.... listen.... Was that the sound of the ropes hitting rock or of the ends snapping against themselves in empty space?

Soon I would realize that we should have gone right where I went left. I'd committed us to a terrible free-hanging rappel, impossible to reverse. We'd gotten sucked into a sustained vertical corner system that angled further left, with no stances and no ledges. Every time we pulled the ropes we descended deeper and further the wrong way, until we hit a hanging snowfield interrupting the vertical rock walls. I set an anchor in a rock outcrop and rappelled the steep little snowfield to its end. Just over the lip, I shined my headlamp.

Swirling gray roiled upward from thousands of feet below, and between breaks in the clouds the beam of my light disappeared into absolute nothingness. I locked off the rope, backed myself up, and ran side to side across the edge of the snowfield, swinging back and forth, scanning my headlamp over the vertical rock below searching for cracks, searching for anchors, searching for anything to make our next rappel.

I went back up the ropes to wait for daylight. Craig was shivering. We were out of food and there was nowhere to lie down, but I've always figured you can survive almost anything for one night.

Pellets of precipitation intermittently tapped our ultralight tarp, and we huddled close for warmth on a tiny butt-sized ledge, our lightweight sleeping bags wrapped around us and the tarp rigged to try to block the wind. We shivered and rocked back and forth, waiting several hours for daylight so we could see if we had a chance. If we could somehow traverse back across to join the correct descent route.

A MONTH AFTER we made it down from Fitz Roy, after countless days of sleeping ten- and twelve-hour nights, I was limping less again. Sometimes I feel like one of those old boxers who can't let go, who keeps coming back, thinking *this time* it will be different.

I was sick of interviewing people and tired of controversy. Plenty of people were sick of me, too. It would have been easier if I'd have let it go and didn't bother.

It was late February and my two-month trip was winding down. Most of the visitors had gone, some of the shops had closed, and the locals' stress seemed to drift away like the changing leaves. Some mornings, frost coated the hilltops. A handful of happy climbers remained, keeping an eye on the Internet forecast for one last opportunity.

From the front door of my rented cabin, fifty feet of dirt road led to a side trail that eventually intersects the main trail into the Torre Valley, and I hiked it every day that my leg allowed. Each day I felt better, popped fewer painkillers, and started to dream a little more.

Along the way I entered brief, intermittent forests where sunlight slatted and slipped through the *lenga* canopy. Where the wind flattened their tops and thickened their trunks and branches to where some of them looked like overgrown bonsais, grown stout to withstand the wind. A grove stood maybe fifty feet tall for a section, and sheltered a flourishing underbrush, and I imagined myself in a coastal rain forest. A short distance farther, the landscape changed and the unprotected and wind-scoured vegetation grew to only waist-height. Shorter ñire trees rose about, looking strong and proud, adapted to their environment, and flecks of autumn leaves— orange, yellow, and green—fluttered across the trail.

Back in town, I walked to a bakery for empanadas. Out front, a pack of dogs napped in the yard. I entered, placed my order, and as I waited I noticed the photos. As with many places in town, photos of the mountains graced the walls. A bunch were from Colin Haley— I knew not only from the photo credit, but because I immediately recognized a couple of the shots from our Cerro Torre climb. I smiled and studied a familiar image, and my mind drifted.

I COULD HARDLY BELIEVE how many hard climbs got done in the 2012–13 season. Dozens of people at the same time climbed routes that not long ago were considered testpieces, lines that made news if they were climbed once a season. When we started up the Afanassieff—the route was first established in 1979 and received its second ascent only in 2007—we shared it with a dozen or more climbers, a potentially dangerous situation due to rockfall hazard. Then again, there are more people around to help if things go wrong.

Everything changed so fast. But you can't blame people for coming to experience the very thing that you also love.

"There is so much vibrant energy and motivation here, so much upward momentum. It is hard not to feel that we are living a special moment for the climbing in this area," Rolando Garibotti wrote of the 2012–13 season. "This massif is no longer the mythical 'great range' where the likes of José Luis Fonrouge, Casimiro Ferrari, Jim Donini, Silvo Karo, Ermanno Salvaterra, and many others made history. Today, instead, it is a phenomenal playground where hundreds of climbers are having deeply fulfilling experiences. We may shed a few tears for what has been lost, but it is hard not to have a big smile on one's face for what is happening."

Standards are skyrocketing. The "kids" are taking the climbing world by storm. The Southeast Ridge of Cerro Torre saw renewed attention—several climbers told me that when the bolt ladders were in place, the beautiful line held no interest for them. Young Slovenians Luka Krajnc and Tadej Krišelj, however, were the only climbers to succeed, and they didn't use any of the (remaining) bolt ladders. They said it wasn't especially hard and that the route was fantastic. It was actually the second significant climb of their trip, and their first trip to the massif. About two weeks earlier they'd rolled into El Chaltén on the early bus under perfect weather, and then hastily repacked their bags and asked the hostel owner for directions to the trailhead.

Four days later they were on the summit of Fitz Roy after putting up a difficult new route in perfect style. They left no fixed gear behind; anyone can go repeat it in its natural state. On their routes, they climbed in alpine style, placed no bolts, and didn't use Jumars—a clear next-step progression that has been happening among top climbers, where the leader and follower both climb, rather than the second jumaring the rope with the heavy pack. If you're good enough and go light enough—if you're confident in the weather remaining clear—you don't need to jumar.

One evening at a group dinner Luka told me one of the things he loves about alpinism. It's how the mountains strip away the bull-shit—something rare in a world of hype and misrepresentations—how when you're actually there, you and your partner on a route, just you and your abilities, the truth always shows. "You can't lie," he said.

An all-Argentine team—Gabriel Fava (no relation to Cesarino), Wenny Sánchez, and Roberto Treu—established a difficult new route (or major variation, depending on definitions) on the west face of Cerro Torre in perfect alpine style. They were the first fully Argentine team, and Sánchez is the first woman, to put up a new line on the Torre.

Colin Haley and Chad Kellogg [Kellogg was killed by rockfall while descending Fitz Roy in early 2014] repeated Cerro Torre's Corkscrew linkup, the second ascent—but the first without using Maestri's bolt ladders. They took only twenty-four hours round-trip.

For comparison, by the end of the 2007 season only seven teams had climbed to the summit of Cerro Torre without using the Compressor Route's bolts to reach the top. As of March 2012, that list had grown to twenty-two. But from November 2012 through February 2013, more than a hundred people summitted Cerro Torre via the Ragni Route. And Austrian hardman Markus Pucher free soloed the route in the mind-blowing time of three hours and fifteen minutes.

While the warm summer and lack of severe storms resulted in unprecedented conditions—very little rime, mostly straight-ahead, spectacular ice climbing on the Ragni Route—such climbing was unheard of, even unthinkable, just a few years earlier.

Still, forever the critic, I wonder when someone will step away from routes they know they can do and tackle the challenges that climbers like Ermanno Salvaterra and Silvo Karo laid down on Cerro Torre's south and east faces; for all the speed, the linkups, and free climbing abilities, sometimes it seems there's a gap between the hardcore alpinism of the '80s and '90s, and the stylish, dainty jaunts of today.

To a couple of the young guns in Chaltén I posed the questions: south face? east face? with a gentle prod. Every time they shook their heads in admiration and awe for those routes and the climbers who did them, and admitted that they aren't quite ready. But I bet they will be soon.

In the blink of an eye I feel old. Yet the magic of the mountains remains as open to me as to anybody. We have so many magnificent landscapes to experience, so many wonders to accept, unravel, and then leave unscarred.

Crossing the Río de las Vueltas, about twelve miles from today's El Chaltén, in early 1959. Fava collection

APPENDIX I SELECTED CERRO TORRE ASCENT TIMELINE

The ultimate ideal in alpine climbing is to make the first ascent of a difficult, previously unclimbed mountain in perfect style. Next best is establishing a new route on a mountain. What constitutes a legitimate new route is debatable, but in the Chaltén Massif, over time, this seems to have stuck: Climb previously virgin terrain to the junction of an existing route and, even without continuing to the summit, it's considered a new route.

Summarized below are the most significant ascents and attempts on Cerro Torre. "Most significant" is, by definition, subjective.

1958
West Face
Italians Walter Bonatti and Carlo Mauri attempt the west face.

East Face
Italians Bruno Detassis and team (including Cesare Maestri) approach the east face. Deeming it suicidal, Detassis prohibits his climbers from even attempting the tower.

1959
North Face/Ridge
Starting from the east, Austrian Toni Egger and Italian Cesare Maestri, with support from Cesarino Fava, make supposed first ascent of the mountain. Egger dies in process.

1968
Southeast Ridge
An Anglo-Argentine team attempts the southeast ridge over several months, before retreating a thousand feet below the summit.

1970
West Face
Carlo Mauri returns to the west face with a large Ragni di Lecco team. They retreat some six hundred feet below the summit.

page 372 photos (from left)
Dörte Pietron, Dani Ascaso, Mikey Schaefer

page 373 photos (from left)
Mikey Schaefer, Ben Ditto, Kelly Cordes

Southeast Ridge
Over the course of two expeditions—one winter, one summer—Cesare Maestri leads teams up the southeast ridge. Sponsored by an industrial equipment company, he hauls up their gas-powered air compressor and drills some four hundred bolts. He fails to reach the summit, but the line becomes known as the Compressor Route.

1974
West Face
Italians Daniele Chiappa, Mario Conti, Casimiro Ferrari, and Pino Negri, of the Ragni di Lecco club, establish the Ragni di Lecco Route and make what is now known to be the true first ascent of Cerro Torre.

1979
Southeast Ridge
Americans Steve Brewer and Jim Bridwell make a rapid ascent of the Compressor Route, complete to the summit, becoming the first to climb it since its installation.

1981
East & North Faces
Englishmen Phil Burke and Tom Proctor climb high on the east and north faces, retreating only a hundred feet below the junction of the upper west ridge (Ragni Route).

1985
Southeast Ridge
Italians Paolo Caruso, Maurizio Giarolli, Ermanno Salvaterra, and Andrea Sarchi make the first winter ascent of the peak via the Compressor Route.

Swiss climber Marco Pedrini makes Cerro Torre's first solo ascent, via the Compressor Route.

1986
East Face
Slovenians Matjaž Fistravec, Janez Jeglič, Silvo Karo, Franček Knez, Pavle Kozjek, and Peter Podgornik put up a difficult big-wall mixed climbing route, Peklenska Direttissima (Hell's Direct) using fixed ropes but placing only five bolts, all at belays. Seven hundred feet below the top, they join the Compressor Route and continue to the summit.

1988
South Face
Slovenians Janez Jeglič and Silvo Karo climb a desperate new big-wall route on the intimidating and cold south face, before traversing the hanging ice field high on the face to join the Compressor Route (a thousand feet below the summit), from where they descend.

1994
South Face

François Marsigny (France) and Andy Parkin (United Kingdom) are the first to climb an ephemeral line of ice (Los Tiempos Perdidos) on the far left side of the south face, leading to the Col of Hope. They retreat below the summit and suffer a true epic.

Slovenians Janez Jeglič, Marko Lukič, and Miha Praprotnik climb a comparatively short, though extremely difficult, big-wall route (What's Love Got To Do with It) on the south face that veers off at mid-height to join the Compressor Route and descend.

Northwest Face

Italians Maurizio Giarolli, Elio Orlandi, and Odoardo Ravizza attempt the northwest face and north ridge from the west, retreating a thousand feet below the summit. They claim a new route, since they joined the supposed 1959 Egger-Maestri.

1995
South Face

Italians Roberto Manni, Ermanno Salvaterra, and Piergiorgio Vidi establish an incredibly difficult new route (Infinito Sud) up the center of the south face, hauling an aluminum box for shelter as they go, to wait out storms, rather than relying on extensive fixed ropes. Upon joining the southeast ridge a thousand feet below the summit, they descend.

1999
North Face

Austrians Franz Niederegger and Toni Ponholzer make an impressive attempt up the center of the north face (approached from the east). They climb to within three hundred feet of the Ragni Route before retreating.

2004
East Face

Italians Alessandro Beltrami, Giacomo Rossetti, and Ermanno Salvaterra establish a brilliant big-wall route (Quinque Anni ad Paradisum), joining the Compressor Route seven hundred feet below the top and continuing to the summit.

2005
North Face/Ridge
Alessandro Beltrami (Italy), Rolando Garibotti (Argentina), and Ermanno Salvaterra (Italy) become the first to climb Cerro Torre from the north, naming their route El Arca de los Vientos.

2007
South & West Faces
Americans Kelly Cordes and Colin Haley become the first to continue Los Tiempos Perdidos to the summit, via linking it to the upper Ragni Route.

2008
Southeast Ridge & West Face
Norwegians Ole Lied and Trym Atle Saeland start up the southeast ridge, use part of the Compressor Route, then traverse the hanging ice field on the south face to connect to the upper Ragni Route to the summit (Corkscrew linkup).

2008
Torre Traverse
Rolando Garibotti and Colin Haley make the first ascent of the Torre Traverse, enchaining Cerro Standhardt, Punta Herron, Torre Egger, and Cerro Torre.

2012
Southeast Ridge
Hayden Kennedy (United States) and Jason Kruk (Canada) become the first to climb the southeast ridge by fair means to the summit. They remove 120 of Maestri's Compressor Route bolts on their descent.

Austrian David Lama, climbing with countryman Peter Ortner, free climbs the southeast ridge.

page 374 photos (from left)
Kelly Cordes, Rolando Garibotti, Ben Ditto

page 375 photos (from left)
Colin Haley, Mikey Schaefer, Mikey Schaefer

APPENDIX II THE PLAYERS

ALESSANDRO BELTRAMI (1981–) An Italian climber, who lives in a village near Maestri, and member of the team whose 2005 new route on Cerro Torre's northern aspect finally put to rest the 1959 myth.

WALTER BONATTI (1930–2011) Widely admired and accomplished Italian alpinist, attempted Cerro Torre in 1958 with Carlo Mauri.

JOHN BRAGG (1947–) American alpinist, made the 1976 first ascent of Torre Egger, and a rapid repeat of the Ragni Route on Cerro Torre a year later.

JIM BRIDWELL (1944–) An all-time great, Yosemite pioneer, American climber who made the first complete ascent of the Compressor Route in 1979.

PHIL BURKE (1950–) Strong British climber, made one of Cerro Torre's finest efforts on the east and north faces in 1981.

BEN CAMPBELL-KELLY (1943–) British climber, made several trips to Patagonia. In 1974 found some of Toni Egger's remains.

MARIO CONTI (1944–) A member of the 1974 Ragni di Lecco (Italy) team that made the first ascent of Cerro Torre.

JIM DONINI (1943–) American alpinist, made the 1976 first ascent of Torre Egger, during which the first hard evidence against Maestri's 1959 claim emerged. Still an active climber in his 70s, still a frequent Patagonia climber.

FOLCO DORO-ALTÁN (1930–1999) Argentine adventurer and climber, Italian émigré, explored the ice cap three times in the 1950s. Likely originator of the idea to climb Cerro Torre.

TONI EGGER (1926–1959) Cutting-edge Austrian alpinist, climbed with Maestri and Fava on Cerro Torre in 1959. Died, reportedly on the descent, his body not recovered.

CESARINO FAVA (1920–2008) Italian immigrant to Argentina, assisted Maestri on his trips to Cerro Torre. Helped Egger and Maestri on the lower parts of the 1959 claimed first ascent before retreating, and always corroborated Maestri's accounts. Helped Maestri with establishing the Compressor Route.

CÉSAR FAVA (1966–) Son of Cesarino, lives in El Chaltén, Argentina.

CASIMIRO FERRARI (1940–2001) Italian alpinist, leader of the 1974 Ragni di Lecco team that made the first ascent of Cerro Torre.

JOSÉ LUIS FONROUGE (1942–2001) Pioneering Argentine alpinist, made the first ascent of the Supercanaleta on Fitz Roy, in alpine style, in 1965. Attempted the southeast ridge of Cerro Torre in 1968.

ROLANDO GARIBOTTI (1971–) One of the Chaltén Massif's greatest climbers, with unparalleled knowledge of its climbing. World's foremost expert on Cerro Torre's history. Member of the 2005 team that first climbed Cerro Torre from the north; dismantled the 1959 lie. Born in Italy, raised in Argentina.

CHRIS GEISLER (1973–) Canadian alpinist who, in 2011, with Jason Kruk, nearly completed the long-sought first fair-means ascent of Cerro Torre's southeast ridge.

COLIN HALEY (1984–) American alpinist, one of the Chaltén Massif's most accomplished climbers in recent years.

SILVO KARO (1960–) Slovenian climber, phenomenally accomplished around the globe, including in Patagonia.

HAYDEN KENNEDY (1990–) American next-generation all-arounder, adept in all aspects of the craft. Removed about 120 of the Compressor Route's bolts after making the first fair-means ascent of the southeast ridge in 2012.

JASON KRUK (1987–) Canadian alpinist, outstanding all-around climber. In 2012, removed about 120 of the Compressor Route's bolts after making the first fair-means ascent of the southeast ridge.

DAVID LAMA (1990–) Austrian climber, from a sport and competition climbing background, transitioned into alpinism with phenomenal success, including his 2012 first fair-means free ascent of Cerro Torre's southeast ridge.

CESARE MAESTRI (1929–) The famed "Spider of the Dolomites," claimed the first ascent of Cerro Torre in 1959 with Toni Egger, with help from Cesarino Fava. Now considered one of mountaineering's biggest lies. Returned in 1970 with a gas-powered compressor and drilled some four hundred bolts into the mountain (the Compressor Route). Still widely respected in Italy.

CARLO MAURI (1930–1982) Great Italian alpinist and adventurer. Attempted Cerro Torre in 1958 with Walter Bonatti.

REINHOLD MESSNER (1944–) Regarded as the greatest mountaineer in history. Lives in South Tyrol, Italy. Although he hasn't climbed in Patagonia, he thoroughly researched the 1959 Maestri affair and wrote a book about Cerro Torre.

ELIO ORLANDI (1954–) Long-time Patagonia climber, still active, and lives in Italy.

ERMANNO SALVATERRA (1955–) Cerro Torre's most devoted and accomplished climber. Lives in Italy, and is one of the climbers who made the 2005 ascent that slammed-shut the 1959 myth. Still active and climbing hard.

ZACK SMITH (1977–) Talented all-around American climber, with several trips to Patagonia. In 2007, he and Josh Wharton made an impressive attempt at Cerro Torre's southeast ridge by fair means.

MIRELLA TENDERINI (1935–) Respected author, editor, and translator in Italy, specializing in climbing and adventure. Knows everybody involved in the old stories.

JOSH WHARTON (1979–) Cutting-edge American alpinist, Patagonia veteran. In 2007, he and Zack Smith made a valiant attempt at Cerro Torre's southeast ridge by fair means.

BRIAN WYVILL (1949–) British climber who made several trips to Patagonia, including the 1974 expedition that first found Toni Egger's remains.

APPENDIX III CLIMBING GLOSSARY

AID CLIMBING
A.k.a. "artificial climbing," advancing upward via direct aid (such as pulling on the gear) from placing pieces of protection. A climber resorts to aid climbing when the natural terrain has become too difficult—too steep, too devoid of features—to climb free (using only one's hands and feet). Free and aid climbing techniques are sometimes combined in pitches of difficult climbing.

ALPINE CLIMBING
Alpinism, or alpine climbing, has long been synonymous with mountaineering. In recent times, however, the term usually implies more technical climbing in the mountains, or alpine regions. In the central Chaltén Massif, there are no nontechnical summits. The climbing is true alpinism, requiring technical expertise on sustained rock, ice, or snow—often all three—to reach even the easiest summit.

ALPINE STYLE
Climbing in a small, self-sufficient team, eschewing fixed ropes and pre-supplied camps. Beginning at the bottom and climbing to the top in one push (often with on-route bivies), carrying all necessary supplies. The opposite of expedition-style or siege-style climbs.

ANCHOR
Can be a single piece of protection, but usually multiple pieces joined together at the beginning and end of a pitch, to create a bombproof belay or rappel point.

BELAYING
Holding the rope while your partner climbs, with the rope fed through a belay device, which gives a powerful mechanical advantage to arrest a fall.

BOLT
A permanent form of protection where a hole is drilled into the rock and a metal bolt is driven in. The hole may be drilled with a motorized drill ("power drill") or with a hand drill. In alpinism, where weight carried is a concern, it's almost always a hand drill, if at all. In alpinism power drilling is usually considered poor form, and even hand drilling is typically considered a last resort.

BOLT LADDER
Bolts successively placed within arm's reach, so that a climber's étriers can be simply clipped to each consecutive bolt to aid climb the rock as if climbing a ladder.

BOULDERING
A form of unroped climbing where the focus is on difficult sequences close to the ground, usually no more that ten or twenty feet high. Crash pads and/or spotters help break a fall.

CAM
Formally known as spring-loaded camming devices (SLCDs), cams are removable pieces of protection with retractable lobes that expand against the sides of the rock. They are quick and easy to place and remove, and extremely strong when placed in dry, solid rock.

CARABINER
A high-strength aluminum loop, with a spring-loaded gate, used for a multitude of climbing tasks; most importantly to clip the rope to protection.

COL
A geographic low point, like a saddle or a pass, between two peaks.

ÉTRIER
A.k.a. aider. A portable ladder, usually made of nylon webbing, used to stand in when aid climbing. Older versions often had steps made of wood or aluminum.

EXPANSION BOLT
A bolt that expands inside the drilled hole, giving it superior holding power. Most modern bolts have expansion properties.

EXPEDITION STYLE
A.k.a. siege style. Climbing with use of extensive fixed ropes, pre-stocked camps, and usually in large teams. Typically a slow and laborious method of climbing mountains. Among modern alpinists, such tactics are generally considered bad style and outdated.

FAIR MEANS

Climbing "fairly," rather than utilizing any and all means to reach the top. A philosophy more than a strict definition, and thus subjective, since external aids can range from insulated clothing to a helicopter ride. The term dates back to Victorian mountaineer Albert Mummery and was popularized in modern times by Reinhold Messner, with his renouncing supplemental oxygen and siege tactics on the highest peaks.

FIXED ROPE

Climbing pitches and leaving ropes secured to the anchors. A rope may be temporarily fixed after a single pitch of climbing, if the second is following using ascenders (versus climbing on second). But fixed ropes are most often used on extremely difficult terrain and/or expedition style climbs, with several hundred (or thousands) feet of rope fixed to save time on return attempts, since the climbers don't have to re-lead the pitches—instead, they can ascend the already fixed ropes (a.k.a. fixed lines).

FOLLOWING OR SECONDING

Climbing with the rope above you (a top-rope). The opposite of leading. Assuming the person above, who just led the pitch, is belaying properly, following is usually low-stress because there's little risk of injury if you fall. You'll only fall a few feet, and gently, due to rope stretch.

FREE CLIMBING

Contrary to popular lingo, free climbing is not climbing without a rope. Climbing unroped is called free soloing. Free climbing simply means climbing without direct aid—i.e., using only one's hands and feet (not the protective gear) for upward progress. The rope and protective gear are present only to safeguard against a fall.

FREE SOLOING

Climbing unroped. A fall is usually fatal.

ÍCE SCREW

A tubular, threaded metal screw with teeth on one end and a hanger for clipping the rope on the other, usually ranging from four to nine inches long. Placed in ice for protection.

JUMAR

A mechanical ascender, used for going up a fixed rope. Many brand names exist, but Jumar was one of the first and thus its name is used like Kleenex for facial tissues. When jumaring the ascender clamps onto the rope, and slides upward in one direction while locking in the other to prevent sliding back on the rope.

LEAD CLIMBING

The leader, climbing on the "sharp end" of the rope, climbs upward, trailing the rope, placing protection as often as he or she feels necessary, and clipping it to the rope, based on confidence and the opportunities offered by the terrain. Leading is a constant game of judgment and self-assessment. It's much faster to place less protection and run out the rope, but it's more dangerous. Leader falls are at least twice the distance climbed above the last piece of protection (assuming the protection is good enough to hold), plus rope stretch (climbing ropes necessarily stretch to absorb the impact of a leader fall).

MOUNTAINEERING

A historically broad term for climbing, back when most climbing was done in the mountains. In recent times, the term often denotes lesser-technical climbing in the mountains, while alpinism tends to refer to more technical mountain climbing.

NUTS

Removable, wedge-shaped pieces of aluminum, also known as chocks or stoppers (the latter is a specific product name, but often used generically), that seat in natural constrictions in the rock, protecting the climber.

ONSIGHTING

Climbing a pitch without falling, without prior knowledge, sight unseen, first try. The ultimate in lead climbing purity.

PITCH

A given length of climbing, up to the length of the rope used. Since the lead climber might stop before the rope runs out, based on opportune belay stances and anchor/protection opportunities, most pitches are somewhat less than a full rope length. The standard rope today is sixty meters (two hundred feet) though different lengths of rope are sometimes employed.

PITONS

Also called pegs or pins, they're steel wedges that climbers hammer into cracks and narrow seams in the rock. Pitons were the primary form of climbing protection for decades, but are used sparingly today, only when the rock offers no alternative. Repeatedly placing and removing pitons permanently scars the rock.

PRESSURE BOLTS OR PRESSURE PITONS

Old-style bolts without expansion properties; essentially glorified rivets; "nails" in Argentine-Italian climber slang. A hole is drilled, and a metal stud (with a hanger for clipping) is pounded in.

PROGRESSION BOLTS

Bolts in a climbing pitch, as opposed to bolts at belay anchors. In the case of the Compressor Route, Maestri's progression bolts were contentious, as they were mostly placed as extensive bolt ladders, without regard for minimal usage or any intention of linking natural features.

PROTECTION

Protection is gear placed in the rock (or ice or snow), to which the climbing rope is clipped with a carabiner, as a safeguard against a fall. Often shortened to "pro" in climber jargon (sometimes called "gear"). While free climbing, pro is only placed as a backup, and is never weighted (unless, of course, the climber falls). Modern pro is extremely lightweight and reliable, and usually removable without damaging the rock. Examples of pro include cams, nuts, bolts, pitons, and ice screws.

RAPPEL

A.k.a. abseil. A means of descending a rope using a belay/rappel device, which utilizes friction and mechanical braking power to descend.

RIME

A unique snow-ice composite that holds together enough to grow into wild shapes, sometimes massively thick and often sculpted by the wind. Although it sticks to seemingly impossible surfaces, like smooth vertical rock, it typically disintegrates when touched, making it terrifying and difficult to protect and to climb. In the Torre group, enormous rime mushrooms guard the summits.

RUNOUT

Stretches of climbing without opportunities for adequate protection. Herein the mental game escalates. The leader has to decide whether to retreat, or whether to continue climbing while risking a big fall. Imagine doing extremely demanding and precise physical movements, while facing consequences of death or serious injury if you fail. The true masters climb equally well—some even better—when the stakes are high.

SHARP END

See lead climbing.

SHORT-FIXING

A speed-climbing technique where the leader finishes a pitch, pulls up the remaining rope and ties it to the anchor. The climber then begins leading the next pitch with a loop of slack and no real belay while the followers jumar (ascend) the ropes. Sometimes the leader improvises a temporary self-belay. When the followers reach the anchor they put the leader on proper belay. A model of efficiency and, thus, speed; not found in any safety manuals.

SIMULCLIMBING

Both climbers climbing together at the same time, roped, with protection placed between them. No proper belay is used, but the climbers try to minimize slack in the rope while moving together. Mostly used on easy and moderate terrain, as it's not as safe as regular belayed climbing. But it's fast.

SNOW MUSHROOMS

Huge mushroom-shaped formations of snow or rime. Often unstable, and thus unsafe; difficult to climb around, through, or over.

SOLOING

Climbing alone, sometimes using self-belay methods, sometimes free soloing.

SPORT CLIMBING

A very popular form of climbing, usually conducted at crags close to the road with well-bolted, gymnastic climbs, where the focus is on doing extremely difficult moves on safe, relatively short routes.

TOP-ROPING

Climbing with the rope above you, as in following or seconding.

DIFFICULTY RATINGS

Different ways of categorizing difficulty exist in different climbing cultures. For the most part, the higher the number within the grading or rating system, the harder it gets.

AID RATINGS
Based on the difficulty of securing gear placements, onto which the climber directly rests his or her body weight, and also the reliability of those placements in case of a fall. It begins at A0 (resting on or pulling up on a perfectly solid placement) and tops out at A5 (moving upward on extremely difficult and insecure placements). Clean aid tactics involve aid climbing without hammering pitons or drilling the rock, and begin with a C (C1, C2, etc.). Being a closed scale, the rating for a given pitch may shift over time as the tools or technique progress. It can be confusing, but the higher the number, the sketchier and trickier it gets.

ICE RATINGS
Difficulty rated on the WI (water ice) or AI (alpine ice) scale. The difference is mostly academic, based on the source of the moisture that freezes. The scale theoretically starts at the bottom, but grade 1 ice is horizontal, such as an icy sidewalk.

Essentially the scale starts at 2, which is easy enough that a good climber can ascend it without ice tools—just balancing on the cramponed feet.

Grade 3 gets a bit steeper, averaging seventy degrees, with perhaps short steeper sections.

Grade 4 ice usually averages seventy to eighty degrees, and requires two ice tools and technical proficiency; it might include short vertical steps.

Grade 5 is sustained vertical ice, or at least eighty degrees (which feels vertical). True vertical is ninety degrees, telephone-pole vertical, as opposed to the common mainstream perception of vertical (which is usually about forty-five degrees).

Grade 6 ice is incredibly sustained vertical, without the slightest "cheat" in the angle, the sort of thing that keeps going and going. WI6 or AI6 will often include overhanging bulges, where the ice formed thicker in one spot but lesser just below.

In most places, grade 6 is the top end. Rare ice climbs get a difficulty rating of 7 or higher. In addition to steepness, the technicality of the ice is a factor. Thick, high-quality ice is comparatively easy. Climbing on unstable ice, or a glazed-over surface, where perhaps the ice is a half-inch thick, even if the angle is less than vertical, can be extremely demanding and thus elicit top-end ratings.

MIXED RATINGS
Similar to ice ratings, but with the letter M preceding the number. Top M-grades go into the double digits, because the primary difficulties are often cold rock, overcome by hooking one's ice tools and crampons onto tiny edges. Rock can be dramatically overhanging, while ice rarely forms steeper than vertical.

ROCK RATINGS
The predominant system referenced in this book for free climbing rock is the Yosemite Decimal System, though different systems are used throughout the world. Terrain goes from class 1 (basically a sidewalk) to class 6 (aid climbing). Second-class terrain is hiking. Third-class terrain is scrambling. Fourth-class terrain is exposed scrambling; stuff that serious climbers might still consider scrambling, but non-climbers would consider more serious, as a fall would likely be highly injurious or fatal.

Fifth class is technical terrain by climber standards, the things where nearly all climbers want a rope because it's hard enough that they could fall, and an unroped fall (i.e., free solo climbing) would be fatal. But class-five climbing gets massively subdivided. After a decimal point is another number.

Starting with 5.10 (pronounced "five-ten"; extremely technical by most standards and moderately hard by highly skilled climber standards), the ratings further subdivide into letters a through d (d being the most difficult). Thus, a climb rated 5.11d is harder than a climb rated 5.11b. The + and - system also exists, as a more general version of the letter subdivision. Thus, 5.10+ might be akin to 5.10d, either of which are easier than 5.11. But only a hair easier than 5.11a, and a lot easier than 5.11d. The current top end is 5.15c. It is an open-ended scale and thus always growing.

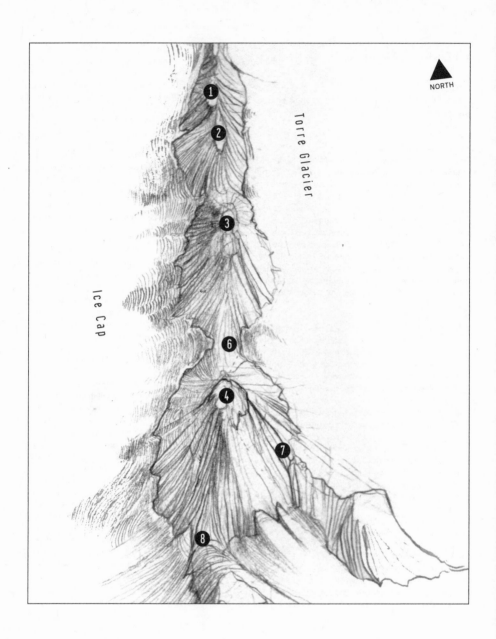

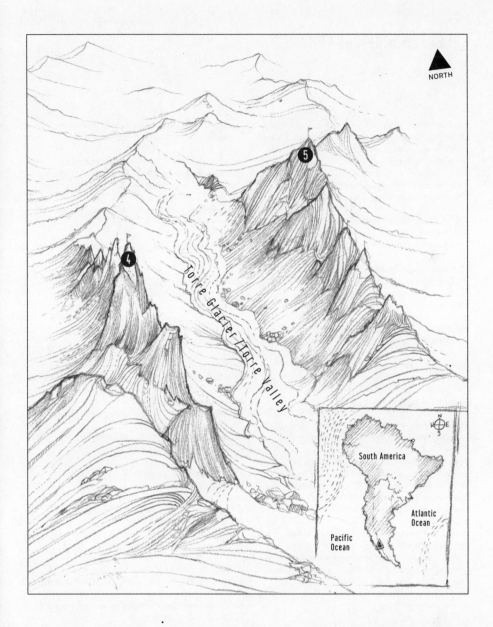

1 Cerro Standhardt
2 Punta Herron
3 Torre Egger
4 Cerro Torre
5 Fitz Roy
6 Col of Conquest
7 Col of Patience
8 Col of Hope

Maps: Jeremy Collins

SELECTED BIBLIOGRAPHY

American Alpine Club. "Reinhold Messner Speaks at Outdoor Retailer." February 6, 2012. http://inclined .americanalpineclub.org.2012/02/reinhold-messner -at-outdoor-retailer/.

Arko, Vojslav. "Cerro Torre, The First Ten Ascents." *The American Alpine Journal*, 1986.

Austin, David. "Mesca-Dawn: A Remembrance of Bill Denz." *Alpinist*, May 9, 2013. http://www.alpinist .com/doc/web13s/wfeature-bill-denz.

"The Backfire Effect." *You Are Not So Smart: A Celebration of Self Delusion*, June 10, 2011. http://youarenotsosmart.com/2011/06/10 /the-backfire-effect/.

Bates, Robert H. "In Memoriam: Richard L. Burdsall, 1895–1953." *The American Alpine Journal*, 1953.

Beal, Peter. "Cerro Torre and the Mountain as a Work of Art." *Mountains and Water*, February 6, 2012. http://www.mountainsandwater.com/2012/02 /cerro-torre-and-mountain-as-work-of-art.html.

Bearzi, Michael, and Ken Wilson. "Cerro Torre 1959 Revisited." *Mountain Review*, August 1994.

Beaumont, Peter. "Climbers Anger Italians by Removing Bolt 'Ladder' From Cerro Torre Peak." *The Guardian*, February 16, 2012. http://www .theguardian.com/world/2012/feb/16/climbers -italians-bolt-ladder-cerro-torre.

"Because of Some Old Nails: Letters from Argentine Climbers on the 2012 Cerro Torre Controversy." From: Compañy, Ricardo and Adriana Estol; Carlos Comesaña; Club Andino El Chaltén meeting minutes excerpt; Jorge Ackermann; Luciano Fiorenza; José Bonacalza; Matias Villavicencio; Sebastián de la Cruz. *Alpinist*, Summer 2012.

Beckwith, Christian. "Shingu Charpa's North Ridge Remains Unclimbed." *Alpinist*, March 30, 2007. http://www.alpinist.com/doc/ALP19/newswire -shingu-charpa-unclimbed-ukrainians.

Beckwith, Christian, and Katie Ives. "The Restoration of the Impossible." *Alpinist*, Summer 2007.

Bisharat, Andrew. "Cerro Torre: The Interviews." [Six-part series with Lincoln Else, Jorge Ackermann, Carlos Comesaña, Tomás Aguiló, Rolando Garibotti, and David Lama.] *Evening Sends*, March 19, 2012. http://eveningsends.com/climbing/cerro-torre-the -interviews/.

Bisharat, Andrew. "The Tyranny of History." *Rock and Ice*, April 2012.

Bonatti, Walter, and Robert Marshall. *The Mountains of My Life*. Modern Library ed. New York: Modern Library, 2001.

Bragg, John. "Cerro Torre Revisited." *Rock and Ice*, July 1984.

Bragg, John. "Torre Egger." *The American Alpine Journal*, 1976.

Bragg, John. "Torre Egger." *The American Alpine Journal*, 1977.

Brewer, Steve. "Cerro Torre—Alpine Style." *Climbing*, January–February 1980.

Bridwell, James D. "Cerro Torre—Alpine Style." *The American Alpine Journal*, 1980.

Bridwell, Jim. "Jim Bridwell, His Cerro Torre Point of View." *PlanetMountain*, March 13, 2012. http://www.planetmountain.com/english/News /shownews1.lasso?l=2&keyid=39298.

Bridwell, Jim, and Keith Peall. *Climbing Adventures: A Climber's Passion*. Merrillville, Ind.: ICS Books, 1992.

Buffet, Charlie. "Cerro Torre: Le sommet du mensonge." *Le Monde*, May 9, 2006.

Buffet, Charlie, and David Roberts. "Cesare Maestri: The Legend Roars." *National Geographic Society*, April 2006. http://www.nationalgeographic.com /adventure/0604/whats_new/cesare-maestri.html.

Burgess, Adrian. "Cerro Torre, First British Ascent." *The American Alpine Journal*, 1996.

Burke, Phil. "Cerro Torre East Face." *Mountain*, May–June 1981.

Buscaini, Gino, and Silvia Metzeltin. *Patagonia: Terra Magica per Viaggiatori e Alpinisti*. Milano: Corbaccio, 1998.

Cahall, Fitz. "The Climber: David Lama." *National Geographic Society*, 2013. http://adventure .nationalgeographic.com/adventure/adventurers -of-the-year/2013/david-lama/.

Cameron, Gwen. "Clear Weather Leads to Binge-Climbing in Patagonia." February 28, 2011. http://www.alpinist.com/doc/web11w/newswire -patagonia-cerro-torre-fitz-roy-pollone/2.

Campbell-Kelly, Ben. "Cerro Standhardt Attempt." *The American Alpine Journal*, 1976.

Campbell-Kelly, Ben. "A Patagonia Handbook." Expedition report, 1975.

Campbell-Kelly, Ben. "A Time to Remember." *Mountain Life* 19, 1975.

Carretto, Guido. "Cerro Torre Enigma: Maestri Speaks." *Mountain*, May 1970.

Cassin, Riccardo. "The Conquest of the Alps: Fascinating Past and Future Continuity." In *Voices From the Summit: The World's Great Mountaineers on the Future of Climbing*. Washington, D.C.: Adventure Press, National Geographic, in association with the Banff Centre for Mountain Culture, 2000.

Castaldi, Lorenzo. "The Beauty, the Tribe and the Choppers." *Alpinist*, February 21, 2012. http://www.alpinist.com/doc/web12wreaders -blog-the-beauty-and-the-choppers.

Centro Andino El Chaltén. "Acta de la Asamblea Llevada a Cabo por el Centro Andino El Chaltén." *La Cachaña*, January 26, 2012. http://www.lacachania .com.ar/noticia.php?id_nota=229&id_seccion=6.

"Cerro Torre Attempt by Club Alpino Italiano, Belledo Section" and "Cerro Torre, Ascent by Southwest [sic] Face." *The American Alpine Journal*, 1971.

"Cerro Torre Bolt Chopping, the Debate in Italy." *PlanetMountain*, February 9, 2012. http://www.planetmountain.com/english/News /shownews1.lasso?l=2&keyid=39140.

"Cerro Torre: A Mountain Desecrated." *Mountain*, September 1972.

"Cerro Torre, la montaña más visitada." *La Cachaña*, February 4, 2013. http://www.lacachania.com.ar /noticia.php?id_nota=526.

"Cerro Torre North Face Mystery—Salvaterra's forum-post: 'The doubt of Maestri's claims still remains.'" *Explorer's Web*, November 30, 2005. http://www .explorersweb.com/everest_k2/news.php?id=1224.

"Cerro Torre, Patagonia." *The American Alpine Journal*, 1959.

"Cesarino Fava, el Pata Corta." *Centro Cultural Argentino de Montaña*. http://www.culturademontania .com.ar/Historia/HIS_cesarino_fava.htm.

Chouinard, Yvon. "A Word…" *Patagonia, Inc.*, February 15, 2012. http://www.thecleanestline.com/2012/02 /a-word-.html.

Chouinard, Yvon. *Climbing Ice*. San Francisco: Sierra Club Books, 1978.

Cicogna, Antonella. "Maestri non salì sul Cerro Torre." *La Gazzetta dello Sport*, November 22, 2005.

Comesaña, Carlos. "No se pueden dejar las cosas como están porque son 'historia.'" *Desnivel*, February 8, 2012. http://desnivel.com/alpinismo /carlos-comesana-se-muestra-a-favor-de-la-retirada -de-los-clavos-de-maestri-de-la-via-del-compresor.

Cominetti, Marcello. "K&K operazione Cerro Torre 'Il giorno prorompe in tutta la sua bellezza, spazzando via i fantasmi della paura della notte.'" February 12, 2012. http://marcellocominetti.blogspot.com/2012 /02/k-operazione-cerro-torre-il-giorno.html.

Conti, Mario. "Cerro Torre: The Bolt Chopping and Its History as Seen Through the Eyes of Mario Conti." *PlanetMountain*, February 2, 2012. http://www.planetmountain.com/english/News /shownews1.lasso?%22l=2&keyid=39120.

Cordes, Kelly. "Cerro Torre by Fair-Means." Video. *Patagonia, Inc*, August 21, 2012. http://www.youtube .com/watch?v=E_nSYJcDJNQ.

Cordes, Kelly. "Cerro Torre, David Lama and Red Bullshit." June 25, 2010. http://kellycordes.wordpress .com/2010/06/25/cerro-torre-david-lama-and -red-bullshit/.

Cordes, Kelly. "Cerro Torre: Deviations from Reason." *Patagonia, Inc.*, February 6, 2012. http://www .thecleanestline.com/2012/02/cerro-torre-deviations -from-reason.html.

Cordes, Kelly. "Cerro Torre Rebooted." *The American Alpine Journal*, 2012.

Cordes, Kelly. "Cerro Torre's Cold Case." *National Geographic Society*, April 2006. http://www .nationalgeographic.com/adventure/photography /patagonia/cerro-torre-maestri.html.

Cordes, Kelly. "Fantasyland: A Deranged Trip Up Cerro Torre." *Climbing*, July 2008.

Cordes, Kelly. "Shingu Charpa, North Ridge, Attempt." *The American Alpine Journal*, 2007.

Crew, Peter. "The British Cerro Torre Expedition." *The Alpine Journal*, 1968.

Crocket, Ken, and Simon Richardson. "Revolutions (1970–1985)." In *Ben Nevis: Britain's Highest Mountain*. 2nd ed. Edinburgh: Scottish Mountaineering Trust, 2009.

Crouch, Gregory. "Cerro Torre Epics: Three Wild Stories from Patagonia." *Climbing*. http://www.climbing.com /climber/wind-madness-cerro-torres-epic-hall-of -fame-no-224/.

Crouch, Gregory. "The Compressor Route Chopped...More Thoughts." January 20, 2012. http://gregcrouch.com/2012/the-compressor -route-chopped-more-thoughts.

Crouch, Gregory. *Enduring Patagonia*. New York: Random House, 2001.

Dalbagni, Gianni. "La Dura Conquista del Cerro Torre." *Corriere degli Italiani*, 16 articles beginning March 23, 1959.

Dauer, Tom. *Cerro Torre: Mythos Patagonien*. Zürich: AS Verlag, 2004.

"David Lama Frees the Compressor Route, While Kruk & Kennedy's Bolt Chopping Is Hotly Debated." *PlanetMountain*, January 23, 2012. http://www .planetmountain.com/english/News/shownews1 .lasso?l=2&keyid=39061.

De Agostini, Alberto María. *Andes Patagónicos, Viajes de Exploración a la Cordillera Patagónica Austral*. Buenos Aires: [Impr. de L.L. Gotelli], 1941.

De La Cruz, Sebastián. "Carta de Sebastián De La Cruz, Primer Argentino en Subir al Torre." *La Cachaña*, January 30, 2012. http://www.lacachania.com.ar /noticia.php?id_nota=201&id_seccion=3.

Dickinson, Leo. "Cerro Torre—The Eleventh Failure." *The American Alpine Journal*, 1973.

Dickinson, Leo. "The Devil in the Detail." *The British Mountaineering Council*, August 4, 2006. http://www.thebmc.co.uk/the-devil-in-the-detail.

Dickinson, Leo. "Round Eleven on Cerro Torre." *Mountain*, September 1972.

Donini, Jim. "Cerro Torre—The Lie and the Desecration." *Climbing*, April 2009.

Donini, Jim. "The Torre Egger Climb." *Mountain*, September–October 1976.

Douglas, Ed. "Achille Compagnoni." *The Guardian*, May 17, 2009. http://www.theguardian.com /sport/2009/may/18/obituary-achille-compagnoni.

Douglas, Ed. "Special Report." *The Guardian*, May 6, 2006. http://www.theguardian.com/sport/2006 /may/07/features.sport5.

Douglas, Ed. "Stealing Beauty." *The British Mountaineering Council*, February 11, 2005. https://www.thebmc.co.uk/stealing-beauty.

"El Cerro Torre y la Torre de Babel." *Centro Cultural Argentino de Montaña*, April 2012. http://www .culturademontania.com.ar/Noticias/NOT_cerro_torre _y_torre_babel_042012.htm.

"Exclusive Interview: David Lama." *UKClimbing*, December 2012. http://www.ukclimbing.com/articles /page.php?id=5147.

Fava, Cesarino. "Basta, va bene se dico che ho inventato tutto?" *La Provincia*, November 30, 2005.

Fava, Cesarino. "Confessioni i Cesare Fava detto Cesarino/RISPOSTA AI NOVELLI TORQUEMADA." *L'Adige*, November 27, 2005.

Fava, Cesarino. *Patagonia Terra di Sogni Infranti*. Torino: Centro di Documentazione Alpina, 1999.

Fava, Mariana. "Carta de Mariana Fava." *La Cachaña*, January 25, 2012. http://www.lacachania.com.ar /noticia.php?id_nota=194.

Ferrari, Casimiro. "Cerro Torre Climbed!" *Mountain*, September 1974.

Ferrari, Casimiro. *Cerro Torre: Pared Oeste*. Barcelona: RM, 1983.

Fowler, Charlie. "Cerro Torre & The Enigma of Cesare Maestri." *Rock and Ice*, July 1984.

"Free Climbing: David Lama on the Record About Cerro Torre." *Red Bull*, February 22, 2012. http://www.redbull.com/cs/Satellite/en_INT/Article /David-lama-interview-021243166676734.

Frimer, Jeremy. "Jirishanca." *The American Alpine Journal*, 2004.

"Fué Vencido el Cerro Torre, Pero se Corbró una Víctima." *La Opinión Austral* [Río Gallegos], February 27, 1959.

Fyffe, Allen. "The Changing Styles of Scottish Winter Climbing." *Mountain*, November 1974.

Gadd, Will. "David Lama, Red Bull, Patagonia." *Gravsports*, June 2, 2010. http://gravsports.blogspot .com/2010/06/david-lama-red-bull-patagonia.html.

Gadd, Will. "Lama, Red Bull, Cerro Torre." *Gravsports*, July 13, 2010. http://gravsports.blogspot.com /2010/07/lama-red-bull-cerro-torre.html.

Gardien, Claude. "The State of the Art: The Alps, a Glance at Modern Alpine Style." *The American Alpine Journal*, 2001.

Garibotti, Rolando. "Cerro Standhardt, Torre Egger and Cerro Torre," in "Unclimbed." *Alpinist*, Autumn 2003.

Garibotti, Rolando. "Cerro Torre—An Impossible Mountain." *Alpinist*, February 21, 2012. http://www .alpinist.com/doc/web12w/petition-in-favor.

Garibotti, Rolando. "Cerro Torre, Attempt [by Austrian climbers]." *The American Alpine Journal*, 1999.

Garibotti, Rolando. "Chaltén Massif, Summary." *The American Alpine Journal*, 2009.

Garibotti, Rolando. "Chaltén Massif, Summary." *The American Alpine Journal*, 2010.

Garibotti, Rolando. "Chaltén Massif, Summary." *The American Alpine Journal*, 2011.

Garibotti, Rolando. "Correo de lectores de Rolando Garibotti." *La Cachaña*, January 21, 2012. http://www .lacachania.com.ar/noticia.php?id_nota=186.

Garibotti, Rolando. "The Expert's Opinion," in "Murder of the Possible." *Rock and Ice*, July 2007.

Garibotti, Rolando. "Mountain Profile: Fitz Roy." *Alpinist*, Winter 2003–2004.

Garibotti, Rolando. "A Mountain Unveiled: A Revealing Analysis of Cerro Torre's Tallest Tale." *The American Alpine Journal*, 2004. http://pataclimb.com/knowledge /articles/pdf/amtunveiled.pdf.

Garibotti, Rolando. "Patagonia Online Climbing Guide." http://pataclimb.com/.

Garibotti, Rolando. "The Restoration of Impossibility." *Alpinist*, Summer 2012.

Garibotti, Rolando. "The State of the Art: Patagonia, Looking Back, Toward the Future." *The American Alpine Journal*, 2001.

Garibotti, Rolando. "Torre Traverse." *Patagonia, Inc.*, Fall 2008. http://www.patagonia.com/us/patagonia .go?assetid=33809.

Garibotti, Rolando. "The Torre Traverse: The Only Way Out Is Up." *Alpinist*, Autumn 2008.

Garibotti, Rolando. "The Torre Traverse: A Two-decade-old Patagonian Dream Is Realized." *The American Alpine Journal*, 2008.

Garibotti, Rolando. "The View from the Top." *National Geographic Society*, April 2006. http://www .nationalgeographic.com/adventure/0604/whats _new/cerro-torre-garibotti.html.

Garibotti, Rolando, and Dörte Pietron. *Patagonia Vertical: Chaltén Massif Climbing Guide*. Ljubljana: Sidarta, 2012.

Geldard, Jack. "An Interview with Rolando Garibotti about the Torre Traverse." *UKClimbing*, February 2008. http://www.ukclimbing.com/articles/page .php?id=819.

Giarolli, Maurizio. "Cerro Torre, West Face Attempt, Crystals in the Wind." *The American Alpine Journal*, 1995.

Gillman, Peter. "Climbing Controversies." *The Alpine Journal*, 2007.

Goodwin, Stephen. "Lino Lacedelli: Mountaineer Whose Ascent of K2 in 1954 Was Shrouded in Controversy." *The Independent*, November 24, 2009. http://www.independent.co.uk/news/obituaries /lino-lacedelli-mountaineer-whose-ascent-of-k2-in -1954-was-shrouded-in-controversy-1826470.html.

Grosselli, di Renzo M. "Carlotta e l'anarchico delle Dolomiti: Cesare Maestri, l'inverno del più grande rocciatore di tutti i tempi." *L'Adige, Trento*, December 24, 2005.

Gutmann, Martin. "Mountain Profile: The Eiger, Part II (1939–2012), The Theater of History." *Alpinist*, Winter 2012–2013.

Haley, Colin. "Cerro Torre, David Lama and Red Bull." January 22, 2011. http://colinhaley.blogspot.com /2011/01/cerro-torre-david-lama-and-redbull.html.

Haley, Colin. "Clarifications About Cerro Torre, David Lama and Red Bull." January 27, 2011. http://colinhaley.blogspot.com/2011/01/clarifications -about-cerro-torre-david.html.

Haley, Colin. "The Corkscrew." January 31, 2013. http://colinhaley.blogspot.com/2013/01/the -corkscrew.html.

Haley, Colin. "David Lama and Cerro Torre—Good News." January 30, 2011. http://colinhaley.blogspot .com/2011/01/david-lama-and-cerro-torre-good -news.html.

Haley, Colin. "The Removal of Cesare Maestri's Bolt Ladders on Cerro Torre." February 4, 2012. http://colinhaley.blogspot.com/2012/02/removal-of -cesare-maestris-bolt-ladders.html.

Haley, Colin. "Sueños del Torre: A 4,500-foot Ice Climb Linking the South Face and West Ridge of Cerro Torre." *The American Alpine Journal*, 2007.

Haston, Dougal. "Cerro Torre—Defeat." *Mountain Craft*, Special Issue, Autumn 1968.

Heppenstall, Alan. "Further Thoughts on the Cerro Torre Problem." *Mountain*, March–April 1975.

Houston, Charles S., and Robert H. Bates. Footnote, p. 11. In *K2, the Savage Mountain: The Classic True Story of Disaster and Survival on the World's Second Highest Mountain*. 1954. Reprint, Guilford, Conn.: Lyons Press, 2009.

"How Mr. Burdsal (*sic*) Met His Death." *The Standard* [Buenos Aires], March 3, 1953.

"Jason Kruk—Cerro Torre Unleashed." February 15, 2012. http://squamishclimbing.com/2012/02/15/jason-kruk-feature-interview/.

"Jirishanca and Yerupajá Chico, Cordillera Huayhuash, and Ascents in the Cordillera Raura." *The American Alpine Journal*, 1958.

Kalous, Chris, and Hayden Kennedy. "Episode 6: Hayden Kennedy: Alpine Taliban or Patagonian Custodian™? (Part 1)." Audio interview. *The Enormocast*, March 1, 2012. http://enormocast.com/episode-6-hayden-kennedy-alpine-taliban-or-patagonian-custodian-part-1/.

Kalous, Chris, and Hayden Kennedy. "Episode 7: Hayden Kennedy: Alpine Taliban or Patagonian Custodian™? (Part 2)." Audio interview. *The Enormocast*, March 14, 2012. http://enormocast.com/episode-7-hayden-kennedy-alpine-taliban-or-patagonian-custodian-part-2/.

Karo, Silvo. "Cerro Torre Crazy." *Mountain*, January–February 1989; republished as "Cerro Torre's South Face." *The American Alpine Journal*, 1989.

Karo, Silvo. "Patagonia: Terra Mystica." In *Voices from the Summit: The World's Great Mountaineers on the Future of Climbing*. Washington, D.C.: Adventure Press, National Geographic, in association with the Banff Centre for Mountain Culture, 2000.

Kearney, Alan. *Mountaineering in Patagonia*. Seattle, Wash.: Cloudcap, 1993.

Kennedy, Hayden. "By Fair Means." *The American Alpine Journal*, 2012.

Kennedy, Hayden. "Into the Fire." *Alpinist*, Summer 2012.

Kennedy, Hayden, and Jason Kruk. "Kennedy, Kruk Release Statement." *Alpinist*, January 26, 2012. http://www.alpinist.com/doc/web12w/newswire-kruk-kennedy-statement.

Kennedy, Michael. "Letter to My Son." *Alpinist*, Spring 2012.

Kern, Steffen. "Scharfes Ende: Wider den Torrerismus!" *Klettern*, May 2012.

Kölliker, Alfred. *In den Einsamkeiten Patagoniens*. Stuttgart: Strecker und Schröder, 1926.

Konnikova, Maria. "I Don't Want to Be Right." *The New Yorker*, May 19, 2014. http://www.newyorker.com/online/blogs/mariakonnikova/2014/05/why-do-people-persist-in-believing-things-that-just-arent-true.html.

Kopp, Christine. "Vertical Dreams: Italy's Lecco Spiders." *Alpinist*, Summer 2003.

Kruk, Jason. "Cerro Torre." *The Canadian Alpine Journal*, 2011.

Kruk, Jason. "Cerro Torre. By Fair Means." October 13, 2011. *Gripped*. http://gripped.com/articles/cerro-torre/.

Kruk, Jason. "Cerro Torre Redux." *The Canadian Alpine Journal*, 2012.

Kruk, Jason. "Cerro Torre SE Ridge Attempt." February 18, 2011. http://jasonthekruk.blogspot.com/2011/02/geisler-and-i-had-epic-week-up-in-torre.html.

Kruk, Jason. "What Happened in Patagonia?" May 23, 2012. http://jasonthekruk.blogspot.com/2012/05/what-happened-in-patagonia.html.

"Kruk y Hayden, 'non gratos' para los andinistas de El Chaltén." *Desnivel*, January 27, 2012. http://desnivel.com/alpinismo/cerro-torre-jason-kruk-y-hayden-kennedy-non-gratos-para-los-andinistas-de-el-chalten-por-quitar-los-clavos-de-maestri.

Labate, Vicente. "Cerro Torre: Patagonian Democracy." *PlanetMountain*, September 14, 2007. http://www.planetmountain.com/english/News/shownews1.lasso?l=2&keyid=35788.

Lacedelli, Lino, and Giovanni Cenacchi. *K2: The Price of Conquest.* 2004. Reprint, Seattle, Wash.: Mountaineers Books, 2006.

Lama, David. "Cerro Torre Free." *The American Alpine Journal,* 2012.

Lama, David. "David Lama on Cerro Torre—Photostory." *Red Bull,* January 26, 2012. http://www.redbull.com /cs/Satellite/en_INT/Article/david-lama-reports -from-the-top-of-cerro-torre-021243154189176.

Lama, David. "David Lama: Flashback on a Patagonian Dream." *Red Bull,* January 31, 2012. http://www .redbull.com/cs/Satellite/en_INT/Article/david-lama -reflects-on-his-way-to-the-top-of-021243156479862.

Lama, David. "Free." *Alpinist,* Summer 2012.

"Lama Speaks Out on Compressor Debacle." *Alpinist,* July 28, 2010. http://www.alpinist.com/doc/web10x /newswire-lama-speaks-compressor.

Lambert, Erik. "Dozens of Bolts Added to Compressor Route." *Alpinist,* June 1, 2010. http://www.alpinist.com /doc/web10s/newswire-david-lama-compressor-bolts.

Lambert, Erik. "Great Mountains of the World: Cerro Torre." *Adventure Journal,* July 2012. http://www .adventure-journal.com/2012/07/great-mountains -of-the-world-cerro-torre-2/.

Lambert, Erik. "Near Boltless Ascent of Compressor Route." *Alpinist,* February 21, 2007. http://www .alpinist.com/doc/ALP18/newswire-cerro-torre -compressor-wharton-smith.

"Lamento in Trento." *Alpin,* July 2009.

Lane, Keese. "Lama's Bolts Cut: It Begins Again." *Alpinist,* November 16, 2010. http://www.alpinist.com /doc/web10f/newswire-flash-bolts-cut.

"Laurea honoris causa a Cesare Maestri." *Trentino Corriere Alpi,* May 22, 2012. http://trentinocorrierealpi .gelocal.it/cronaca/2012/05/22/news/laurea -honoris-causa-a-cesare-maestri-1.5112020.

Lavigne, Joshua. "Bryn Carlyle Norman, 1982–2012." *The Canadian Alpine Journal,* 2012.

Lavigne, Joshua, and Sharon Wood. "Carlyle Norman Accident Report." *Alpinist,* January 30, 2012. http:// www.alpinist.com/doc/web12w/newswire-carlyle -norman.

"L'incompiuta del Cerro Torre." *La Repubblica Sport,* December 3, 2005.

Lovison, Stefano. "Pataclimb, When Toponymy Hides a Crusade." *Alpine Sketches,* January 23, 2012. http:// alpinesketches.wordpress.com/2012/01/23/pataclimb -when-toponymy-hides-a-crusade/.

Lovison, Stefano. "Taliban on Cerro Torre." *Alpine Sketches* and *PlanetMountain,* February 9, 2012. http://www.planetmountain.com/english/News /shownews1.lasso?l=2&keyid=39140.

MacDonald, Dougald. "Cool Fair Means Ascents on Cerro Torre." *Climbing,* January 2013. http://www .climbing.com/news/cool-fair-means-ascents-on -cerro-torre/.

Maestri, Cesare. *Arrampicare è il Mio Mestiere.* 4th ed. Milano: Garzanti, 1972.

Maestri, Cesare. "Il Cerro Torre." *Club Alpino Italiano Rivista Mensile,* July–August 1961.

Maestri, Cesare. "The Cerro Torre Enigma: Maestri Speaks." *Mountain,* May 1970.

Maestri, Cesare. "The Conquest of Cerro Torre." Translation of 1960 *La Montagne* article, *Mountain Craft,* Special Issue, Autumn 1968.

Maestri, Cesare. "La Conquete Du Cerro Torre." *La Montagne & Alpinisme,* April 1960.

Maestri, Cesare. "La Conquista del Cerro Torre." *Bollettino Società Alpinisti Tridentini,* March–April 1959.

Maestri, Cesare…. *E se la Vita Continua.* Milano: Baldini & Castoldi, 1997.

Maestri, Cesare. *Il Ragno delle Dolomiti.* Milano: Rizzoli, 1981.

Maestri, Cesare. "The South-East Ridge of Cerro Torre." *Mountain,* July 1971.

Maestri, Cesare. "E Venne la morte Bianca." *L'Europeo*, April 12, 1959.

Maestri, Cesare, and Fernanda Maestri. *Duemila Metri della Nostra Vita: Le Due Facce del Cerro Torre*. Torino: Centro di documentazione alpina, 2002.

Mason, Vittorino. "Cesarino Fava: Little Big Man." *L'Eco delle Dolomiti*, Number 5. http://www .ecodelledolomiti.net/Num_5/Num_5_Eng/Fava _5Eng.htm.

Mauri, Carlo. "Cerro Torre: The West Face." *Mountain*, September 1970.

Maxim, Paul. *Bold Beyond Belief: Bill Denz, New Zealand's Mountain Warrior*. 2nd ed. Wellington, N.Z.: Maxim Books, 2013.

Messner, Reinhold. "Direttissima oder Mord am Unmöglichen." *Alpinismus*, August 1968.

Messner, Reinhold. *Grido di Pietra: Cerro Torre, la Montagna Impossibile*. Milano: Corbaccio, 2009.

Messner, Reinhold. "The Murder of the Impossible." *Mountain*, May 1971.

Morandi, Carlo. "Cesare Maestri, una vita per l'ascesa." *University of Verona*, 2012. http://www .univrmagazine.it/sito/vedi_articolo.php?id=1626.

"Mountain Interview—Reinhold Messner." *Mountain*, May 1971.

Multiple Cerro Torre Reports. *The American Alpine Journal*, 1996.

"Nach der Kompressor-Route: David Lama im Interview." *Klettern*, 2012. http://www.klettern.de /community/leute/david-lama-interview.653109.5.htm.

Norman, Carlyle. "The Sound of Silence." *Highline*, December 23, 2011. http://highlineonline.ca /2011/12/23/the-sound-of-silence/.

Orlandi, Elio. "Cerro Torre, Attempt." *The American Alpine Journal*, 1999.

Orlandi, Elio. "La teoria del rancore e la ruggine della polemica, di Elio Orlandi." *PlanetMountain*, April 4, 2012. http://www.planetmountain.com/News /shownews1.lasso?l=1&keyid=39385.

Parkin, Andy. "Lost in Patagonia." *High Mountain Sports*, September 1994.

"Patagonia: Cerro Torre." Information section in *Mountain*, May 1971.

"Patagonia: Cerro Torre." Information section in *Mountain*, May–June 1981.

"Patagonia: Cerro Torre." Information section in *Mountain*, January–February 1989.

"Patagonia: Torre Egger/Cerro Torre." Information section in *Mountain*, September 1970.

"Patagonia's Big Year." *Mountain*, September 1974.

Petit, Arnaud. "It's Tough Being Ahead of Your Time." *Piolets d'Or*, 2012. http://www.pioletsdor.com/index .php?option=com_content&view=article&id=217: cerro-torre-lavis-darnaud-petit&catid=56:actu -montagne&Itemid=1&lang=en.

"Piolets d'Or, Special Mention to Kennedy, Kruk, Lama and Ornter." *PlanetMountain*, March 22, 2013. http:// www.planetmountain.com/english/News/shownews1 .lasso?l=2&keyid=40721.

Potts, Mary Anne. "Maestri Unbolted Update: Climber David Lama Frees Cerro Torre's Compressor Route." *National Geographic Society*, February 2, 2012. http://adventureblog.nationalgeographic.com /2012/02/02/maestri-unbolted-update-climber -david-lama-frees-cerro-torres-compressor-route/.

Procknow, Hillary. "Remembering Cesarino Fava." *Alpinist*, April 30, 2008. http://www.alpinist.com /doc/web08s/wfeature-cesarino-fava-tribute.

Pullan, Brandon. "Carlyle Norman," in "Homage." *Alpinist*, Spring 2013.

Rébuffat, Gaston. *On Ice and Snow and Rock*. Paris: Librairie Hachette, 1959 and 1970. Reprint, New York: Oxford University Press, 1971.

Roberts, David. "The Hardest Mountain in the World." In *Great Exploration Hoaxes*. New York: Modern Library, 2001.

Roberts, David. "K2: The Bitter Legacy." *National Geographic Society*, September 2004. http://adventure.nationalgeographic.com/2004/09/k2/david-roberts-text.

Roberts, David. "Patagonia's Cerro Torre Gets the Chop: Maestri Unbolted." *National Geographic Society*, January 29, 2012. http://adventureblog.nationalgeographic.com/2012/01/29/patagonias-cerro-torre-climbing-controversy-maestri-unbolted/.

"Rolando Garibotti Interview." *Climb*, January 27, 2012. http://www.climbmagazine.com/news/2012/01/rolando-garibotti-interview.

Roy, Adam. "Chopped." *Outside Online*, January 25, 2012. http://www.outsideonline.com/outdoor-adventure/the-gist/Chopped.html.

Sacks, Samantha. "The Revision of History." *Alpinist*, Winter 2005–2006.

Salkeld, Audrey. "The Buxton Talk-in." *Mountain*, March 1974.

Salvaterra, Ermanno. "The Ark of the Winds." *Alpinist*, Summer 2006.

Salvaterra, Ermanno. "Boom of Ascents on the West Face of Cerro Torre, Ermanno Salvaterra's Point of View." *PlanetMountain*, December 20, 2008. http://www.planetmountain.com/english/news/shownews1.lasso?l=2&keyid=36503.

Salvaterra, Ermanno. "Cerro Torre's North Face: Putting to Rest the 1959 Mystery." *The American Alpine Journal*, 2006.

Salvaterra, Ermanno. "Cerro Torre, Winter Ascent." *The Alpine Journal*, 1986.

Salvaterra, Ermanno. "Mia Patagonia." *Alpinist*, Autumn 2004.

Salvaterra, Ermanno. "The Torre Traverse at Last." *Alpinist*, August 13, 2008. http://www.alpinist.com/doc/web08x/wfeature-a25-torre-traverse.

"Salvaterra, Cerro Torre and Maestri." *PlanetMountain*, November 24, 2005. http://www.planetmountain.com/english/News/shownews4.lasso?l=2&keyid=34978.

Sbarra, B. J. "Cerro Torre for Dummies (& Non-Alpinists)." *Splitter Choss*, February 15, 2012. http://www.splitterchoss.com/2012/02/15/cerro-torre-for-dummies-non-alpinists/.

Schaffer, Grayson. "Torre, Torre, Torre." *Outside Online*, April 9, 2012. http://www.outsideonline.com/outdoor-adventure/climbing/Torre-Torre-Torre.html.

Schneider, Steve. "A Route Worth Keeping," in "Murder of the Possible." *Rock and Ice*, July 2007.

"A Season in Patagonia." Multiple authors. *Alpinist*, 2002.

Selters, Andrew. "The Ice Revolution." In *Ways to the Sky: a Historical Guide to North American Mountaineering*. Golden, Colo.: AAC Press, 2004.

Signorelli, Luca. "1954: Italia K2." *Alpinist*, Winter 2011–2012.

Signorelli, Luca. "Beyond the Shadows." *Alpinist*, Summer 2012.

Smith, Zack. "Cerro Torre, Southeast Ridge, Attempt by Fair Means." *The American Alpine Journal*, 2007.

"A Snowball's Chance in Hell." *Red Bull*, November 17, 2009. http://www.redbull.com/cs/Satellite/en_INT/Article/A-Snowballs-Chance-in-Hell-021242793048040.

Spreafico, Giorgio. *Cerro Torre—La Sfida*. Bergamo: Sesaab, 2013.

Spreafico, Giorgio. "Cesarino, l'ultima stoccata e la difesa di Trento"; "Daniele Chiappa rompe il silenzio: 'Non credo più a quella scalata'"; "Lugano accende un faro sul giallo del Cerro Torre." *La Provincia*, May 10, 2006.

Spreafico, Giorgio. *Enigma Cerro Torre*. Torino: CDA & Vivalda, 2006.

Spreafico, Giorgio. "I Ragni nel '74 i primi in vetta al Cerro Torre." *La Provincia*, June 29, 2005.

Spreafico, Giorgio. "Il Cerro Torre non svela il suo segreto." *La Provincia*, November 16, 2005.

Spreafico, Giorgio. "Maestri ha scelto la via del silenzio Affida la sua risposta a un avvocato" and "Vi spiego perché non credo al Cerro Torre del '59." *La Provincia*, November 30, 2005.

Spreafico, Giorgio. "Quel Grido di Pietra scalato dai dubbi." *La Provincia*, May 13, 2006.

Spreafico, Giorgio. "Salvaterra, Garibotti e Beltrami scalano il versante Nord a 46 anni dalla controversa prima salita: 'Nessuna traccia'" and "Maestri non è mai stato lì, un capolavoro quello dei Ragni." *La Provincia*, November 23, 2005.

Spreafico, Giorgio. "Tre 'detective' per il mistero del Cerro Torre Salvaterra e Garibotti, i grandi contestatori della via di Maestri nel '59, tentano la Nord con Beltrami" and "L'alpinistà trentino racconta le motivazioni speciali di questa sua appassionante sfida: stile alpino integrale, niente tende e un Gps per mappare la parete impossibile. 'Ma se trovo uno di quei vecchi chiodi lo sbatto in faccia al mondo. E a me per primo.'" *La Provincia*, October 5, 2005.

Stefanello, Vinicio. "Alpinism and Climbing in 2012— Part 1." *PlanetMountain*, January 2, 2013. http:// www.planetmountain.com/english/News/shownews1 .lasso?l=2&keyid=40453.

Stefanello, Vinicio. "Ciao, Cesarino Fava." *PlanetMountain*, April 23, 2008. http://www .planetmountain.com/english/News/shownews .lasso?l=2&keyid=36130.

Stefanello, Vinicio. "Fabio Giacomelli Killed by Avalanche at Cerro Torre." January 7, 2010. http:// www.planetmountain.com/english/News/shownews1 .lasso?l=2&keyid=37169.

Surette, Jim. "Ice Revolution." *Granite Films*, February 3, 2012. http://www.granitefilms.com/2012/02/03 /ice-revolution-with-rick-wilcox/.

Swenson, Steve. "Mountain Profile: K2, Part I (1856–1954)." *Alpinist*, Winter 2011–2012.

Synnott, Mark. "Cliffhanger: On a Deadly Route in Patagonia, Two Hotshot Climbers Seek Truth— and the Summit." *Outside*, March 2004.

Synnott, Mark. "The Maestri Enigma." *Climbing*, May 1999.

"Tell David Lama's Sponsors to Stop Their Support of His Bolting Actions on Cerro Torre." *Change.org, Inc.*, January 2011. http://www.change.org/petitions /tell-david-lamas-sponsors-to-stop-their-support -of-his-bolting-actions-on-cerro-torre.

Terray, Lionel. *Conquistadors of the Useless: From the Alps to Annapurna*. 2001 ed. London: Bâton Wicks, 2001.

"To Os or Not to Os." *National Geographic Society*, May 18, 2012. http://ngm.nationalgeographic.com /everest/blog/2012-05-18/to-os-or-not-to-os.

Tompkins, Douglas. "Carta de Douglas Tompkins a Carlos Comesaña." *La Cachaña*, February 9, 2012. http://www.lacachania.com.ar/noticia.php?id_nota =219&id_seccion=3.

"Tragedy in Patagonia—Carlyle Norman (1982–2012)." *Gripped*, January 19, 2012. http://gripped.com/news /jan-19-2012-tragedy-in-patagonia-carlyle -norman-1983-2012/.

Trento Film Festival. "Reinhold Messner, Cerro Torre e il Grido di Pietra." 2009. http://www.youtube.com /watch?NR=1&feature=endscreen&v=eZqwFARGTCU.

Twight, Mark. "Discourse: Chop the Bolts!" http:// www.marktwight.com/discourse.php?id=39.

"Un Nuevo Capítulo Para el Polémico Cerro Torre." *La Cachaña*, January 21, 2012. http://www.lacachania .com.ar/noticia.php?id_nota=185&id_seccion=1.

"Walter Bonatti." *The Telegraph*, September 14, 2011. http://www.telegraph.co.uk/news/obituaries/8763567 /Walter-Bonatti.html.

Wharton, Josh. "A Route Worth Chopping," in "Murder of the Possible." *Rock and Ice*, July 2007.

Wilson, Ken, et al. "Interview with Cesare Maestri." *Mountain*, September 1972.

ACKNOWLEDGMENTS

In writing this book I relied heavily on Katy Klutznick, who volunteered her exceptional editorial skills, and whose love and encouragement saw me through when I wanted to quit. As I reflect on the depth of her support my words fail me, so I will keep it simple. To Katy, my love: Thank you.

This book also would not have been possible without Rolando Garibotti, who knows more about Cerro Torre and the Chaltén Massif than anyone in the world and who I feel fortunate to have as a friend. Rolo generously offered me his encyclopedia of knowledge and information, from that which resides in his brain to scans of documents and translations, as well as his magnificent photos. And, I should note, every time that he lent me information from his brain, and I double-checked to be sure he wasn't letting emotion influence the facts, it checked out. Every time. Never in my life, including my dozen years helping edit the *American Alpine Journal*, during which I corresponded with the finest experts in various mountain ranges around the world, have I known anybody more dialed than Rolando Garibotti. Furthermore, far beyond this book, his contributions to climbing and conservation in the Chaltén Massif deserve the gratitude of all climbers. To Rolo: Good effort.

Gregory Crouch closely read my final manuscript and added valuable suggestions as well as encouragement and inspiration along the way. I am grateful for his help. The many margaritas I owe him cannot possibly convey my thanks, but we can try.

I conducted in-person interviews in seven different countries during the two years I spent working on this book. Many, many people helped me. Among those, Mirella Tenderini deserves special gratitude. Not only for her insight, knowledge, and for arranging interviews for me, but for her friendship, the great conversations over wine, and for being an inspiration.

I thank my sister Jill for her steady supply of support and encouragement and for her comments on the manuscript, which helped make this accessible to an audience much wider than climber dudes.

My thanks to John Dutton, Linda Kay Norris, Karla Olson, Haruna Madono, and Rick Ridgeway at Patagonia books for making this book happen.

Yvon Chouinard inspires me for reasons too numerous to list. Thank you for being such a badass, YC.

Others I wish to thank, in alphabetical order because it's probably fairest, include (but not limited to):

Jason Albert, The American Alpine Club Library & Katie Sauter, Christian Beckwith, Alessandro Beltrami, Sevi Bohórquez, Matteo Della Bordella, Bean Bowers (RIP), John Bragg, Cian Brinker, Charlie Buffet, Alex Buisse, Miguel Burgos, Phil Burke, Tommy & Becca Caldwell, Luca Calvi, Gwen Cameron, Ben Campbell-Kelly, Doug Chabot, Carolina & Esteban Codo, Jeremy Collins, Carlos Comesaña, Mario Conti, Rob Coppolillo, Cristobal & Raul Costa, Marcello Costa, Marcos Couch, Seba de la Cruz, Dad & Carter & Tanya, Tom Dauer, Scott DeCapio, Kyle Dempster, Leo Dickinson, Ivo Domenech, Jim Donini, Justin DuBois, Valentina Eccher, Stefanie Egger, Lincoln Else, Terry Erickson, Adriana Estol, Adrián Falcone, César Fava, Marisa Field, Sandro Filippini, Alyssa Firmin, Diane French, Karl Gabl, (SB) Dan Gambino, Paul Gagner, Mike Gauthier, Chris Geisler, Ron Gomez, Stephen Goodwin, Mike Graham, Lindsay Griffin, Colin Haley, Steve Halvorson, John Harlin III, Matt Hartman, Tom Hornbein, Alexander & Thomas Huber, Markus Huber, Katie Ives, Silvo Karo, Joel Kauffmann, Alan Kearney, Peter Kelleher, Chad Kellogg (RIP), Hayden & Julie & Michael Kennedy, Kasey Kersnowski (Dude), Florian Klingler, Carin Knutson, Luka Krajnc, Tadej Krišelj, Jason Kruk, Vicente Labate, David Lama, Joshua Lavigne, Sebastián Letemendia, John Long, Dougald MacDonald, Cesare Maestri, Paul Maxim, José Luis Mendieta, Reinhold Messner, Alessandro Modia Rore, Simone Moro, Bernard Newman, Carlyle Norman (RIP), Elio Orlandi, Fabio Palma, Marcos Paz, Sebastián Perrone, Korra Pesce, Dörte Pietron, Marko Prezelj, Joy Ramirez, Corey Rich, Ermanno Salvaterra (Mr. Cerro Torre), (Crampon) Craig Scariot, Mikey Schaefer, Luca Signorelli, Zack Smith, Juan Pedro Spikermann, Giorgio Spreafico, Vincent Stanley, Jim Surette, Jack Tackle, Chris Trimble, Natalia Westberg, Josh & Erinn Wharton, Rick Wilcox, Freddie Wilkinson, Jim Woodmencey, Brian Wyvill, and Baba Yaga.

Last, but nowhere near least of all, I thank my climbing partners, who have contributed to the most powerful memories of my life. Thank you for sharing the mountains with me.

Kelly Cordes

INDEX

One percent of the sales from this book go to the preservation and restoration of the natural environment.

Colophon
Photo: Kelly Cordes

Front Cover
Cerro Torre. Photo: Mikey Schaefer

Inside Front and Back Covers
Front The Chalten Massif. Map: Jeremy Collins
Back The Torre group. Map: Jeremy Collins